Italian Regionalism

Italian Regionalism

History, Identity and Politics

Edited by
Carl Levy

BERG
Oxford · Washington, D.C.

First published in 1996 by
Berg
Editorial offices:
150 Cowley Road, Oxford, OX4 1JJ, UK
22883 Quicksilver Drive, Dulles, VA 20166, USA

Berg is an imprint of Oxford International Publishers Ltd.

Library of Congress Cataloging-in-Publication Data

A catalogue record for this book is available from the Library of Congress.

British Library Cataloguing-in-Publication Data

A catalogue record for this book is available from the British Library.

ISBN 1 85973 131 7 (Cloth)
1 85973 156 2 (Paper)

Typeset by JS Typesetting, Wellingborough, Northants.
Printed in the United Kingdom by WBC Book Manufacturers, Bridgend,
Mid Glamorgan.

Contents

Acknowledgements

The chapters in this volume are revised versions of papers originally given for the annual conference of the Association for the Study of Modern Italy held on 20/21 November 1992 in London. I would like to thank the assistance of the executive committee of the Association for the Study of Modern Italy. I would also like to thank Dr Francesco Villari, the former Director of the Italian Cultural Institute in London, and the staff of the Institute, for hosting the conference on 20 November 1992. They provided an excellent venue and a memorable supper. Dr John Foot of Churchill College, Cambridge and Dr John Dickie of University College London were very helpful in providing some valuable information. Finally, Mrs Shirley Angel of the secretarial office of the Department of Social Policy and Politics, Goldsmiths College kindly assisted in the preparation of this manuscript. It goes without saying that the editorial product is solely my own responsibility.

Carl Levy
Goldsmiths College
University of London

Notes on Contributors

Percy Allum is Professor of Italian Politics at the University of Reading. Among his publications are *Politics and Society in Postwar Naples* (1973); *Italy: Republic without Government?* (1973); *Italia tra crisi ed emergenza* (1979); (with I. Diamanti), *'50/'80. Vent'anni* (1986); *Democrazia reale. Stato e società civile nell'Europa occidentale* (1991); *State and Society in Western Europe* (1995).

Anna Cento Bull is Professor in Italian Studies at the University of Bath. Her research interests focus on small firms and industrial districts, the process of industrialization in Italy, and more recently, the Northern League. Publications include: (with P. Corner), *From Peasant to Entrepreneur. The Survival of the Family Economy in Italy* and (with M. Pitt and J. Szarka), *Entreprenurail Textile Communities. A Comparative Study of Small Textile and Clothing Firms* (1993).

Martin Clark is Reader in Politics at the University of Edinburgh. Author of *Antonio Gramsci and the Revolution that Failed* (1977), and of *Modern Italy 1871–1982* (1985; 2nd edn 1996), he has contributed two chapters on Sardinia since 1847 to Vol. 4 of M. Guidetti (ed.), *Storia dei Sardi e della Sardegna* (1990), and has edited the writings of Mazzini and Cattaneo on Sardinia (1994).

John A. Davis currently holds the Emiliana Pasca Noether Chair in Modern Italian History at the University of Connecticut. Author and editor of several publications, including *Conflict and Control. Law and Order in Nineteenth-Century Italy* (1988), he is writing a book on 'The Crisis of the *Ancien Regime* in Southern Italy', and preparing the volume on Italy in the Oxford History of Europe. He is also co-editor of *The Journal of Modern Italian Studies*.

Ilvo Diamanti teaches political sociology at the Universities of Padua and Urbino; and is a member of the Editorial Board for the review, *Il Progetto*. Amongst his publications are (with P. Allum), *'50/'80. Vent'anni* (1986); (with A. Parisi), *Elezioni a Trieste* (1991); (with G. Riccamboni), *La parabola del voto bianco* (1992); *La Lega. Geografia, storia e sociologia di un nuovo soggetto politico* (1993); and (with

R. Mannheimer) (eds), *Milano a Roma. Guida all' Italia elettorate del 1994* (1994).

Joseph Farrell teaches Italian Studies at the University of Strathclyde in Glasgow. He writes regularly on Italian politics for the *Scotsman* newspaper, and has done several radio documentaries on the same subject for the BBC. He is also a regular contributor to other news and current affairs programmes. He has translated several novels and plays, and has just completed a study of the Sicilian writer Leonardo Sciascia for Edinburgh University Press (1995).

David Hine is an Official Student (Tutorial Fellow) and Senior Censor at Christ Church College, Oxford. He is the author of numerous articles and chapters on Italian politics and government, and *Governing Italy. The Politics of Bargained Pluralism* (1993).

Anna Laura Lepschy is Professor of Italian at University College London. Among her publications are (with G. Lepschy), *The Italian Language Today* (1977); *Tintoretto Observed* (1983); *Narrativa e teatro fra due secoli* (1984).

Giulio Lepschy is Professor of Italian at the University of Reading and Fellow of the British Academy. Among his publications are *A Survey of Structural Linguistics* (1970); *Saggi di linguistica italiana* (1978); *Nuovi saggi di linguistica italiana* (1989). He is an editor of a *History of Linguistics* (1990 and 1993).

Carl Levy is Lecturer in European Politics at Goldsmiths College, University of London. He is the author of many articles and chapters on comparative European labour movements, the history of European social and political thought, the politics of the higher educated and Italian anarchism. He is editor of *Socialism and the Intelligentsia 1870–1914* (1987) and joint editors of *The Future of Europe* (1996). He is completing for Berg, *Gramsci and the Anarchists* and for Polity, *Gramsci*.

Adrian Lyttelton is Professor of Contemporary European History at the University of Pisa. From 1979 to 1990 he was Professor of History at the John Hopkins Centre in Bologna. His publications include *The Seizure of Power: Fascism in Italy 1919–1929* (1973; 2nd edn 1988); (ed.), *Italian Fascisms* (1983); and numerous other chapters on the political and social history of modern Italy.

Miriam Voghera obtained a degree in Philosophy of Language at the University of Rome and a Ph.D. in Italian Linguistics at the University of Reading. Among her publications are (with A.M. Thornton), *Come dire. Storia, grammatiche e usi della lingua italiana* (1985); *Sintassi e intonazione dell'italiano parlato* (1992); (and with T. De Mauro *et al.*), *Lessico di frequenza dell'italiano parlato* (1993).

List of Abbreviations

ALL DEM	Democratic Alliance
AN	National Alliance
CCD	Christian Democratic Centre
DC	Christian Democrats
DN	National Right
DP	Proletarian Democrats
FI	Fonza Italia (Berlusconi)
LA RETE	The Network
MSI	Italian Social Movement (neo-Fascists)
PCI	Italian Communist Party (later PDS)
PDIUM	Italian Democratic Party of Monarchist Unity
PDS	Democratic Party of the Left (previously PCI)
PDUP	Democratic Party of Proletarian Unity
PLI	Italian Liberal Party
PNM	National Monarchist Party
PPI	Italian Popular Party
PRC	Party of Communist Refoundation
PRI	Italian Republican Party
PRS	Sardinian Radical Party
PSd'AZ	Sardinian Party of Action
PSDI	Italian Social Democrat Party
PSI	Italian Socialist Party
PSIUP	Italian Socialist Party of Proletarian Unity
VERDI	Greens.

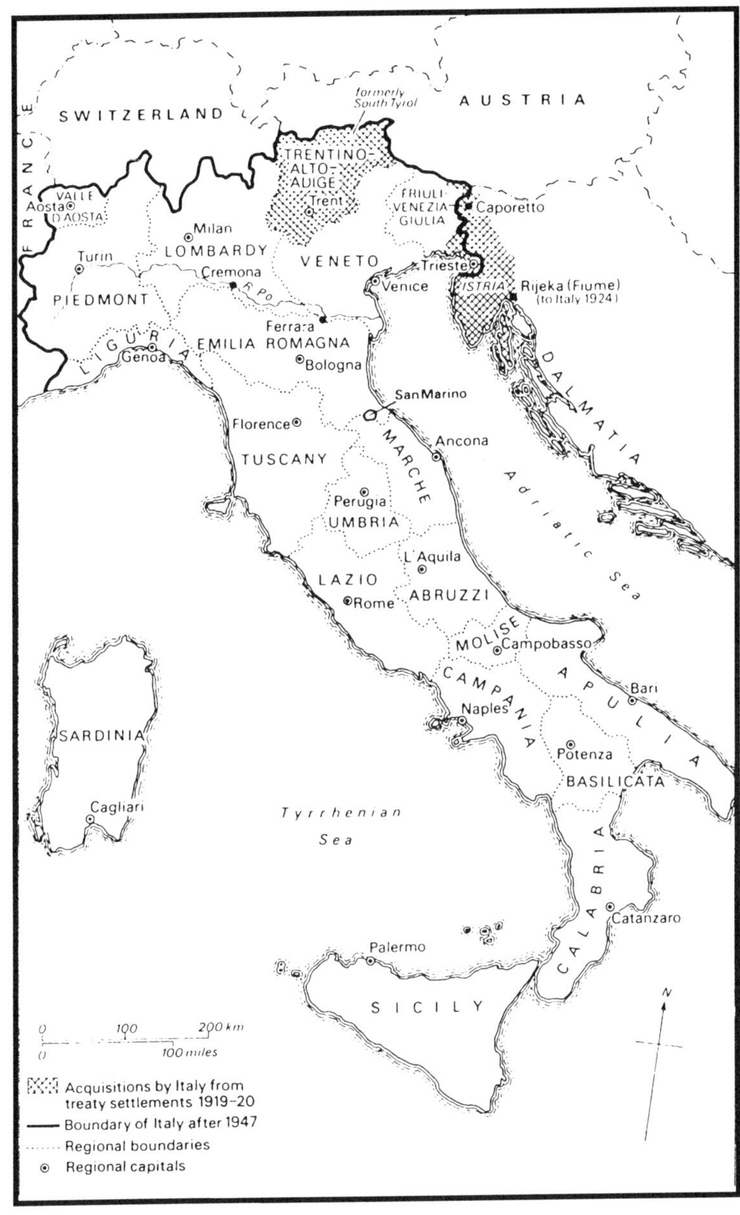

Regional Italy since 1919 (adapted from C. Duggan, *A Concise History of Italy*, Cambridge, 1994, p. 197)

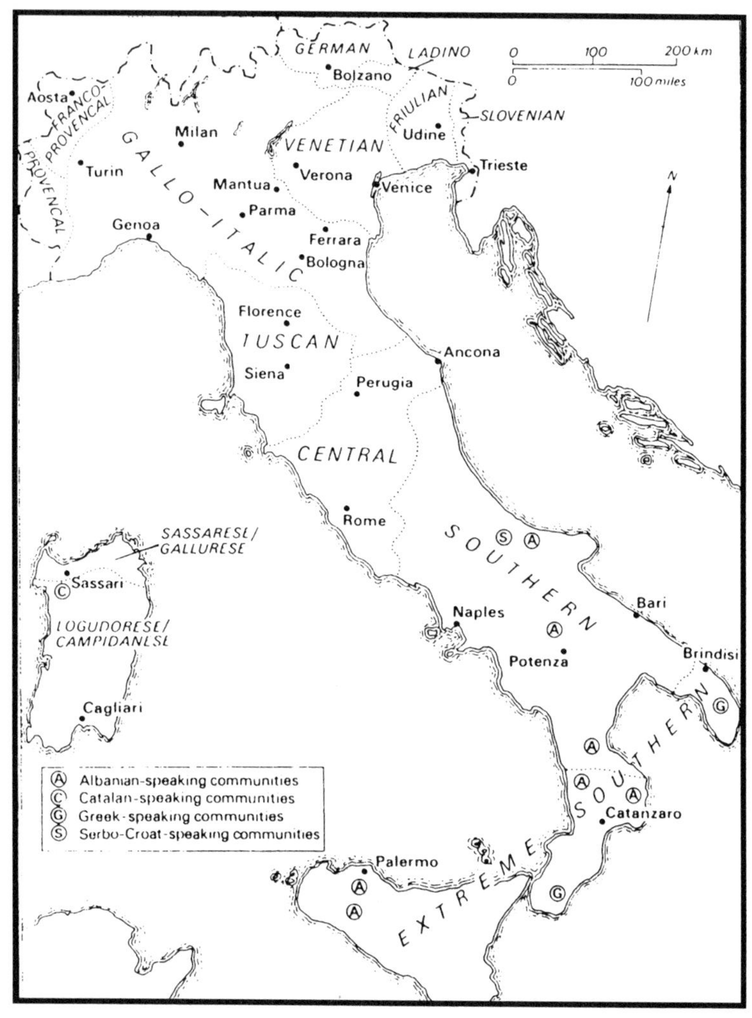

The Dialects and Languages of Italy (adapted from C. Duggan, *A Concise History of Italy*, Cambridge, 1994, p. 29)

—1—

Introduction: Italian Regionalism in Context

Carl Levy

The importance of regionalism for the history of modern Italy seems obvious to even the most casual observer of her politics and culture. But the real nature and implications of regional identity, and the politics and government of regionalism, are far from clear. The intention of this book is to clarify this ill-defined field by examining in Part I – History: The Construction of Regional Identities – how regional identities have been constructed in Italy from the nineteenth century to the present. In Part II, contributors to this book examine how regional government has functioned in the Italian Republic and the nature of political regionalism in the 1980s and 1990s – Regionalism in the Italian Republic: Centre and Periphery under Strain. The main themes of this book are therefore the political and cultural processes involved in the formation of regional identity and the more mundane governmental, political and economic constraints which have shaped this process since the *Risorgimento*.

Regionalism has been a newsworthy item in Italy in the 1980s and 1990s. One has only to look at the rapid transformations in Italian politics since 1989. The establishment of the Berlusconi government in May 1994 and its rapid replacement at Christmas by a government of technicians is to a great extent explained by the activities of the Northern League in the 1980s and early 1990s. Berlusconi came to power in the aftermath of the *Tangentopoli* and *Mafia* scandals which discredited the Christian Democrats, the Socialists and the smaller lay parties. Meanwhile, the end of the Cold War and the collapse of the socialist bloc transformed the Communist Party into two new parties: the PDS (*Partito Democratico della Sinistra*), the larger reformist party, and *Rifondazione Comunista*, a smaller party composed of Leninists and remnants of the New Left. The newly installed hybrid first-past-the-post and proportional representation electoral system set the seal on the older party system. The short-lived Berlusconi administration brought to power the most right-wing government in Italian post-war history. It was composed of two regionally based parties: the populist regionalist Northern League and the centralist, but largely southern supported, *Alleanza Nazionale* (composed of the neo-fascist *Movimento Sociale Italiano* and largely southern remnants of the Christian Democrats and their centrist allies), as well as Berlusconi's curious *Forza Italia*. Using the resources of Fininvest, Berlusconi carried out a media blitz and turned his infant movement into a one-man catch-all party of the middle classes and of a significant proportion of the youth vote (Bellu & Bonsanti 1993; Diamanti & Mannheimer 1994; Lyttelton 1994; Gundle & Parker 1995).

Berlusconi's programme, endorsed by the Northern League, seemed to promise an Italian version of Thatcherism, and even aspects of the right-wing corporatism of the *Movimento Sociale Italiano* were publicly jettisoned by Gianfranco Fini, the youthful leader of the *Alleanza Nazionale* (Ignazi 1994; Valentini 1994). After the decisive victory of Berlusconi's coalition in the spring elections, it was thought by many observers that he would engage in a Thatcherite programme of privatization, deregulation and welfare cuts. However, his government rapidly collapsed due to the unresolved problems of corruption and conflicts of interest that led to disputes with the President over constitutional issues and the judiciary investigating his business affairs. The mass mobilization of the trade unions against aspects of his pension reforms, and the notice that he was under judicial investigation, undermined Berlusconi's government. But it was the Northern League which finally deserted his coalition in a vote of no confidence and destroyed his government. The Northern League had undermined the hegemony of the Christian Democrats in their northern bastions of Lombardy and the Veneto, and it was the Northern League which prevented Berlusconi from consolidating a new right-wing coalition. Although, later in this introduction, I shall return to similar points raised in the second half of this book, it is important to emphasize the novelty of a regionalist party setting the Italian political agenda.

But if the little-expected 'Northern Problem' helped accelerate the demise of the Christian Democrat-dominated post-war Republic, it was the far better-known Southern Problem (*La Questione Meridionale*) that has been one of the chief areas of concern for foreign and Italian observers for the past century. Indeed the Southern Problem had been exacerbated by the combined effects of the deep recession of the early 1990s and the liberalization of the Italian economy. Liberalization and privatization have resulted in the gradual termination of subsidies to state industry in the South, a drive to reform a welfare state that has used invalidity pensions in the South to disguise long-term unemployment, and the winding up of the Fund for the South (Furlong

1994: 231–52). New threats were also posed by organized crime in Naples (the *Camorra*), Calabria (*'ndrangheta*), Apulia (*Sacra Corona Unita*) and Sicily (the *Mafia* or the *Cosa Nostra*) (Bevilacqua 1993: 123–36; Gambetta 1993; Lupo 1993).

Although, as John Davis shows in his chapter, the nature of the Southern Problem has been distorted by social scientists and historians generally, and in a different context, advocates of the Northern League, the gap in economic performance between North and South remained. If the average GDP in the European Community in 1991 equalled 100, the GDP of Northern and Central Italy was 122, that of the South 68.9. Indeed, Northern and Central Italy had a higher per capita GDP than Germany (113.8), France (108.9) and the UK (106.3). In the same year, if the South received 53 per cent of the capital transfers from the Italian state, it only paid 20 per cent of the national direct tax revenues, 29 per cent of all indirect revenues, and 16 per cent of national social security contributions. Finally, in 1991 unemployment stood at over 15 per cent in Sicily, Calabria, Basilicata, Campania and Molise. In most of Piedmont, Lombardy, Emilia-Romagna and the Veneto it was below 5 per cent and in the rest of the North generally between 5 per cent and 10 per cent (Graham 1994; also see Wolleb & Wolleb 1990; Boccella 1994).

These dismal facts however are not surprising. The Southern Problem has been discussed since the late nineteenth century, but no one in the early or even mid-1980s would have predicted that by the late 1980s and early 1990s a major movement claiming Northern identity as its distinguishing characteristic would be undermining the bastions of Christian Democrat and Socialist power. Indeed, in the introduction to his study of the Northern League, Ilvo Diamanti, who with Percy Allum, contributes a chapter in this volume, rather sheepishly admitted that he missed the first stirrings of this mass movement in own Venetian backyard (Diamanti 1993: viii).

In the first section of this volume, the authors examine to what extent regional or local identities have affected the formation of the Italian nation-state. Journalistic discussion concerning the rise of the Northern League has contained an unstated assumption that a latent Lombard or Venetian regional identity was an unproblematic given. While historians argue that since the Italian nation-state was a relatively recent development, arising from the fortuitous combination of European diplomacy, Piedmontese initiative and nationalist conspiracy, older varieties of vibrant localistic or regional identities were suppressed but never completely eradicated (Duggan 1994). The author of an interesting account of the invention of the Italian, Giulio Bollati (1983), claimed in an interview in 1994 (Martinat 1994) that a nationally based

Italian culture had never really developed until the economic miracles of the 1960s and 1980s started to homogenize the populations of Italy (also see Ginsborg 1990). The precarious settlement of Liberal post-*Risorgimento* Italy had been placed under strain by the shocks of the First World War. The Fascist regime had left Italy in 1945 divided between a North radicalized by civil war and the Resistance and an Allied-occupied monarchist and largely conservative South. Although Bollati did not believe that regional tensions would tear Italy apart, he did stress that national unity was still a rather fragile plant.

A variation on this argument could be also employed to explain why the Christian Democrat-dominated party system collapsed. This anti-communist but welfare-oriented coalition, it could be argued, never produced a national civic culture (Cartocci 1994). It is certainly true that the Christian Democrats were *de facto* a coalition of regionally based political bosses (Leonardi & Wertman 1989; Franzina 1994: 139–40; Allum and Diamanti's chapter in this volume). Although the PCI was based on different ideological premises and always sought to represent the working classes of the 'industrial triangle', it too was in some respects an even more regionally dependent party of the red subcultural centre (Mannheimer & Sani 1987; Hellman 1988; Caciagli 1993; McCarthy 1993). Furthermore, as David Hine argues in his chapter, the increased importance of regionalism in the late 1980s and early 1990s, seemed to be linked (at least temporarily) to the fact that the collapse of the 'First Republic's' party system had mutated ideological cleavages so that political representation might be mediated through regionally specific political parties (see also Calise 1993; Sani 1993).

The problem with this plausible composite genealogy of regionalism, is that the historical evidence shows that regionalist parties (as opposed to regionally rooted parties with national and catch-all pretensions) have had only fleeting importance in the history of modern Italy. Regional government was not established in Italy until after the Second World War and except for the special regions, most of Italy did not experience regional government until the 1970s. The highly centralized Napoleonic system of Rome-appointed and -directed provincial prefects was employed by the rulers of Liberal Italy as their eyes and ears and to mediate between municipal and provincial interests and, at times, to promote strictly limited self-government. Parliamentary deputies and the mayors of larger cities also acted as mediators between local interests and Rome (Romanelli 1988; Duggan 1994: 139–41). Fascism and the Republic did not greatly alter this political arrangement.

Adrian Lyttelton asks the obvious question in his chapter: why did regionalism fail to sustain itself in post-*Risorgimento* Italy? Why in a new nation-state composed of a collection of former city-states and kingdoms, and the inheritor of a variety of legal and political systems imposed by the Habsburgs, the Pope and the Bourbons, did regionalist parties fade so quickly? Why, in a country with a population in which perhaps only 2.5–10 per cent spoke 'standard' Italian and in which the rest of the population spoke not other dialects but closely related and different Romance languages (discussed in their chapter here by Giulio Lepschy, Anna Laura Lepschy and Marian Voghera), did regionalist movements and parties based upon language differences or other cleavages become scarce by the 1890s?

Only in the past decade or so have historians become interested in the question of how Italy was created as a cultural and social entity.While the contributions of Bollati (1983), Lanaro (1988) and Duggan (1994) have charted how new national identities were developed in the nineteenth and twentieth centuries, there have been few in-depth studies of the political fortunes of regionalism in Italy before 1945 (Romanelli 1979; Donzelli 1985, 1989; Riall 1993, 1994: 63–82). Indeed, it is curious how the massive multi-volume history of the regions published by Einaudi only fitfully addresses this theme. In much of these volumes the region is used to tell the national history from these specific geographical settings.

Adrian Lyttelton, however, examines in some detail the reasons why regionalist politics largely died out in the North and Centre by the 1890s. The key to this problem is, Lyttelton notes, the region as such was not the focus of local identity in the North and Centre. Rather, the small or large city and its surrounding countryside, or the former state, served as the pole around which regionalist politics were organized in the 1860s and 1870s. Attempts by Minghetti and others to create a regionally devolved form of government in the 1860s came to nothing. Cattaneo's dream of a federal Italy seemed to be undermined by the failures of 1848. In the 1860s, federally minded liberals were prepared to endorse centralization to secure the unexpectedly rapid unification of the Italian peninsula. There was also, of course, the other liberal obsession: good and progressive local government. Cavour, for instance, was sympathetic to the demands of the Lombards to keep their own local governmental traditions, but in practice many liberals did like local government dominated directly or indirectly by conservative landlords, smallholders and peasants more concerned with low taxes and less with the creation of a modern local infrastructure.

In other areas of Northern and Central Italy, such as Umbria or Emilia, there was little regional identity. Indeed, municipalism undermined regionalism in the case of Emilia-Romagna when Modena feared that Bologna's claim to be a regional capital would threaten its prestige. In a region such as Tuscany, a distinctive culture of free trade and private enterprise was respected by the new Italian state but the regionally specific Catholic dynastic party faded in importance after 1876. In the more distinctively regional Veneto, only incorporated into Italy in 1866, Catholicism rather than regional differences became the major political cleavage.

Lyttelton argues that the combined effects of the agrarian and industrial revolutions, and the migratory flows which accompanied them, undermined regional identities in the North and Centre by the early twentieth century. The territorially defined red and white subcultures of the Po Valley were populated by migrants, and in any case did not coincide with regional boundaries as such. In the end, the schemes for regional devolution were superseded by other plans to deepen the autonomy of the provinces but at the same time assert their role as the sinews of the newly centralized Italian nation-state (Romanelli 1988; Duggan 1994: 138–41). But centralized government, Lyttelton argues, was always predicated on the idea that the central state was permeable by local élites. From the 1880s onwards, if Church/State and class conflicts became national conflicts rather than regionally specific ingredients of a territorial cleavage, regional patterns of industrialization did reveal that certain regionally based industrial élites (Liguria) were more dependent on state intervention than others (Lombardy and Piedmont). Later the élites of the peasants' leagues of Emilia permeated the Giolittian state. This theme of the permeable state is a constant in the history of modern Italy, as we shall see when we review Hine's discussion of the nature of regional government in the Italian Republic. Certainly it is a theme also present in John Davis's chapter.

If regionalism in the North and Centre was something of a damp squib during the era of Liberal Italy, this is not to argue that regional tensions did not exist. In his chapter, John Davis summarizes the new historical debate surrounding *La Questione Meridonale*. In terms of regional identity Davis notes how it has become increasingly difficult to draw boundaries between North and South. Just as Lyttelton stresses in his chapter the differences within the North and Centre, Davis demonstrates that the cumulative effect of this exciting new historiography is to cast doubt on an entity known as the South. (For a good summary see Donzelli 1990.)

The South did not produce substantial regionalist movements founded on ethno-linguistic cleavages. Martin Clark's chapter on Sardinia demonstrates the weakness of this sort of autonomous movement. In Sicily, although a Sicilian autonomy movement was present during the Liberal era, largely as a reaction to effects of certain economic decisions carried out by Rome, the 1866 revolt in Palermo or the controversy over the *Mafia* in the late nineteenth century were not directly linked to Sicilian separatism (Lupo 1993: 19–66). The revolt in 1866 was tied to the specific problems of Palermo and it should be recalled that with the accession to power of Crispi, Sicily had a native son in Rome (Lupo 1993: 49–51). The *Fasci Siciliani*, the mass social movement of the 1890s, was only separatist in the fevered imagination of Crispi (Duggan 1994: 167). Sicilianism was largely an artificial creation which could never override the clear differences between an eastern Sicily of small landholders and a western Sicily of great estates (Balistreri 1994b: 211).

More generally in the South, many of the intellectuals in the forefront of nationalism and liberalism were centralizers and looked to Rome and the Italian state to solve their problems. The involvement of Southern intellectuals in early-twentieth-century syndicalism (Furiozzi 1992) did not lead to calls for greater autonomy for the South, but praise of the North, with Milan becoming one of their first successful political bases. Southern civil society, they argued, would be modernized through the processes of capitalist industrialization and mass politics pioneered in the North.

Another controversy that Davis discusses, and which will reappear in chapters devoted to regionalism under the Republic, is the extent to which Southern society lacked the appropriate institutions and civil society to support a modern entrepreneurial capitalism. The new Southern historiography challenges the extent to which the *Mezzogiorno* had been burdened with 'pre-modern' institutions. The archetypal economic and social institution of the Southern countryside, the *latifondo*, has now been re-evaluated in a new light. Some scholars now claim that it was a thoroughly rational way of exploiting the resources of the countryside (Petrusewicz 1989). Neither is the protectionist *Blocco Storico* of state-protected *latifondisti* and Northern industrialists credible. On several occasions Davis has shown how factious Southern landowners found little enthusiasm for tariffs. In fact, like much else in the politics and economics of the South between 1870 and 1945, seemingly common interests were cross-cut by other conflicting objectives (Davis 1988: 343–59). If certain commercial interests in the South saw closer ties with Northern capital useful, others believed that Northern capital would displace their position in the economic and political market-places. Davis's carefully balanced survey of the new Southern historiography demonstrates that the idea of a united Southern identity was always a myth, except perhaps in the minds of certain publicists and social scientists from the North *and* the South. Indeed, it was precisely the divisions amongst Southern interest groups that might explain why they were so ineffectual at getting Rome to address the Southern Problem in a more effective way.

There have been a plethora of recent studies devoted to the issue of why a substantial part of the South has never experienced self-sustaining capitalist development. Much of this literature is related to the discussion of industrial districts and their relationship to regional or local governmental facilitation of small and middle-sized entrepreneurship based upon the methods of flexible specialization. This argument is given an historical gloss by Putnam (1993: 121–62; also see Trigilia 1992) who claims that only those areas of Northern and Central Italy which experienced the centuries of communal self-government, of late medieval and Renaissance civic republicanism, have been truly successful in creating the self-supporting economic miracle of the 'Third Italy'. We shall return to this discussion – here I would only like to note how Davis has staked out a new and interesting interpretation that deserves greater research. Comparative studies of nineteenth and twentieth-century entrepreneurs in the North and the South demonstrate that Southern entrepreneurs were more dependent on state and public intervention. But it is perhaps the absence of an orderly civil society in the South, caused in part by the particularly rapid decay of traditional forms of deference and paternalism in the first half of the nineteenth century, that undermined the self-confidence of local autonomous elites and forced them either to seek the protection of the new Italian state (Cassese 1977) or, as others have argued, pay the costly premiums for the commodity of enforced trust peddled by the *Mafia* (Gambetta 1993; Lupo 1993). Therefore areas of the South, it is argued, experienced 'modernization without growth'. Conversely, recent studies of the emergence of modern capitalism in the North stress the role of traditionalist forms of deference and paternalism, particularly evident in the pluri-active rural family, aiding the rise of small, medium and large-scale entrepreneurs, who depended little upon the state and were suspicious of public intervention in the market-place and civil society (Cento Bull & Corner 1993; Lanaro 1993; Duggan 1994: 119). This unusual combination of the traditional and the modern, resonates in the regionalism of the late-twentieth-century North (see Cento Bull's chapter in this volume).

The first section of this book also examines the connections between language, territory and regional identity. It is a commonplace in the literature on regionalism to equate regional identity with a strong ethno-linguistic identity (Petrosino 1991; Melucci & Diani 1992). But to what extent has this been the case in Italy?

Anna Laura Lepschy, Giulio Lepschy and Miriam Voghera address this question by examining linguistic variety in Italy. Except for the peripheral areas (Valle d'Aosta, Trentino-Alto Adige and to some extent Friuli-Venezia Giulia), this has not played a predominant role in Italian regionalism. In Sicily and Sardinia, as we shall see, language and dialect have not been as important for the development of autonomous or separatist movements as one might suppose. But the contributors to this chapter do show that even today Italian is in fact just one language amongst many spoken in Italy (De Mauro 1994). Regional dialects are not offspring of a mother tongue but separate if related Romance languages tied closely to the standard Italian which developed from Tuscan. In this sense this chapter gives something of a fillip to those in the *Lega Lombarda* and *Liga Veneta* who argued that their native tongues were languages not dialects (Leonardi & Kovacs 1993: 61). It may also explain the greater visibility of ethno-linguistic arguments amongst the militants of the *Liga Veneta* (Diamanti 1992). However, it may not explain that much since the languages of the red subcultural areas did not generate strong support for the Leagues there; although it has been argued (Shore 1993) that the very red subculture itself can be classified as a politically determined form of ethnicity.

The authors of this chapter also point to the small but distinctive communities of Greek, Albanian, German, Croat, Slovene, Occitain and Franco-Provençal speakers scattered throughout the peninsula. The connection between French or German-speaking communities and regional identity contains interesting paradoxes. It is worthwhile recalling that in areas where either bilingualism (Valle D'Aosta) or, as the authors of this chapter put it, 'linguistic apartheid' (Trentino-Alto Adige), is in operation, the standardized versions of French or German are quite different from the Franco-Provençal or Bavarian used by speakers in these communities.

Although the use of dialects or closely related Romance languages has fallen in the past twenty years due to the effects of mass media and education, it is still important to remind ourselves that even in 1991 less than half the population used standard Italian regularly with friends and colleagues, and a third used solely their own dialect or language at home (also see De Mauro 1994). The authors of this chapter conclude that Italy is now largely a bilingual country whereas even in the 1960s it had remained effectively multilingual, consisting of speakers of closely related or utterly foreign languages. One effect of the emergence of this much larger group of Italian speakers has been the transformation of written and spoken Italian from the stilted and pompous to new, more spontaneous and colloquial forms. And in their own distinctive ways, both the Leagues and Berlusconi have demonstrated the ability to tailor their message to the linguistic conventions of modern spoken Italian (see Allum & Diamanti; Farrell and Levy in this volume).

Lepschy, Lepschy and Voghera also analyse the shifting objectives of the linguistic policy of the Italian state. Essentially the policy was to stress the centralization and homogenization of language during the Liberal and Fascist periods. The Fascists merely took this policy to extremes by enforcing monolingualism in the ethno-linguistic peripheries, purging foreign words from dictionaries and officially suppressing 'dialects'. All of these efforts were ineffective. Under the Republic the rights of the languages in the ethno-linguistic peripheries were protected, but there was a much more ambiguous response to the dialects and languages of Italy itself, including Sard. It was not until 1991 that the Chamber of Deputies attempted to pass a law which would have allowed the use of languages such as Sard in the classroom. This was not approved by the Senate and it seems unlikely that this question will be reopened in the near future.

The number of Sard speakers has always been controversial, now estimated to range from several hundreds of thousands to over one million. In his chapter, Martin Clark examines the history of Sardinia, the one obvious case where language and an autonomy movement might have fused. Clark argues that over the past 150 years demands for Sardinian autonomy were filtered through the modernization plans of the Kingdom of Piedmont and the various political regimes of the modern Italian nation-state. Autonomy in Sardinia meant three different things. In its first incarnation, Clark argues, autonomy meant resistance to the destruction of an older moral economy which had little sense of an ethno-linguistic political counter-community. The second version of autonomy demanded a slower Sardinian-directed form of modernization. In its third incarnation, autonomy meant quite the reverse, an enthusiastic embrace of all things modern. Clark argues that except for the first version of autonomy, Sardinian advocates of some form of 'home rule' have carefully nurtured their ties with Rome. From the building of railways in the nineteenth century to chemical factories in the twentieth, Sardinian politicians have used autonomy as a form of clientelist politics. The aim was to control the funds originating from Rome, not to dispense with them altogether. From the Sardinian Party of Action in the immediate post-First World War era to the episode of Sard-Fascists in the 1920s, to the largely Christian Democrat-directed politics of the Republic, regional politics, and later regional government, have been a method through which local political élites and Rome could advance each other's political objectives.

The dismal record of post-war modernization is charted in some detail by Clark, but he points out that the role of agitation for the recognition of the Sard language had perhaps only a fleeting effect during the ethnic revival when it was spurred on by intellectuals in the 1960s and 1970s, and is now largely an unimportant factor in Sardinian politics. With the rural unrest and organized kidnappings of the 1960s, 1970s and 1980s, Sardinia witnessed a revival of the first form of autonomy, while the third form – aggressive modernization – merely resulted in disastrous and ecologically damaging attempts at creating a self-sustaining capitalist economy. The traditional pastoral economy, now supported by the European Union, still dominates the island.

It is useful to compare Sardinian and Sicilian regionalist politics (Butera 1981; Finlay *et al.* 1986; Aymard & Giarrizzo 1987), since both islands were granted special regional status in 1948 and, as Clark argues, the Sardinians were granted their autonomy because of the example of the Sicilian dispensation. As I have already noted, regionalism in Sicily was apparent during the Liberal era, and the supporters behind it were a coalition of certain large and medium-sized landholders, elements associated with organized crime and some urban intellectuals. The point to stress is that Sanfedism (the Bourbon and Catholic traditionalist opposition to the new Italian nation-state active on the southern mainland) was never strong here and regionalism was quickly assimilated into Roman politics. Although there was a certain resentment of the Fascist regime's ruthless drive against the *Mafia* (Duggan 1989; Lupo 1993: 147–58), the 1943–8 period is probably the era in which the strongest movement for Sicilian autonomy and independence was evident (Finlay *et al.* 1986: 213–17; Mangiameli 1987).

The collapse of the Fascist regime and the rise of the Communists in the North dismayed the older monarchist liberal élite of Sicily. Elements amongst this élite became sympathetic to the independence movement precisely because they feared the spread of social radicalism to the island. Recent work on the history of the *Mafia* has also shown that it too was an important influence within the military arm of the Sicilian independence movement (EVIS) (Lupo 1993: 161–6). The power of the pre-Fascist élite lay with a distinctive group of *latifondisti*. Unlike Sardinia, as Clark reminds us, Sicily had a large, relatively autonomous élite not so closely bound to Roman politics. In Sardinia the local village-based landed élite was politically inconsequential compared to the urban-based middle-class white-collar workers whose jobs were dependent on Roman patronage. So whereas the Sicilian independence movement was a serious social force, Sardinian nationalism was in fact fairly weak.

To what extent the *Mafia* acted or acts as a unified group remains controversial but it is now largely accepted that the revival of the *Mafia* in Sicily in the post-war period can be traced to this episode of Sicilian separatism (Catanzaro 1992; Lupo 1993: 160–9). Once the Christian Democrats guaranteed that Sicily would get autonomy and the Communists were excluded from national government, the independence movement fractured and disappeared. The *Mafia* distanced itself from the activities of the bandit Giuliano who had been an ally in the Sicilian independence movement, and indeed the Christian Democrats in Rome and Sicily always differentiated between the 'nebulous' culture of *mafiosità*, which they claimed could not be pinned down to a confederation of criminal groups, and banditry which could be wiped out (Finlay *et al.* 1986: 217–20; Lupo 1993: 171–5). Even if the *Mafia* has been an extremely factious entity, all contending *cosche* (clans) wanted a balkanized and weak central government which would allow them to be guarantors of trust.

But the *Mafia* was not averse to the modernization of the island, and it was by no means a mere creature of the great landlords. It benefited from the land reforms of the 1950s and the emergence of various industrialization plans carried out by the regional and central governments. A new class of small landowners became clients of *Mafia* protection, while regional government funds and projects allowed the *Mafia* to become a modern enterprise. Regional government and narco-dollars transformed the Sicilian *Mafia* into a major player in the national and international economy and an influential power in Italian politics (Arlacchi 1983; Gambetta 1993).

I have tried to pinpoint some of the differences found between the Sardinian and Sicilian case. If, as we have seen, both modern Sardinia and Sicily have experienced banditry, Sardinia has never possessed the Sicilian forms of organized crime. However, there are still similarities in the type of relationships maintained with Rome by Sicilian and Sardinian politicians. Both insular groups of leading politicians sought to maintain their privileged roles as dispensers of Roman patronage on their respective islands. In Sicily the Christian Democrats became increasingly entangled with *Mafia* politics. Sicily provided a major base for Andreotti within the factional politics of the Christian Democrats, and with its assurance of virtual continuous government in Rome, factions within the Christian Democrats were essential for the control of political power in the Italian state (Chubb 1982; Finlay *et al.* 1986: 219–20; Centorrino & Hoffmann 1988; Bevilacqua 1993: 123–34; Duggan 1994: 259–61, 269, 276–9). The *Mafia* guaranteed votes to the Christian Democrats on the island and regional industrial development projects ('cathedrals in the desert') guaranteed patronage for local politicians and money and power for the *Mafia*. The sustained assault on *Mafia* power by the judiciary in the 1980s and early 1990s, the ensuing unprecedented violent counter-attack, followed by the mobilization of Sicilian voters in *La Rete* and the Progressives, undermined and then destroyed the regional power of the Christian Democrats. It is hard to predict what will occur in the next few years, but the assassination of judges and Christian Democrat politicians were messages sent by the various and by no means unified *cosche* of the Sicilian *Mafia* that they would not tolerate a unified effective central state meddling in their business. It is probably the case that the various contentious factions of the *Mafia* do not want to support a new separatism to guarantee their interests; they much prefer a weak Italian state (Catanzaro 1993: 146–9). The challenge for the advocates of greater devolution is to see to what extent greater Sicilian 'home rule', without the sustained mobilization of the anti-*Mafia* movements of the early 1990s, will only result in organized crime regaining the terrain it undoubtedly lost as Christian Democratic hegemony unravelled. But even as the Christian Democrats collapsed, regionally based parties have not been able to replace them. Neither the Sardinian nationalists nor the Sicilian *La Rete* could withstand the successful sweep by Berlusconi's *Forza Italia* in 1994. The need in the minds of Sardinian and Sicilian voters to remain closely aligned with the most powerful forces in Rome still held sway even after the collapse of the party system of the 'First Republic' (Allum 1994; Diamanti 1994b).

In the second section of this book – Regionalism in the Italian Republic: Centre and Periphery Under Strain – the contributors examine in detail the role of regionalism and regionalist politics during the Republic. There is naturally a danger in dealing with subjects that are in rapid transition, but here I would like to cover three issues: first, the nature of regional government in Italy during the past two decades and second, a review of the vast literature on the leagues in light of the events in the early and mid-1990s. Finally, I make some concluding remarks about Northern intolerance and Southern identity, which I argue is perhaps one of the most important political challenges confronting the Italian Republic.

In his chapter, David Hine analyses the shape and features of regional government in Italy. Five special regional governments were created in the immediate post-war era to defuse separatist and/or ethno-linguistic tensions: Sardinia, Sicily, Valle d'Aosta, Trentino-Alto Adige and Friuli-Venezia Giulia (although the last region mentioned did not come into operation until 1964, after post-war controversies with Yugoslavia were settled). The remaining fifteen regions became a reality in 1970, but only became viable institutions in the late 1970s and 1980s.

David Hine argues that the real exercise of power by regional governments is limited (also see Putnam 1993; Voci 1994). From being a tool of the half-hearted indicative planning of the 1960s and 1970s, the regions acquired willy-nilly the potential for greater control of grass-roots urban and industrial planning, the ability to shape local tourism and protect the environment, and were delegated responsibilities from Rome for administering planning for the National Health Service, as well as transport and agricultural policies. If the devolution of powers to the regions and the establishment of the Permanent Committee of the Regions means these relatively new institutions still does not give them the equivalent clout of the state governments in the USA or the *Länder* in Germany, the cumulative effects of these changes have propelled a highly centralized form of government towards a form of regionalism which may become increasingly federalist (Pitruzella 1994).

One severe limit to this rosy scenario, however, is that even if the regions are now accepted as a permanent part of the Italian system of government by electors and politicians alike, Hine demonstrates that regionalism has always lived in that symbiotic relationship with the central state we had cause to note in the Sardinian and Sicilian cases. Furthermore, the administration of the regions has suffered because of reliance upon the clientelistic procedures of national party politics to staff regional government (Putnam 1993: 49–50). In addition, without more substantial sources of autonomous revenue, elections to the regional councils will be seen as a type of bargaining between local élites and Rome. As Hine shows, even if regional government may become more stable through the reforms of regional system of elections and regional government formation, regional politicians may have to remain 'political entrepreneurs' (Hine 1993a: 260) in order to drum up resources from the centre. Therefore, the limits of the autonomous legitimacy of regional government are not only few independent sources of revenue and the lack of linkage between revenue expenditure by regional government and regional electors, but the widespread belief by voters that regional elections are mere dress rehearsals for the real battles fought in Rome. The proposed reforms of regional government's fiscal powers are still too unclear to argue confidently that the new procedures for the selection of regional representatives and the formation of regional government will be enough to increase their legitimacy in the eyes of the electorate. Indeed, the success of the Northern League in the early 1990s, may have confirmed a general suspicion that even in a movement which celebrated devolution and federalism, local and regional politics were merely a stepping-stone to power-sharing in Rome.

Hine analyses the proposals for regional reform put forward in the early and mid-1990s in detail, while Farrell and Levy discuss suggested changes by the Northern League and certain ministers in the short-lived

Berlusconi government. These boil down to types of fiscal federalism which give either regional or city governments greater tax-raising powers. One of the central problems, however, for the regionally based leagues was that local or urban identity may still be stronger than a regional focus.

In certain cases such as Basilicata, regional identity was the product of regional government itself (Leonardi *et al.* 1987a: 71), and its economy has been at the mercy of the misused government funds given to the region after the earthquake of 1980 and by the assistance of Rome in getting Fiat to site its most modern automobile factory in Melfi (Sinisi 1994). Two of the authors in the volume in the Einaudi history of the regions devoted to Apulia address in separate chapters the same theme of weak identity (Masella 1987; Salvemini 1987). Indeed, the peasant of the Salentino was incomprehensible to the inhabitant of Bari or Foggia (Salvemini 1994: 196). Apulia was always dependent on the central state in order to build and maintain the vital aqueducts and assist in land reclamation, while in the post-war era it was one of the chief recipients of agricultural and industrial aid from the Fund for the South (Salvemini 1994: 197–200). Calabria, too, did not have a strong regional identity, and the major struggle at the beginning of regional government was not over greater powers demanded by a regionally conscious electorate but over which city would be the regional capital and get the central government funds and jobs for a new regional bureaucracy. The famous revolt of Reggio Calabria in 1970–1, graphically retold by James Walston (1988: 198–214), exposes how the pressures of clientelist politics, organized crime and neo-fascism in Reggio Calabria were brought into play during this struggle with its rivals Cosenza and Catanzaro (also see Bevilacqua 1994). Elsewhere on the southern mainland, Abruzzo has had a weak regional identity because, whereas parts of the region can economically be considered as an extension of the 'Third Italy', on the whole the local economy is very dependent upon transfer payments from Rome and extra-regional economic forces (Mazzonis 1994). On the other hand, Molise gained its regional institutions only in 1963 through a movement of the local intelligentsia. Whereas Molise had no regional identity until the occupation by the French during the Napoleonic era, since 1963 its regional identity has grown (Martelli 1994). But the regional identity of Campania has always been overladen by older historical memories. Under the Bourbons the area had been divided into three zones (Terra del Lavoro, Principato Ulteriore and Principato Citeriore), but throughout its history and most certainly during the Republic, Naples has overwhelmed any regionally specific identity (Galasso 1994).

In other regions identity may be in flux. Gibelli (1994) argues that

Ligurian identity is declining as its economy is affected by deindustrialization. With the port of Genoa in crisis and the heavy industry of its hinterland undermined by privatization, Ligurian identity may be swallowed up by its dynamic neighbours. In the future the economic and social importance of Provence in France, Piedmont (but this region too may be threatened by deindustrialization (Jocteau 1994)), Lombardy, Emilia and Tuscany might undermine Liguria's *raison d'être* (Gibelli 1994). Umbrian regional identity, too, is challenged by, as Lyttelton mentions in his chapter here, the lack of an historic past and the present dynamism of its neighbours, Tuscany and Lazio (Covino 1994). Until the last twenty-five years, it appeared that Lazio itself would be swallowed up by Rome, but perhaps with the rise of provincial centres a local balance will foster a stronger regional identification in the future (Gurreri 1994).

Even in the ethno-linguistic peripheries the identity of local populations with regional government is far from straightforward. In Friuli-Venezia Giulia, the Friulian language and culture has generated local electoral lists which joined with the leagues, but the city of Trieste has been a case in itself. Italophone Istrian refugees from Yugoslavia and a Slovene minority have heightened the importance of the far right. In Trieste, the fear that Italian identity could be questioned has meant that the neo-fascists always produced a respectable electoral showing. Indeed, there has always been a tension between provincial Friuli and Trieste. Whilst Friuli has had a strong localist political culture, Trieste, even with its linkage to a tradition of *Mitteleuropa*, has always depended on the Italian state (Flores 1994). Valle d'Aosta was given special regional status to prevent French annexation, but since 1948 internal migration and urbanization has undermined its francophone culture. Although Valle d'Aosta as a special region has more autonomy than the ordinary regions, the collapse of Alpine agriculture means that this region has been heavily dependent on the Italian government to help promote tourism and fund its public tertiary sector (Cuaz 1994). In Trentino-Alto Adige, because of the Italian/German linguistic cleavage, this special region has been effectively ruled by two provinces. The Italian speakers tend to be strongly supportive of the central state; German speakers autonomists. However, in this setting of intensely localistic cultures, the provincial governments can sometimes ride roughshod over local authorities and the rights of the other linguistic group, the Ladino speakers, can be overlooked (Coppola 1994).

This brief survey of the nature of regional identity in Italy shows that certain regions may be suffering from an identity crisis while others have never overcome deeply etched historical local identities that weakened regional identity in the first place. As a result of this, regional government reform, Trigilia (1991) argues (and this is a point also endorsed by Hine), might benefit not from acquiring more tasks but through the paring down to those appropriate duties best carried out at this level of government. But even in the model red-belt regional governments such as Emilia-Romagna and Tuscany, a light-touch management and coordination of local and municipal government on the one hand, and local and regional interests groups on the other, is far from easily accomplished (Trigilia 1986: 316–80; Trigilia 1991; also see Nava 1994). Even after over twenty years of regional government and over a decade of League politics, municipal loyalties remain, as Lyttelton noted for the nineteenth century, more significant than putative regional ties. And as Farrell and Levy argue here, it may be that greater powers to municipalities and cities could be a more effective long-range form of devolution (Rotelli 1993: 142–7; Voci 1994: 93–9).

To what extent has the European Union created the scope for the deepening of regional government in Italy? With the importance of the region emphasized through the policy of cohesion and the establishment of the consultative Committee of the Regions in the Treaty on European Union, it would seem natural to assume that Italian regions might use Brussels as an ally to deepen their powers (Battini 1994). However, in general the powers of the regions, although increased since the 1980s, have been limited to consultative meetings between the government in Rome and representatives of the regions. More significantly, the presidents of the regions do take part in cabinet meetings when important decisions adopted by the EU Council or Commission are discussed. At these meetings the presidents are allowed to voice their non-binding opinions (Grottanelli de Santi 1992: 188). Finally, the special statute regions (Valle d'Aosta, Trentino-Alto Adige, Friuli-Venezia Giulia, Sardinia and Sicily) have a wider latitude in implementing European Union decisions than do the other ordinary regions.

However, if we turn from constitutional theory to the implementation of European Union policies, the situation is far from satisfactory. It was only through the pressure of the European Community's regional aid programmes, known as Community Support Frameworks (CSFs), that properly targeted developmental plans underwritten by regional and national officials in the South were actually carried out (Leonardi 1992: 234–6). In Sicily, for instance, the implementation of CSFs at the beginning of the 1990s 'represented the first time that regional planning was seriously undertaken in the South as an exercise in bringing into line budgetary allocations, government programmes, and administrative efficiency' (Leonardi 1992: 234). Earlier the regions began to develop effective links with Brussels in the late 1980s through their implementation of the Integrated Mediterranean Programmes (IMPs).

But the IMPs required a consistent policy of regional planning by regional governments in order to spend allocated funds, and revealed the wide variance in regional governments' experience in planning and managerial efficiency (Leonardi 1992: 235).

It may be the case that regional government and administration has attracted a more pragmatic and policy-making type of politician and administrator, but performance has varied widely (Putnam *et al.* 1985; Leonardi *et al.* 1987a; Leonardi, *et al.* 1987b; Nanetti 1988; Leonardi & Nanetti 1990; Leonardi 1992; Leonardi & Nanetti 1994). Putnam (1993: 63–82) has measured the effectiveness of regional governments by checking how far they have delivered services to citizens. The checklist included cabinet stability (vital for long-term policy formulation and implementation), the delivery of information services, the maintenance of day care centres and family clinics, industrial policy, effective expenditure of agricultural and health budgets, the building of social housing and last, but not least, bureaucratic responsiveness. Even if this last crucial benchmark is marred by clientelism and a high degree of incompetence in the eyes of community leaders in the North, nevertheless certain regions in the South (Calabria, Molise and Campania) consistently come out on the bottom in all the criteria listed above, while Emilia-Romagna, Tuscany and Umbria scored the highest results. (It should be added that the implementation of IMPs demonstrated a similar division of regions' managerial capacities: regions such as Umbria, Emilia-Romagna, Tuscany, Veneto, Friuli-Venezia Giulia, the Marche and Lazio which had had experience in regional planning had no difficulty implementing the IMPs; whereas regions such as Sicily, Campania and Calabria, with little or no experience in planning and interregional cooperation, ran into severe problems (Leonardi 1992: 235).)

While Italian public opinion has grown to be supportive of regional government and believes that even with all its failures and incompetence it is better than Roman government, nevertheless many grave difficulties accompany any move in the direction of greater regional devolution or outright federalism. Fiscal federalism might merely sharpen the noticeable differences in the nature and performance of regional governments and increase tensions between the wealthy northern regions and the poorer South in much the same manner that is already present between the richer and poorer *Länder* in the well-developed German version of federalism (Jeffrey & Savigear 1991; Sturm 1992; Harvie 1994). In Italy the poorer regions are dependent on the redistribution of resources from the central government and therefore have sought a closer and cosier relationship with Rome; the northern and central regions have increasingly sought greater independence to pursue their local projects. A future federal Italy might merely fan the general resentment of the South found in the North. It had also been suggested by the Northern League that regions be amalgamated into three more efficient macro-regions (Padania, Etruria and Sud). Farrell and Levy go into some detail about these efforts, however a Fondazione Agnelli report has suggested a consolidation into twelve larger regions would be a more realistic alternative (Balistreri 1994: 221). However the boundaries of larger regions might be drawn, as Hine notes, regionally specific parties such as the Northern League or for that matter the centralist *Alleanza Nazionale*, could intentionally or unintentionally use a federal system to undermine the very legitimacy of the central state itself if adequate checks and balances were not developed. This may, however, be of little immediate importance: one lesson of the failure of the Northern League in 1994 to burst out of the 'Gothic Line' and affect politics in central or southern Italy, is that a majority of the Italy electorate is still attracted to nationally based parties such as Berlusconi's *Forza Italia* which performed well in Sicily and the North (Allum 1994; Mannheimer 1994).

However, the results of the 1994 elections did not mean that the trend towards regionally based parties in Italy, apparent in the late 1980s and early 1990s, had been completely checked. The very collapse of the Berlusconi government within eight months of its formation was closely related to the persistence of new forms of territorially based politics. Not only was the Northern League a disruptive coalition partner,the success of the *Alleanza Nazionale* in the South was linked to the fears expressed by southern voters that neo-liberals and reformers would undermine the system of subsidies from Rome which certain parts of the South needed to survive (Ignazi 1994). Moreover, the Left also did well in parts of the South, and this too was related to its endorsement of retaining parts of the Italian Keynesian state (Allum 1994; Diamanti 1994b). The net effect of these pressures undermined the policies of neo-liberalism represented by Berlusconi's and Bossi's mutually suspicious parties. This is therefore the appropriate point to turn to the final three chapters of this book which deal with the protagonists of greater regional devolution, the leagues.

The early 1990s saw a boom in studies about the *leghe*. Not only do we have some fine global studies in Italian (Mannheimer 1991; Diamanti 1993, 1994a), we also have a vast range of English-language academic and journalistic analyses of uneven quality.[1] These studies focus on three aspects of the sociology, politics and history of the leagues, namely: the origins and development of the leagues; the ideology and ideologists of the leagues, and the sociology of the leagues' activists and voters.

All three chapters in this volume examine the leagues' Thatcherite neo-liberalism, regionalism and intolerance. Farrell, Levy and Cento Bull show how the Northern League shifted the emphasis it placed on its regionally specific 'ethnic' neo-liberalism – a party which represented the 'Northern work ethic', to denying an essentialist Northern ethno-regionalism, by embracing supporters from all of Italy. In the early 1990s Umberto Bossi stressed the need for an alliance of all producers against a Roman parasitical bureaucracy. Therefore, all three chapters on the leagues stress that not only has its ideology been malleable, but a great deal of league politics have been linked to the wills of charismatic personalities. Allum, Diamanti, Farrell and Levy trace in some detail the histories of the leagues which comprised the Northern League and the reader will quickly note that the history of a distinctive league radicalism is linked to the activities of its leaders and ideologists. One of the limitations of the electoral expansion of the Northern League was precisely when their radicalism clashed with the more moderate viewpoints of their followers. But the relationship between the league rank and file and its electorate is interlocked with controversies over the precise definition of league ideology. To what extent was the league phenomenon merely a flash-in-the-pan protest movement of anti-southern racist Northerners? Was the Northern League merely a prototype anti-tax and anti-big government movement whose voters Berlusconi and future Italian neo-liberals can mobilize to create a nationally based conservative party? Allum, Diamanti, Farrell and Levy assess the evidence, but Cento Bull takes the argument one step further by seeking to locate a specific regional environment for the unique aspects of the leagues' ideology which may not merely be explained by universal trends towards low-tax neo-liberalism.

When Berlusconi formed his government in Spring 1994, it quickly became evident that he would face an impossible task of reconciling the Northern League's federalism and neo-liberalism with the centralist and corporatist features of the *Alleanza Nazionale*. Furthermore, the widespread disquiet voiced by the Left and Centre of the political spectrum over the success of the neo-fascists and their influence in the Berlusconi administration also appeared within the Northern League itself. The leadership of the Northern League could neither tolerate the threat that Berlusconi posed to their electoral support nor the 'Southern' character of the *Alleanza Nazionale*. But this was not merely due to cynical politics or an odd form of anti-fascist racism, which identified neo-fascism with the corporatist South. There seemed to be a genuine fear that Berlusconi and Fini might subvert the constitutional order. And there was a definite suspicion of Berlusconi as a Milanese fat-cat who was foreign to the culture of the 'Deep North' of the industrial periphery of Catholic Lombardy and the Veneto.

In their chapter, Allum and Diamanti argue that the Northern League was first and foremost a movement of fiscal revolt similar to others that have shaken up US and Western European politics in the last twenty years. And it is certainly true that a significant proportion of the League's electorate sought out the slicker message advanced by the executives of *Forza Italia* when it became available. But it still remains to be seen the extent to which the landslide victory for the Right was also a victory for intolerance and/or, in the case of the Northern League vote, a unique form of intolerant regionalism.

The *Alleanza Nazionale* (Ignazi 1994; Valentini 1994) ran its campaign with strong undertones against the *extracomunitari* and as Cento Bull shows in her chapter, the supporters of the Northern League have demonstrated a consistent hostility to immigrants from the South or the Third World. The appointment, in 1994, of the Northern League deputy Irene Pivetti as Speaker of the House of Deputies, a Catholic Integralist who is a known anti-semite, did not bode well for the advocates of tolerance (Leney 1994). It also remains to be seen how respectable the *Alleanza Nazionale* will become even after its formal disassociation with Fascism. But there were also other tendencies present before the Berlusconi government collapsed. Roberto Maroni, the *Leghista* Minister of Interior, sacked the Prefect of Vicenza after he allowed a demonstration of extreme right-wing Naziskins and he also visited Sicily to express his support for Progressive mayors under attack by a rejuvenated *Mafia* (Cavallaro 1994: 12).

Nevertheless, the rising tide of intolerance experienced in Italy during the 1980s and early 1990s was an unavoidable fact of political life. As Italy became a nation of immigration in the 1980s, it was more common to detect manifestations of open racism. The brutal and illegal deportation of Albanian 'boat-people' in 1991 sent a message to the public (Vasta 1993). But as Cento Bull demonstrates in her chapter, it may be that dramatic and exogenous events surrounding the increase of migratory flows from the Third World and Eastern Europe to Italy revealed a less easily discernible indigenous intolerant culture. She argues that there is substantial evidence of a widespread culture of intolerance in the white subcultural industrial districts of Lombardy. Cento Bull therefore not only presents new evidence about the origins of the new intolerance which has enveloped Italian politics in the past decade but also adds a new and disturbing contribution to the vast literature about the nature and dynamics of the industrial districts of the 'Third Italy'.

Elsewhere Cento Bull and Corner (1993: 120–51) have analysed the arguments concerning Italian industrial districts. They summarize those concerned with explaining the reasons for the emergence of the 'Third Italy'.[2] Briefly, these include the decentralization of industrial production as a consequence of trade union-induced higher labour costs in the 'industrial triangle' of the 1970s, the distinctive historical relationship between the pluri-active rural family of these districts and family-oriented entrepreneurship, the roles of artisans and skilled workers from towns and cities in providing the entrepreneurial skills needed to exploit the new technologies which supported flexible specialization, and the effects of Christian Democrat policies in fostering small-scale capitalism through a system of soft loans and fiscal advantages.

Furthermore, real industrial districts are not merely industrialized zones in the countryside, but a tissue of small industries producing for niche markets on the world market, using flexible production to meet the consumer demand for customized products not available through the serial production of Fordism. The entrepreneurs in these industrial districts are therefore not subcontractors but independent producers who rely on highly skilled, well-paid and motivated labour. These industrial districts are to be found in the white and red subcultures of Northeast and Central Italy (Trigilia 1986) and as I have mentioned, Putnam (1993) and Trigilia (1992) have both stressed the beneficent effect of the long-standing civic communities of these areas underwriting entrepreneurial cooperation and user-friendly local government (also see Bagnasco 1977, 1988 and Nanetti 1988). Therefore, the presence of civic communities, of local political cultures which support networks and institutions that are reliant on trust between citizens, creates a virtuous circle that generates greater amounts of trust. This network of trust supports the production of those collective goods – the shared costs for the training of highly motivated and skilled labour, marketing and infrastructural developments – which underpins the successful economies of the 'Third Italy'.

But the evidence that Cento Bull presents in her chapter exposes other less-explored aspects of this culture of trust, at least that present in a former white subcultural district. Her interpretation of recent opinion polls and her own limited survey data show that the culture of trust in the Lombard industrial district is based on sustaining an inward-looking and suspicious entrepreneurial community. Cento Bull demonstrates how long-term native pluri-active Lombard families are at the heart of the industrial districts, how dialect is used between social actors carrying out business, and equally, how these 'natives' comprise the networks of trust that keep cooperation alive between small entrepreneurs. Trust is based on an almost ethno-regionalist cleavage and by the projection of an 'other' by these Lombard speaking entrepreneurs. This 'other' is composed of locally resident Southern civil servants and *extracomunitari* immigrants.

Several questions are raised by the findings of this chapter. To what extent do similar intolerant and parochial attitudes inform the pluri-active entrepreneurial families of the red-belt centre? A recent intervention has argued that a deep sense of localism can be found in the Tuscan Left (Caciagli 1993); and although Ramella (1994) claims it was precisely a red subculture which endorsed localism and regionalism on the one hand, and promoted civic solidarity on the other, which restricted the growth of the leagues in Emilia-Romagna and Tuscany, it was also certainly the case that during the 1980s and early 1990s intolerance was not absent from Emilia-Romagna or Tuscany. But there needs to be more in-depth work in the red subcultural area addressing the same problems which Cento Bull has done for Lombardy. Shore's ethnographical work (1993) could be expanded to include a closer investigation of how the changing role of the formerly Communist cooperatives after the fall of the Berlin Wall will affect this culture of trust. Furthermore, the *Mafia* has infiltrated its money-laundering operations into the local banks of the industrial districts of Emilia-Romagna (Nava 1994: 157–8) and this too must affect the local culture of trust. We also need to have more studies of the growth of intolerance towards *extracomunitari* in this area.

Such research would be an important contribution to our understanding of how localist or regionalist politics will affect the evolution of the Italian party system in the future. But if we return to our previous discussion of the leagues, Allum and Diamanti argue in their chapter that there is the potential for a more radical form of separatism to arise in the core membership of the *Liga Veneta* if they feel betrayed by Bossi's politics. In sum, to what extent will the Northern League be torn between a parochial core membership in the Lombard and Venetian heartlands who feel betrayed by the compromises of national politics, a second group of urban Northern League supporters who are attracted to Berlusconi's or another politician's neo-liberalism, and a third area of potential support by some of the Northern League's former left-of-centre voters for a broad federal Left as an effective alternative to the growth of the 'post'-fascist-dominated *Alleanza Nazionale*?

It is difficult to answer these questions but if the Northern and Southern Problems are linked together, changes in the South may shift the emphasis away from the politics of northern regional identity. The events which led to the collapse of the old regime in the North were spurred on by a judicially inspired cleansing of the élites and the electoral breakthroughs of the Northern League. In the South there was a genuine social and political mobilization in the streets of a substantial minority of the population against the collusion of regional and national politicians with organized crime. However, this 'South', to recall John Davis's chapter, is a flexible concept. Not only did a new culture of civic responsibility seem to be emerging in these years, but over a longer period the self-sustaining economic development of the Centre had spilled over to parts of Abruzzo and Molise, so that they can no longer be considered economically as parts of the South (Bevilacqua 1993: 118–20; Boccella 1994: 430). This may mean that solutions to the Southern Problem can be more focused on certain southern regions and this can be accomplished through a national political dialogue. The more nationally orientated political players in 1994 – *Forza Italia* and the PDS – helped dilute the largely regionally specific vote for the *Alleanza Nazionale* (Diamanti 1994b). Indeed the events of 1994–5 suggest that nationally successful political parties still have much life in them. But any further devolution of powers to the regions without a sense of national compact or solidarity would merely reawaken the regionalist politics of the late 1980s and early 1990s which seemed briefly to threaten the very integrity of the Italian state. If the Northern Problem will only be solved when the political economy of Italy and its national system of politics are reshaped, in the South, the creation of public trust in Sicily, Campania, Calabria and Apulia will address some of the ills still associated with the Southern Problem. But much will depend on the extent to which the attempts at the weakening of organized crime will not be reversed and, perhaps, how far vital democratic local and regional government can nurture an emergent if hesitant civic culture in the South.

Notes

1. There is an extraordinary if varied range of studies in English on the Leagues, see Ruzza & Schmidtke 1991–2; Woods 1992; Ruzza & Schmidtke 1993; Gallagher 1993; Leonardi & Kovacs 1993; Pileri *et al.* 1993.
2. For an overview of the vast literature on the Third Italy, see Weiss 1988; Goodman *et al.* 1989; Hirst & Zeitlin 1989; Bianchini 1991; Zamagni 1993: 445–55.

Bibliography

Allum, P. (1994), 'Il Mezzogiorno', in I. Diamanti and R. Mannheimer (eds), *Milano a Roma. Guida all'Italia elettorale del 1994*, Rome, pp.109–16.

Arlacchi, P. (1983), *Mafia, Peasants and Great Estates*, Cambridge.

Aymard, M. and Giarrizzo, G. (eds), (1987), *La Sicilia (Storia d'Italia: Le regioni dall'unità a oggi)*, Turin.

Bagnasco, A. (1977), *Tre Italie. La problematica territoriale dello sviluppo italiano*, Bologna.

—— (1988), *La costituzione sociale del mercato*, Bologna.

Balistreri, G. (1994a), 'Federalismo o regionalismo?', in P. Ginsborg (ed.), *Stato dell'Italia*, Milan, p.221.

—— (1994b), 'Sicilia: la ricerca di una nuova identità', in P. Ginsborg (ed.), *Stato dell'Italia*, Milan, pp.211–15.

Battini, S. (1994), 'L'Influenza dell'integrazione europea', in S. Cassese and C. Franchini (eds), *L'Amministrazione pubblica italiana*, Bologna, pp.143–53.

Bellu, G.M. and Bonsanti, S. (1993), *Il Crollo. Andreotti, Craxi e il loro regime*, Bari.

Bevilacqua, P. (1993), *Breve storia dell'Italia meridionale dall'Ottocento a oggi*, Rome.

—— (1994), 'Calabria: classi dirigenti senza un progetto', in P. Ginsborg (ed.), *Stato dell'Italia*, Milan, pp.205–10.

Bianchini, F. (1991), 'The Third Italy: Model or Myth?', *Ekistics*, 350, Sept./Oct., pp.336–45.

Boccella, N. (1994), 'Mezzogiorno più lontano dal Nord', in P. Ginsborg (ed.), *Stato dell'Italia*, Milan, pp.429–31.

Bollati, G. (1983), *L'Italiano. Il carattere nazionale come storia e come invenzione*, Turin.

Butera, S. (ed.), (1981), *Regionalismo siciliano e problema del Mezzogiorno*, Milan.

Caciagli, M. (1993), 'Tra internazionalismo e localismo: l'area rosso', *Meridiana*, **16**, pp.81–98.

Calise, M. (1993), 'Remaking the Italian party system: How Lijphart got it wrong by saying it right', *West European Politics*, **16**, 4, pp.343–60.

Cartocci, R. (1994), *Fra Lega e Chiesa*, Bologna.

Cassese, S. (1977), *Questione amministrativa e questione meridionale*, Milan.

Catanzaro, R. (1992), *Men of Respect: A Social History of the Sicilian Mafia*, New York.

—— (1993), 'A watershed year for both the Mafia and the State', in S.

Hellman and G. Pasquino (eds), *Italian Politics: A Review*, **8**, London, pp.134–50.

Cavallaro, F. (1994), 'Le bombe della mafia non ci fermano', *Corriere della Sera*, 20 May, p.12.

Centorrino, M. and Hoffmann, A. (eds), (1988), 'La spesa pubblica: il caso della Sicilia', in L. Tamburrino and M. Villari (eds), *Questioni del mezzogiorno: le ipotesi di sviluppo nel dibattio meridionalistico degli anni ottanta*, Rome, pp.73–88.

Cento Bull, A. and Corner, P. (1993), *From Peasant to Entrepreneur. The Survival of the Family Economy in Italy*, Oxford.

Chubb. J. (1982), *A Tale of Two Cities: Patronage, Power and Poverty in Southern Italy*, Cambridge.

Coppola, G. (1994), 'Trentino-Alto Adige: una cultura per difendere la qualità della vita', in P. Ginsborg (ed.), *Stato dell'Italia*, Milan, pp.132–7.

Covino, R. (1994), 'Umbria: uno sviluppo tardivo, ed è subito crisi', in P. Ginsborg (ed.), *Stato dell'Italia*, Milan, pp.168–71.

Cuaz, M. (1994), 'Valle d'Aosta: si puo vivere di solo paesaggio?', in P. Ginsborg (ed.), *Stato dell'Italia*, Milan, pp.120–5.

Davis, J.A. (1988), *Conflict and Control: Law and Order in Nineteenth-Century Italy*, London.

De Mauro, T. (1994), 'Lingua e dialetti', in P. Ginsborg (ed.), *Stato dell'Italia*, Milan, pp.61–6.

Diamanti, I. (1992), 'La mia patria è il Veneto. I valori e la proposta politica delle Leghe', *Polis*, **2**, pp.225–55.

—— (1993), *La Lega. Geografia, storia e sociologia di un nuovo soggetto politico*, Rome.

—— (1994a), 'La Lega', in I. Diamanti and R. Mannheimer (eds), *Milano a Roma. Guida all'Italia elettorale del 1994*, Rome, pp. 53–62.

—— (1994b), 'I Mezzogiorni', in I. Diamanti and R. Mann-heimer (eds), *Milano a Roma. Guida all'Italia elettorate del 1994*, Rome, pp.127–34.

Diamanti, I. and Mannheimer, R. (eds), (1994), *Milano a Roma. Guida all'Italia elettorale del 1994*, Rome.

Donzelli, C. (1985), 'Il concetto storico spaziale di regione: una identificazione controversa', *Passato e Presente*, **9**, Sept.–Dec., pp.30–7.

—— (1989), 'La dimensione regionale e l'Italia contemporanea', in F. Andreucci and A. Pescarolo (eds), *Gli spazi del potere. Aree, regionali, stati: le coordinante territoriali della storia contemporanea*, Florence.

—— (1990), 'Mezzogiorno tra "questione" e purgatorio. Opinione comune, immagine scientifica, strategie di ricerca', *Meridiana*, **9**,

pp.13–53.
Duggan, C. (1989), *Fascism and the Mafia*, New Haven, Conn.
—— (1994), *A Concise History of Italy*, Cambridge.
Finlay, M.I., Smith, D.M. and Duggan, C. (1986), *A History of Sicily*, London.
Flores, M. (1994), 'Friuli-Venezia Giulia: la ricerca del porto perduto', in P. Ginsborg (ed.), *Stato dell'Italia*, Milan, pp.148–51.
Franzina, E. (1994), 'Veneto: una società dinamica al bivio tra globalizzazione e leghismo', in P. Ginsborg (ed.), *Stato dell'Italia*, Milan, pp.138–47.
Furiozzi, G.B. (1992), 'Il meridionalismo dei sindacalisti rivoluzionari', in C. Cingari and S. Fedele (eds), *Il socialismo nel Mezzogiorno d'Italia 1892–1926*, Bari, pp.154–71.
Furlong, P. (1994), *Modern Italy: Representation and Reform*, London.
Galasso, G. (1994), 'Campania: l'eredità della storia', in P. Ginsborg (ed.), *Stato dell'Italia*, Milan, pp.192–5.
Gallagher, T. (1993), 'The Rise of the Regional Leagues in Italy', *Regional Politics and Policy*, **13**, 2, pp.65–87.
Gambetta, D. (1993), *The Sicilian Mafia. The Business of Private Protection*, Cambridge, Mass.
Gibelli, A. (1994), 'Liguria: dopo il declino, l'identità in fratumi', in P. Ginsborg (ed.), *Stato dell'Italia*, Milan, pp.152–6.
Ginsborg, P. (1990), *A History of Contemporary Italy: Society and Politics, 1943–1988*, London.
—— (ed.), (1994), *Stato dell'Italia*, Milan.
Goodman, E., Bamford, J. and Saynor, P. (eds), (1989), *Small Firms and Industrial Districts in Italy*, London.
Graham, R. (1994), 'Elections may not bridge the gap', *Financial Times*, 23 March, p.23.
Grottanelli de Santi, G. (1992), 'The impact of the EC on the Italian form of government', in F. Francioni (ed.), *Italy and EC Membership Evaluated*, London, pp.179–91.
Gundle, S. and Parker, S. (eds), (1995), *The New Italian Republic. From the fall of the Berlin Wall to Berlusconi*, London.
Gurreri, F. (1994), 'Lazio: i tempi lunghi dell'emancipazione dall'Urbe', in P. Ginsborg (ed.), *Stato dell'Italia*, pp.176–81.
Harvie, C. (1994), *The Rise of Regional Europe*, London.
Hellman, S. (1988), *Italian Communism in Transition. The Rise and Fall of the Historic Compromise in Turin, 1975–80*, New York.
Hine, D. (1993a), *Governing Italy. The Politics of Bargained Pluralism*, Oxford.
—— (1993b), 'The New Italian Electoral System', *ASMI Newsletter*, 24, pp.27–34.

Hirst, P. and Zeitlin, J. (eds), (1989), *Reversing Industrial Decline?*, Oxford.

Ignazi, P. (1994), 'Alleanza nazionale', in I. Diamanti and R. Mannheimer (eds), *Milano a Roma. Guida all'Italia elettorale del 1994*, Milan, pp.43–52.

Jeffrey, C. and Savigear, P. (eds), (1991), *German Federalism Today*, Leicester.

Jocteau, G-C. (1994), 'Piedmonte: nelle città-fabbrica lo spettro della deindustrializzazione', in P. Ginsborg (ed.), *Stato dell'Italia*, Milan, pp.116–19.

Lanaro, S. (1988), *L'Italia nuova*, Turin.

—— (1993), 'Le élites settentrionale', in special issue of *Meridiana*, **16**, January, pp.9–40.

Leney, F. (1994), 'Jackboot-in-mouth ails Italy's right', *The Independent*, 24 April, p.8.

Leonardi, R. (1992), 'The Regional Reforms in Italy: From Centralized to Regionalized State', *Regional Politics and Policy*, **2**, 1–2, pp.217–46.

Leonardi, R. and Kovacs, M. (1993), 'The Lega Nord: the Rise of a New Italian Catch-All Party', in S. Hellman and G. Pasquino (eds), *Italian Politics: A Review*, **8**, London, pp.50–65.

Leonardi, R. and Nanetti, R.Y. (eds), (1990), *The Regions and European Integration: The Case of Emilia-Romagna*, London.

—— (eds), (1994), *The Regions and European Integration: The Case of Tuscany*, London.

Leonardi, R., Nanetti, R.Y. and Putnam, R.D. (eds), (1987a), *Il Caso Basilicata*, Bologna.

—— (1987b), 'Italy. Territorial Politics in the Postwar Years: The Case of Regional Reform', *West European Politics*, **10**, 4, pp.88–107.

Leonardi, R. and Wertman, D.A. (1989), *Italian Christian Democracy: The Politics of Dominance*, London.

Lupo, S. (1993), *Storia della mafia dalle origini ai giorni nostri*, Rome.

Lyttelton, A. (1994), 'Italy: The Triumph of TV', *The New York Review of Books*, 11 August, pp.25–9.

McCarthy, P. (1993), 'The Italian Communists Divide – and Do Not Conquer', in G. Pasquino and P. McCarthy (eds), *The End of Post War Politics in Italy. The Landmark 1992 Election*, Boulder, Co., pp.31–49.

Mangiameli, R. (1987), 'La regione in guerra (1943–50)', in M. Aymard and G. Giarrizzo (eds), *La Sicilia (Storia d'Italia: Le Regioni dall'Unità a oggi)*, Turin, pp.485–600.

Mannheimer, R. (1994), 'Forza Italia', in I. Diamanti and R. Mannheimer (eds), *Milano a Roma. Guida all'Italia elettorale del*

1994, Milan, pp.29–43.
—— (ed.), (1991), *La Lega Lombarda*, Milan.
Mannheimer, R. and Sani, G. (1987), *Il mercato elettorale*, Bologna.
Martelli, S. (1994), 'Molise: prudente transizione al nuovo', in P. Ginsborg (ed.), *Stato dell'Italia*, Milan, pp.187–91.
Martinat, G. (1994), 'Italiani prava gente', *La Repubblica*, 21 May, p.25.
Masella, L. (1987), 'La difficile costruzione di una identità (1880–1980)', in L. Masella and B. Salvemini (eds), *La Puglia (Storia d'Italia. Le regioni dell'Unità a oggi)*, Turin, pp.281–438.
Mazzonis, F. (1994), 'Abruzzo: un modello vincente con due nei, clientelismo e provincialismo', in P. Ginsborg (ed.), *Stato dell'Italia*, Milan, pp.182–6.
Melucci, A. and Diani, M. (1992), *Nazioni senza stato*, Milan.
Nanetti, R.Y. (1988), *Growth and Territorial Politics: The Italian Model of Social Capitalism*, London.
Nava, P. (1994), 'Emilia-Romagna: a una svolta la cultura dei servizi', in P. Ginsborg (ed.), *Stato dell'Italia,* Milan, pp.156–9.
Petrosino, D. (1991), *Stati, nazioni, etnie*, Milan.
Petrusewicz, M. (1989), *Latifondo: Economia morale e vita materiale in una periferia dell'Ottocento*, Venice.
Pileri, S., Schmidtke, O. and Ruzza, C. (1993), 'The League and the Crisis of Italian Politics', *Telos*, 96, pp.86–100.
Pitruzzella, G. (1994), 'I poteri locali', in P. Ginsborg (ed), *Stato dell'Italia*, Milan, pp.472–6.
Putnam, R.D., Leonardi, R. and Nanetti, R.Y., (1985), *La pianta e le radici*, Bologna.
Putnam, R.D. (1993), *Making Democracy Work. Civic Traditions in Modern Italy*, Princeton, N.J.
Ramella, F. (1994), 'L'area rossa', in I. Diamanti and R. Mannheimer (eds), *Milano a Roma. Guida all'Italia elettorale del 1994*, Milan, pp.99–108.
Riall, L. (1993), 'Elite Resistance to State Formation: The Case of Italy', in M. Fulbrook (ed.), *National Histories and European History*, London, 1993, pp.46–68.
—— (1994), *The Italian Risorgimento. State, Society and National Unification*, London.
Romanelli, R. (1988), *Il commando impossibile. Stato e società nell'Italia liberale*, Bologna.
—— (1979), 'Il sonno delle regioni', *Quaderni Storici*, 41, pp.778–81.
Rotelli, E. (1993), *Una democrazia per gli italiani*, Milan.
Ruzza, C.E. and Schmidtke, O. (1991–2), 'The Making of the Lombard League', *Telos*, 90, pp.43–56.

—— (1993), 'The Roots of Success of the Lega Lombarda: Mobilization Dynamics and the Media', *West European Politics*, **16**, 2, pp.1–23.

Salvemini, B. (1987), 'Prima della Puglia. Terra di Bari e il sistema regionale in età moderna', in L. Masella and B. Salvemini (eds), *La Puglia (Storia d'Italia: Le Regioni dall'Unità a oggi)*, Turin, pp.5–218.

—— (1994), 'Puglia: vecchi e nuovi equilibri regionali', in P. Ginsborg (ed.), *Stato dell'Italia*, Milan, pp.196–200.

Sani, G. (1993), 'The Anatomy of Change', in G. Pasquino and P. McCarthy (eds), *The End of Post-War Politics in Italy*, Boulder, Co., pp.108–20.

Shore, C. (1993), 'Ethnicity as Revolutionary Strategy: Communist Identity Construction in Italy', in S. MacDonald (ed.), *Inside European Identities*, Oxford, pp.27–53.

Sinisi, A. (1994), 'Basilicata: un laboratorio per il Mezzogiorno del 2000', in P. Ginsborg (ed.), *Stato dell'Italia*, Milan, pp.201–4.

Sturm, R. (1992), 'The Changing Territorial Balance', in G. Smith, W.E. Paterson, P.H. Merkl and S. Padgett (eds), *Developments in German Politics*, Basingstoke, pp.119–36.

Trigilia, C. (1986), *Grandi partiti e piccole imprese*, Bologna.

—— (1991), 'The Paradox of the Region: Economic Regulation and the Representation of Interests', *Economy and Society*, **20**, 3, pp.306–27.

—— (1992), *Sviluppo senza autonomia*, Bologna.

Valentini, C. (1994), 'Alleanza Nazionale: la componente "storica" del Polo delle libertà', in P. Ginsborg (ed.), *Stato dell'Italia*, Milan, pp.677–80.

Vasta, E. (1993), 'Rights and Racism in a New Country of Immigration: The Italian Case', in J. Wrench and J. Solomos (eds), *Racism and Migration in Western Europe*, Oxford, pp.83–98.

Voci, P. (1994), 'Il decentramento amministrativo e le autonomie locali', in S. Cassese and C. Franchini (eds), *L'Amministrazione pubblica italiana. Un profilo*, Bologna, pp.85–99.

Walston, J. (1988), *The Mafia and Clientelism. Roads to Rome in Post-War Calabria*, London.

Weiss, L. (1988), *Creating Capitalism*, Oxford.

Wolleb, E. and Wolleb, G. (1990), *Divari regionali e dualismo economico*, Bologna.

Woods, D. (1992), 'The Rise of Regional Leagues in Italian Politics', *West European Politics*, **15**, 2, pp.56–76.

Zamagni, V. (1993), *Dalla periferia al centro*, Bologna.

Part I

History: The Construction of Regional Identities

–2–

Shifting Identities: Nation, Region and City

Adrian Lyttelton

The real problem posed by Italian regionalism is why there was so little of it. In both political and cultural terms, down to 1922, it was a weak and declining force. In continental Italy, it never inspired a significant political movement between the 1870s and 1945. This needs some explanation, in light of the general consensus on the need for devolution after 1945, and still more when set against the rise of the aggressive populist regionalism of the *leghe*.

Northern regional identities were not simply 'invented' or artificial entities, as some critics maintained. The territorial states of the sixteenth to eighteenth centuries each had their distinctive style of government, and 'political personality'. These differences in state traditions were decisive for the constitution of regional identities. According to Carlo Cattaneo, the most lucid and coherent exponent of regionalism, its rationale lay in the existence of different legislative systems, which corresponded to different stages of civilization. Tuscany, Lombardy and Sicily were 'greater and no less real beings' than their constituent provinces and cities. The imposition of a centralized system was wrong and in a way false, because it meant trying to create overnight 'a new mode of inheritance and ownership and making contracts and living in the family and in the commune' (Pavone 1964: 338). Cattaneo, however, distinguished between strong regions and weak regions, large and small. In regions such as Piedmont, Liguria, Lombardy and the Veneto, or Tuscany, there might be border problems, but the existence of a solid core corresponding to the territorial states of the past could not be put in doubt. With the exception of Piedmont, where Turin achieved pre-eminence only through its role as a dynastic capital, the regions mentioned had all been shaped by the action of a dominant city. One can think of regionalism as a force radiating out from the capital city and diminishing in intensity as one moved away from it. The Lombard region had only a tenuous existence outside the borders of the old state of Milan; the modern boundaries of the region were quite different from what they had been in earlier centuries.[1] For the conservatives of the influential newspaper *La Perseveranza* the 'end of Lombardy' (*finis longobardiae*) essentially meant the loss of Milanese primacy, and the reduction of the capital to the rank of a mere provincial *capoluogo*, formally on a par with the insignificant Sondrio (Vigezzi 1975: 269).

There were two kinds of limits on regional identity. One was the historic rivalry between cities, which had certainly not been annulled by the regional states. It was a conflict of identities, which did not exclude a similarity of social constitution. The other, less well-known but of considerable significance, was the existence of peripheral areas partially or wholly refractory to the model of social organization and discipline imposed by the city-state. For example, while the northern part of the old state of Siena belonged to the 'core area' of Tuscany, where urban landownership and the *mezzadria* system prevailed, the southern areas comprised the Maremma, still largely uncultivated and plagued by malaria, and the mining towns of Monte Amiata: wild backlands, the home of cowboys, bandits, prophets and other strange phenomena alien to the urbane traditions of Tuscan civilization. In general, the mountains were a zone apart, which resisted identification with the society and politics of the lowlands. In the later nineteenth century they were strongly affected by emigration. In united Italy, these differences of social structure tended to complicate and modify regional loyalties. The politically homogeneous subcultures of 'red Tuscany' or 'the white Veneto' did not coincide with the boundaries of the historic regions.

In 1861, Cavour's Minister of the Interior, Marco Minghetti, introduced a bill for regional devolution. Yet Minghetti's own claims, as a Bolognese, to speak for a coherent region were highly problematic. The 'provinces of Emilia', were in a different category from Lombardy and Tuscany. United in 1859 for reasons of contingent political necessity, they comprised three different political entities: the duchies of Parma and Modena, and the Romagna, formerly part of the Papal States. In central Italy, Umbria and the Marche were also regions with a weak identity and no tradition of unity and self-government. There was, indeed, a 'historic Umbria', which could trace its origins back to pre-Roman times, and which coincided roughly with the territory of the Lombard Duchy of Spoleto in the early Middle Ages. But this Umbria did not include the modern region's most important city, Perugia, and the lands west of the Tiber, traditionally considered as part of 'Etruria'. The political boundary between Tuscany and the Papal States did not correspond to a cultural or linguistic boundary. From the end of the seventeenth century, it is true, Perugia came to be considered part of Umbria, for descriptive and administrative convenience, but the identification remained tenuous. The Papal style of government did little to foster a common sense of citizenship among its constituent communities, as Pius VII recognized frankly in the preamble to his administrative reforms of 1816: 'Our state still lacked that uniformity which is so useful to public and private interests, since, formed by the successive reunion of different dominions, it presented an aggregate of naturally diverse usages, laws, and privileges' (Grohmann 1989: 20–1).[2] Perugia's status as a regional capital was not recognized by the other cities. In 1860, they protested vigorously against the decision to organize Umbria as a single province (Covino 1989: 508–12).[3] Ironically, while the Italian state refused to grant recognition to the 'strong' regions, in the Umbrian instance it created an administrative unit which in the long run reinforced a hitherto weak regional identity. In the later nineteenth century local intellectuals, with some help from Carducci, worked to create an image of Umbria as an oasis of rural tranquillity with a religious tradition of intense and mystical devotion. In a poor region, tourism was important, and guidebooks helped to diffuse the stereotypes of '*Umbria verde*' and '*Umbria mistica*', conveying the image of a timeless, rural 'land of saints and warriors'. The early twentieth century even saw the fleeting emergence of an 'Umbrian question'; local deputies were roused to action by Sonnino's programme of special legislation for the South to demand similar concessions for their region. This meant admitting what had previously been denied: that 'happy' Umbria was in fact backward and underprivileged. A similar regional agitation took place in the Marche. However, political leaders were careful to insist that demands for tax breaks and other economic incentives did not amount to 'regionalism', a dirty word treated as synonymous with 'separatism'. One can see in the Umbrian case how regional identity expanded to fill a void and to exploit new opportunities, and also how it was fostered by the state's new willingness to intervene in an attempt to redress the growing inequality between advanced and backward areas (Bracco and Irace 1989: 612–19, 642–9; Covino and Gallo 1989: 90–2).

In spite of the claims that could be made for regions, in terms of a shared political past, or of a dominant model of social relations, it would be hard to argue that they were the primary focus for identification, either at the popular level, or among the literate classes. On the one hand, they had recently been weakened by the rise of Italian patriotism. But it is also significant that the evil which Italian patriots had fought went under the name not of regionalism but 'municipalism'. Underneath the surface of the territorial states of the modern period, the vitality of the city-state tradition survived powerfully. Cattaneo, though he did believe in the existence of a Lombard identity, insisted on the survival of the 'minute nationalities' of the individual cities. For Cattaneo's federalist outlook there was no contradiction; city and region were links in a chain of identities reaching up to the nation. Minghetti, though far more cautious in his political conclusions, can be said to have broadly shared this theoretical framework. But both were perhaps too optimistic. National, regional and urban identity could all enter into conflict. As Denis Mack Smith has pointed out, Italian nationalism owed a great deal to the resentments of lesser cities against regional capitals – Brescia against Modena, Leghorn against Florence. Where a whole region had been incorporated into a larger centralized state, however, regionalism and Italian nationalism, at least temporarily, could be allies: this was the case in Liguria and Sicily. It is certainly no accident that these two regions had a critical role in 'making Italy' in 1860. But whereas Liguria remained perhaps the most patriotic of Italian regions, in Sicily the desire for autonomy was frustrated by the centralizing solutions adopted by the new state. However, just as before 1860, Messina and Catania, suspicious of Palermo's pre-eminence, did not show much enthusiasm for separatist or autonomist politics.

To municipal élites in Northern and Central Italy the province appeared as a 'natural' unit, formed through the conquest of the *contado* by the city. Whether this dominion always appeared so natural to the subject peasants, or even to the inhabitants of minor towns, may be doubted, but at least it was a fact of life which could hardly be ignored, except by the inhabitants of distant and mountainous districts. For the peasants, who constituted the great mass of the population, the natural focus of identity would be the village or the parish, and beyond that the local market town; in Tuscany, Emilia and the Marche these numbered between one and two hundred. In the Alps, mountain valleys created their own identities, sometimes based on a distinct dialect. They sustained Italy's most effective military units,and the only ones allowed to enjoy a strictly local recruitment, the *alpini*. One should not imagine, however, that wider regional loyalties lacked all meaning for the peasants. There might be a symbolic attachment to the person of the ruler, or even to a former dynasty, or else a more complex and developed loyalty to the state, as in the territories of the Venetian *terraferma*.[4] The belief that 'the enemy of my enemy is my friend' prevailed, and peasant loyalism could provide a vocabulary for expressing hostility to the nearby towns and their landowners. But where the state authority was external to the region, it was not impossible for the local élites to turn the tables and win peasant support against oppressive central government. This happened in Sicily, and, briefly, in the Veneto in 1848. We do not really know how far the decline of the territorial states had eroded these traditional loyalties by the nineteenth century. What seems certain is that the attitude of the Church was critical in determining the extent and nature of regional sentiment. The strength and direction of regionalism was largely the outcome of the triangular relationship between the Church, the government and the landowning and urban élites. The Veneto and Tuscany, regions which were not markedly dissimilar in terms of economic and social development, nevertheless evolved distinctive and in ways diametrically opposed regional ideologies. Although landlord paternalism was a feature of both, in Tuscany this went with an insistence on the urban and secular traditions of the Renaissance and the Enlightenment, whereas the image of the 'tranquil Veneto' was founded on the alliance between proprietor, priest and peasant, and defined by fidelity to religion and rural mores.

In retrospect, it can seem surprising that the new Italian state was able to impose a centralized system of government on a complex of diverse societies marked by a high degree of local particularism. Only Lombardy in 1859, and Umbria and the Marche in 1860, were the objects of a straightforward 'royal conquest' (and in Lombardy it was by courtesy of the French). Elsewhere, local leaders possessed some degree of autonomy and bargaining power. One explanation must be the memory of the failures of 1848. Federalism might be a fine way of reconciling regional and national feeling, but in Italy's circumstances it had come to seem impracticable as a means of achieving independence. There were still some impenitent federalists, for whom the structure of the new unitary state represented not the creation but the end of Italy, *finis Italiae*, but they had little influence on events. Clemente Busi, a Tuscan democrat who turned legitimist, explained his volte-face by the difference between 1848 and 1859; 1848 had preserved Italian traditions by promoting federalism, but 'the ideas of 1848' could have little hearing from the men of 1859 (Salvestrini 1967: 218). More typically, many liberals, both moderates and democrats, who were attached to the principles of local or regional autonomy, were none the less willing to suspend or forgo them in the interests of unity. Frequently, an initial surrender was confirmed by the argument, which was not without its plausibility, that the new state was too weak and too severely menaced by both internal and external enemies to change its constitution or style of administration. By the time the pressure had lifted, in 1870, a new orthodoxy had crystallized, and the success of the system in overcoming a number of major challenges was a powerful argument for its retention. However, the abandonment of ideas both for regional representation and for greater communal and provincial autonomy was not a separate and peripheral issue which can be divorced from that of the nature of Italian liberalism as a whole. It involved a tacit abandonment of some of liberalism's central tenets: the necessity for checks on the overweening power of government, and the need to ground national identity and state authority on intermediate bodies and 'natural' communities of interest and opinion. The euphoria of unification tended momentarily to eclipse criticism; but even at the time the rejection of Minghetti's proposals prompted pessimistic reflections on the betrayal of liberalism. For Giuseppe Saredo, the author of a brief but eloquent biographical sketch of Minghetti, the defeat of the latter's proposals marked a victory for the 'administrative school', in alliance with democracy, over the 'school of liberty': 'An admirably designed mechanism has been created. . .the various individual and collective personalities have become so many marionettes that move uniformly from one end of the state to the other. . .Nothing has been left to liberty, nothing to responsibility: not men but objects of administration were desired, not men but pupils' (Saredo 1861: 218).

During the period of unification, the regional question was raised in several different forms. First, there was the demand to preserve particular features of the old order in law and administration. This could be viewed as either a permanent or a transitory necessity. Many of those who spoke up for greater autonomy and diversity between 1859 and 1861 agreed that uniformity of legislation and administration was desirable in itself, but objected to 'Piedmontization' and demanded a genuine national synthesis, to which each region would contribute its best practices. Second, there was the attempt to guarantee the institutions of regional capitals: courts of appeal, banks of issue and universities. Third, there was the demand for the formal recognition of the regions, either through a delegation of executive power to regional governors (the *regione amministrativa*), or through the creation of some form of regional representation (the *regione autarchica*). It is important to note that the first two types of regional demand did not necessarily imply the third.

The incorporation of Lombardy was decisive in setting the pattern which was later followed with other regions. The later turn towards centralization has been explained by the problems raised by the conquest of the South. But this explanation cannot, of course, apply in the Lombard case, at a time when the annexation of Naples was not even contemplated. There is little doubt that Cavour was initially sympathetic to Lombard claims for the recognition of their distinctive traditions in administration. Indeed, he generously, or diplomatically, wrote that Piedmont had more to learn than to teach in this respect. But this did not mean that he had any tolerance for the idea of a Lombard representative assembly, nor did his interlocutors among the Lombard moderates want one. Count Giulini, the head of the commission of Lombard notables set up to advise the government on how Lombardy should be administered, confidently attributed to Cavour himself the aim 'to maintain of the present Lombard administrative regime all that the changed political circumstances and the necessities of the war do not require to innovate'. However, Giulini's brief was only to report on the structure of the temporary administration which was to govern until such time as a truly national solution could be worked out.

The report of the Giulini commission underlined these terms of reference with an unmistakable note of Lombard patriotism: Lombardy, together with other lands which might be annexed, would make an important contribution to 'the transformation of the administrative order of the whole state', thanks particularly to its skilfully designed municipal institutions, 'the noble relics of ancient Italian wisdom' (Raponi 1962: 11).

The Lombards argued that the vitality of local institutions, though severely damaged and corrupted by the Austrian police state, had none the less acted to some degree as an effective check on despotism. Unfortunately, Urbano Rattazzi, the Minister of the Interior and true leader of the government which took over after Cavour's resignation, was far less sympathetic to the Lombard point of view. He was probably much more representative of the common opinion of Piedmontese politicians and bureaucrats. Unlike Cavour, he was more sympathetic to the French model of a strong, centralized state than to the English ideal of self-government. As Minister of Justice in 1853 he had been instrumental in strengthening the control of the executive over the judiciary. In 1858, Cavour noted acutely that 'Rattazzi has always been the most conservative member of the cabinet, the most decisive partisan of the principles of authority. . .he is a liberal by conviction, but. . .an absolutist by instinct' (Livorsi 1988: 341). The first blow to Lombard susceptibilities was Rattazzi's abrupt termination of the full powers given to the governor and administration of Lombardy, and their subordination to the Piedmontese ministries. This was a prelude to the extension of the Piedmontese local government system and other features of the Piedmontese law by decree. The use of the full powers granted to the government to secure legislative uniformity without parliamentary discussion was in itself a severe breach in liberal principles, and set an ominous precedent. If Cavour was the architect of Italian political unity, Rattazzi might be termed the engineer who designed the blueprints for the structure of the state. Rattazzi had some excuse for his impatience; during the previous decade, the Turin parliament had repeatedly failed in its efforts to reform the local government law. It was predictable that in a national parliament it would be much harder still to achieve a workable consensus. So, indeed, it was to prove; between 1861 and 1886 fourteen local government bills were drafted, but not one of them even reached the floor of the Chamber of Deputies (Caracciolo 1960: 115). The Lombards had made some attempt to defend their peculiar version of local taxpayers' democracy, expressed by the institution known as the *convocato degli estimati*. In small communes (under 3,000 inhabitants), all property-holders could take part in the communal assembly. Cattaneo waxed lyrical about this form of direct democracy, but recent studies have shown its disadvantages. It is true that through the *convocato* the peasant communities of the mountains could exercise control over their common lands and resist demands for their privatization; but they were equally stubborn in resisting expenditure on health or education. It was 'a democracy of poverty and social stagnation' (Meriggi 1987: 71–5). Popular participation was not always easy to reconcile with progress. On the other hand, in the communes of the Lombard plain the direct representation of taxpayers was simply a cloak for the domination of the large landowners, who could even delegate their functions to substitutes.[5] It is hardly likely that Cavour, who believed that one of the aims of the reform of local government should be to bring pressure on absentee landlords and force them to take a more active and socially responsible role, would have countenanced a similar idea (Pavone 1964: 367–8). The annulment of Lombard regional autonomy was in part due to the half-hearted conservatism of its advocates. However, Cavour was able to use Lombard indignation at Rattazzi's methods to assist his return to power, and to win over important personalities, such as Stefano Jacini, who was to be the most persistent and influential champion of regionalism after 1859. It was widely expected that Cavour would reverse or at least modify the centralizing and 'Piedmontizing' tendencies of the Rattazzi administration.

Tuscany and 'the provinces of Emilia' had a different status from Lombardy. They were not occupied by Piedmontese troops, and their annexation had to be negotiated. Indeed, the terms of the Treaty of Villafranca excluded the annexation of Modena or Tuscany. This situation had contradictory consequences. It gave local leaders potentially greater bargaining power. But it also put pressure on them to create a *fait accompli* which would make annexation possible, and one way of doing this was to assimilate the Piedmontese system of laws and administration. In all these territories, the small ruling groups of moderates were highly conscious of the insecurity of their position and fearful both of external aggression and internal subversion, from either the clerical and legitimist Right or the republican Left. This tended to favour haste and acceptance of the Piedmontese model.

The 'provinces of Emilia', as already indicated, did not form a true region. The autonomist Cattaneo was critical of the grouping together of three areas each with a different 'form and discipline of the state' (Pavone 1964: 341). The Modenese Farini's drive to unify Parma, Modena and the Romagna was not designed to create a viable regional entity, but to aid the process of 'Piedmontization'. This is made clear by Farini's triumphant letter announcing the success of his mission: 'I have thrown down the *campanili*. . .by the New Year from Piacenza to Cattolica the laws, the regulations, and the names will all be Piedmontese.' The aim of this process was to cancel all traces of the old states: 'to reform them into simple provinces, to obliterate their borders, to mingle their interests'(Zanni Rosiello 1965: 68–9). At the time, this policy had the full support of Minghetti, later to be the leading proponent of regional institutions. He wrote that 'we intend to become Piedmontese provinces like Cuneo' (Zanni Rosiello 1965: 51). So in Emilia, if uniformity was imposed, it was not in the first place by Piedmontese authority but by the local moderate leaders. However, already before the union with Piedmont this policy provoked strong protests. A Piacenza correspondent wrote angrily to Farini: 'Who conferred on you the mandate to proceed with unification?', and described the transfer of government to Modena as a *coup d'état* (Zanni Rosiello 1965: 65). If one takes into account the essentially municipal inspiration of these protests (they were strongest in the former subject cities of Piacenza and Reggio), one can see why Minghetti's project for regional devolution ironically met with particularly strong opposition in his own 'region'. At a later stage, the old rivalry between Modena and Bologna came to the fore. A Modenese newspaper wrote that 'all this business [of the region] has been invented in Bologna to make Bologna the centre of Emilia', and to reduce their own city, once the capital of a state, to being 'merely a suburb' of its hated rival (Zanni Rosiello 1965: 250–1).

After the annexation, there was time to reconsider, and doubts about the wisdom of the rapid and complete process of unification on the Piedmontese model began to affect the very men who had carried it out. Farini and Minghetti were no doubt sensitive to the protests of their friends; the influential Count Giuseppe Pasolini wrote to Minghetti in July 1860: 'I will *never* pardon the error sustained by you, that it was necessary to destroy everything old. . .'. It was no excuse to say that the changes had been undertaken to make a Papal restoration impossible; on the contrary, Pasolini believed that 'the inconveniences of the new. . .have revived the desire for the old' (Zanni Rosiello 1965: 230). In October 1860, there was strong opposition to the adoption of the Piedmontese civil code in Parma, Piacenza, and to a lesser degree, in Modena. For the time being, this opposition was successful, and only

Romagna adopted the new civil code. The citizens of the former Duchy of Parma, a state which had a good name for enlightened legislation, did not feel the same urgency for change as the former subjects of the Pope, and resented being treated in the same way. One of the parliamentary deputies from Piacenza asked: 'Why should we be worse off only to do good to the Romagnole provinces?' (Zanni Rosiello 1965: 237). The opposition was less effective because it was divided and motivated by local grievances. However, a common note of criticism of excessive controls, insufficient autonomy and lack of attention to local differences can be heard. In the Romagna, for example, the reorganization of local government by communes was criticized for ignoring the rights of smaller communities, the so-called *luoghi appodati*.

In Tuscany, Bettino Ricasoli was in a far stronger negotiating position than Minghetti or Farini. Tuscany was a 'strong' region with unrivalled cultural traditions. In the eighteenth century, the economic and political reforms of Peter Leopold had made Tuscany into the model state of enlightened absolutism, and the Restoration had marked less of a breach in continuity than elsewhere. It was particularly important for the governing élite to preserve Tuscany's liberal attitude towards free trade and private enterprise. Ricasoli was a convinced advocate of strong central authority. He had admired Napoleon III's system of government, and when he became Prime Minister in June 1861 he was to make the decisive moves to end all projects for devolution. But he used the transition period skilfully to establish Tuscany's special status. He knew that this was necessary to preserve the union of the moderate ruling class and to isolate the legitimist supporters of the Grand Duke. One of the other leaders of the Tuscan moderates, Ubaldino Peruzzi, wrote to Minghetti in June 1859 that the 'true danger' came from 'the possible agreement of the party of autonomy with the dynastic party. . .even the warmest unitarians hold dear to their heart certain ancient and free Tuscan traditions, which are too little known in Piedmont, where the centralized order has remained. . .worsened by militarism' (Salvestrini 1965: 40–1). He thought that unifying reforms should be confined to the abolition of customs barriers and the reorganization of the police. Ricasoli himself was clear that, though Tuscany might accept laws voted by a national parliament, it would refuse to be subjected to 'the laws of Rattazzi' (Pavone 1964: 55–7). In fact, the special status of Tuscany in some respects outlasted the transition period. It kept its own advanced penal code (Peter Leopold had been the first ruler to abolish the death penalty), its mining laws, its appeal court, and not one but two separate banks of issue.

Ricasoli's hostility to regionalism was decisive. If he had thrown his weight behind Minghetti's proposals the pressure to make some concessions would have been strong. Cavour, though we know he remained favourable to Minghetti's ideas up till the moment they were presented to Parliament, carefully avoided using his moral authority in their support. One can only guess at the reasons for his failure to do so. Most probably, he came to recognize that the regions were a divisive issue, likely to weaken the cohesion of the parliamentary majority, and in particular to alienate the Centre-Left of Rattazzi. At the least, therefore, the reform should be postponed to quieter times. Minghetti himself defended his programme without much conviction; his failure to fix the boundaries of the proposed regions, designed to minimize opposition, in fact played into the hands of those who argued that the regions were artificial and unviable. The strength of the opposition is surprising; in committee, the idea of the *regione autarchica* was rejected unanimously, and even the proposal to install regional governors was voted down by 18 to 6. The main reason voiced by opponents was that any recognition of regions would open the doors to federalism and would endanger national unity, so miraculously achieved.

One cannot but feel that these fears were exaggerated, in view of the very modest powers attributed to the regions, and the strong position of the governors.[6] But a number of deputies also attacked the proposal as a danger to the autonomy of the communes and provinces, considered as 'natural' institutions, contrasted with the artificiality of the regions. The proposals to broaden the local suffrage and to make mayors elective instead of having them appointed by the government got a better hearing than the regions, although in the end they were abandoned. This suggests that some of the opponents of the region were genuine in their support for local autonomy. However, in general, the opposition of the deputies reflected the interests and anxieties of a new political class which had won power, but still felt it to be precarious. They were a class of municipal and provincial notables, mostly committed to a national programme; their position as the indispensable mediators between government and civil society, centre and periphery, might be weakened by the creation of an intermediate level of power. The most acute critics of centralization, like Jacini, always insisted that its consequence was not to suppress local interests, but to ensure that they were mediated by the deputies, in or out of Parliament. Paradoxically, it led to a permanent deficit of decision making. The difficulty of reconciling conflicting local interests in the national Parliament meant that important measures were often passed by executive decree, and that the 'provisional' solutions of the period of unification became definitive by default, because it was impossible to achieve a consensus on reform.

In the last major northern region to be annexed, the Veneto, the forces favouring regional cohesion and opposition to the central State were particularly strong. The overwhelming influence of the Church and its firm alliance with the nobility, the landowning class, and even the new industrialists, made the Veneto the most solidly conservative of Italian regions. Quintino Sella, an industrialist and a leader of the Piedmontese *destra storica*, when he was serving as commissar in Udine, remarked in astonishment, 'I always believed I was a reactionary, but here I seem to have become a Jacobin' (Lanaro 1984: 410). There was quite a considerable pro-Austrian protest vote in the first elections after unification, but most of the local ruling class was willing to seek an accommodation. Although there was some attempt, as in Lombardy, to defend the *convocato*, opposition did not focus so much as in Tuscany or Lombardy on questions of organization or local government. Probably the Veneto representatives realized that after the 1865 measures for legislative and administrative unification attempts at revision were not likely to be successful. Instead, there was a fierce opposition to ecclesiastical policy and to financial unification. There was a widespread popular rejection of civil marriage, and the propertied classes protested against fiscal standardization and the consolidation of the public debt. The deputy Augusto Righi recalled with regret 'the sacramental concept which Austrian law had of the bank deposit' (Lanaro 1984: 432).

How far, and why, and in what forms, did regionalism survive after the process of unification was complete? First, there was the widely diffused sense of unease at the character of the new state. Admiration for the novel virtues of Piedmontese liberalism was soon tempered by dismay at the heavy hand of Piedmontese bureaucracy. Like all bureaucracies, it represented an element of continuity and carried over many features of the old regime, which, although relatively efficient, had also been peculiarly invasive. It was rigid, hierarchical, formalist and impersonal. Old Piedmont had been a 'well-ordered police state' (in the eighteenth-century sense of the term), and something of this obsessive concern with control survived the advent of liberalism. Many Italian liberals, by contrast, felt that their revolution had been against bureaucracy, and this was particularly true of the landowning and financial élites of Lombardy and Tuscany, with their strong *laissez-faire* traditions. On the other hand, the subjects of old princely states – not only in Naples but in Parma or Modena – regretted the loss of the intimate, personal relationships between governors and governed under the old regime, and continued to address *suppliche* in the old style to indifferent offices. However, when they learnt the rules of the new Italian game, they soon discovered that *suppliche* and *raccomandazioni* were far from obsolete and the operations of the administration far from wholly impersonal. Only now the most effective channel through which personal appeals reached the bureaucracy was through the local deputies. Their network extended downwards through the *grandi elettori* to the grassroots of society, upwards to the minister, and often 'sideways' to friends in the bureaucracy who frequently exchanged ideas and personnel with the political class.[7]

Clientelism has traditionally been written about in Italy as a wholly negative phenomenon. And looking at Italy today, it is hard to deny its ravages. But one cannot see clientelism in its proper light or understand its strength and persistence unless we see it as a crucial instrument for tying together the threads of Italy's multiple and diverse societies into some kind of knot. It bound local interests to the central state. It was, of course, just this feature of Italy's 'material constitution' after 1860 which horrified thoughtful critics like Jacini. Jacini's functional version of regionalism was essentially designed to break what he saw as a vicious circle by drawing a sharp line of separation between local administration and national politics. A primary aim of Jacini's suggested reforms was to strengthen the decision-making power of Parliament and the central government by relieving it of local pressures and responsibilities. Another objective was what we would now call 'transparency': interests which were 'clearly represented, administered and promoted by their mandatories' (Jacini 1926: 55), at the regional level, would be out in the open, and free local initiative would replace backdoor influence.

Since the 1960s there has been a lively historical debate on centralization, regionalism and local autonomy. The pendulum has now swung back towards the centralizers. One result has been established (if it were ever in doubt): centralization was far from implying a neglect of local interests. The Italian state could be ruthless and harshly oppressive; but essentially in its day-to-day operations it depended on compromise with local élites, even for the preservation of public order, as John Davis has shown (Davis 1988). It was, and has remained, a *permeable* state, more of a sponge than an iron frame.

Higher education is a good example. The new state intervened actively to reinvigorate the stagnant local cultures of academe by bringing in new men, exiles and outsiders. However, the efforts of a succession of education ministers to rationalize the higher education system by reducing the number of universities were unavailing. It proved harder to close a university than to abolish a capital city. The proposal to shut down Siena University even brought together the archbishop and local freemasons (Rossi 1976: 96). However, the state's rather reluctant tolerance undercut regionalism. Universities became key centres of regional culture and identity. But they were not centres of regionalism: in Northern and Central Italy, at least, they were faithful propagators of the national ideal. At most, it might acquire a regional inflection, as in Padua, where the university was always sensitive to the idea of a greater Veneto, extending as far as Trento and Dalmatia, and where D'Annunzio's re-evocation of the maritime glories of the *Serenissima* found a receptive audience.

The unimportance of regionalism as a political force in Liberal Italy does not mean that regional loyalties and interests ceased to play a major part in the structure of politics. De Sanctis noted, in fact, that regional interests had taken their revenge, and that their rivalry threatened to dominate 'national' politics. Unfortunately, the real consistency of regional 'parties' in the Parliament of the 1860s is still largely an unknown subject. However, contemporaries were clear about the importance of two groups. On the one side there was the '*consorteria*', an alliance between Tuscan and Lombard moderates, with the former playing the dominant role; on the other, the Piedmontese *permanente*, formed in opposition to the Tuscans and to the transfer of the capital to Florence. It is important to note that there was a Piedmontese particularism which disliked the submersion of the old Kingdom in the new state. Neither of these two regional groups represented a 'periphery' in revolt against the centre. Instead, they expressed the interests of national capitals and the claims of regional groups to a special place in national politics. The Tuscans, with men like Bastogi and Cambray-Digny, exerted a predominant and not always scrupulous influence over public finance, and the Piedmontese kept a leading role in the army and civil administration.

Regional discontents certainly contributed to the fall of the Right in 1876, when a group of Tuscan deputies went over to the opposition. The issue which finally pushed the Tuscan dissident Right into opposition was the project for state control over the railways, but specifically regional grievances had already created a climate of dissatisfaction. The Tuscans resented the refusal of the state to come to the aid of the bankrupt commune of Florence, and the creation of a new *Corte di Cassazione* in Rome, which was formerly under Florence's jurisdiction. Behind these specific grievances one can sense the Florentine chagrin at the loss of the capital. But it is important to note that the Tuscan rebellion of 1876 marked the end, not the birth, of a cohesive regional bloc; it did not reverse the decline of the *consorteria*. The Venetian Right had more potential to become a true regional opposition, especially in view of its late incorporation and the strong popular support which it could mobilize through the Church.

Why did this not happen, and why in general did regionalism decline as a factor in Italian politics? The first major reason is, I think, to be found in the polarization of politics around the issue of policy towards the Church. After the Syllabus and the declaration of Papal Infallibility, political Catholicism was reduced to a marginal minority in national politics. To a large extent, however, the autonomist opposition of the 1860s was absorbed by the clerical intransigent opposition of the 1870s, along with the relics of legitimism. In fact, the reliance of legitimists on the cause of the Church to revivify their tepid and ill-organized support had begun much earlier. The Grand Duke's 'party' in Tuscany included many of the most influential leaders of the Florentine aristocracy, but between 1859 and 1861, when there were still serious hopes for a restoration, they proved remarkably inept. Only the clergy were able to create a serious political organization, or even to run a viable newspaper. More significant is the conversion of a man such as Vito d'Ondes Reggio. A Sicilian nationalist in 1848, he went into exile in Genoa, where he taught constitutional law, and became a supporter of Cavour. However, as a Sicilian he could not stomach centralization and the abolition of Sicily's traditional liberties; he became one of the most learned and eloquent supporters of regionalism in the 1860s. His position on Church issues had been moderate. But the failure of his autonomist battles, his opposition to the confiscation of Church lands, and finally his dismay at the forcible occupation of Rome, converted him into an intransigent defender of the Papacy. At the first congress of Catholic organizations in 1874 he was the leading speaker. In general, one can say that the Catholic movement in its origins had a strong regional inflection. It was far more deeply rooted in the Veneto, and to a lesser extent, in eastern and northern Lombardy than elsewhere. It is interesting that Brescia and Bergamo – old Venetian provinces absorbed by Lombardy – followed the political model of the '*Veneto bianco*'.

A second reason for the decline of regional politics lay in economic and social change and the restructuring of politics along class lines. It is true that industrialization had contradictory effects. A discussion of regional patterns of industrialization would take me well beyond the bounds of this chapter, but one can at least note the influence of the regional capitals – Turin, Milan and Genoa – in promoting different styles of industrialization. These divergent forms of industrialization interacted in distinctive ways with politics. So Liguria, the home of shipping, shipbuilding and other industries dependent on state patronage, became one of the most 'governmental' regions in politics. Ligurian heavy industry and finance formed a regional lobby of great power, but one which could not afford to antagonize the government for long. On the other hand, Milanese industrialists led the protest in the 1890s against the fiscal extravagance of Crispi's colonial policy.

If one is looking for the roots of contemporary upheavals, then the opposition of what at the time was called 'the state of Milan' to Crispi is particularly significant. This opposition was inspired by pride in Milan's economic and cultural achievements. Milan's claim to be the 'moral capital' was not without its justification. If one looks at the way in which political movements, or models of social organization, as well as economic innovations, were diffused, then Milan was the true capital of Italy at this time. Milan had the first modern newspapers and the first modern department store. The story of the foundation of the Socialist Party can be read as the triumph of the Milanese model of working-class organization over the Mazzinian traditions of Liguria and the revolutionary heritage of the Romagna. But the claim to be the 'moral capital' obviously had a polemical edge; it implied that Rome was the immoral capital. The polemic became much sharper after the bank scandals of 1892, which contributed to establishing the primacy of Milan as a financial centre over her rivals in Turin, Florence and Rome. The banks in these three cities – the successive capitals of Italy – were deeply involved in building speculation and in shady political dealings. The Milanese banks, notoriously cautious and supported by a solid industrial and agricultural base, came through relatively unscathed. As is well known, opposition to Crispi's colonialism temporarily united Left and Right, industrialists and workers. Giuseppe Colombo, perhaps an even more representative spokesman of industry than the more famous Alessandro Rossi of Schio, hoped that Lombardy could provide the impetus for the formation of a new conservatism linked to industry and the application of 'scientific method' to social questions (Ullrich 1975: 199–201).

Yet this remained an episode, although it helped to crystallize permanent attitudes of distrust towards central government and 'politics', and to confirm the Lombard sense of difference and superiority. Colombo and other leaders of the industrialists were enlightened in their attitude to technical progress, but they were unprepared to deal with the social and political consequences of industrialization. They distrusted democracy and feared the entry of the masses into politics. Between 1898 and 1900 they committed themselves to reaction and suffered a decisive defeat, even in Milan itself. They did not regain their political influence until the end of the Giolittian era, and then it was as part of a wider conservative bloc. In this, the industrialists were politically subordinate to the landowners represented by the new Catholic deputies and the heirs of the old *consorteria*. Milanese or Lombard opposition to Rome was instrumental and discontinuous. But as industrialists, conscious of their weakness, tended to retreat from national politics into local government, they developed a kind of anti-political politics, based on the cult of free enterprise and practical 'administration'. This proved an enduring ideology; it can only be understood in relations to its enemies, Rome and the South. Lombard identity had been reformulated just at the time when the South, in the person of Crispi, for the first time became dominant in national politics. One can find parallels on the Left, in Turati's conviction that the Northern working class and the progressive bourgeoisie must form an alliance against the 'feudal' and reactionary South.

In conclusion: Italy was united by education, bureaucracy and patronage and divided by class and religious conflict. Both the positive and negative influences worked to reduce the significance of regional cleavages. On the other hand, industrialization and the rise of mass movements deepened the fissure between North and South. Class politics, moreover, could have their regional overtones, as in the *socialismo bracciantile* of Emilia, or, on the other side, the role of Bologna, Parma and Piacenza as centres of agrarian organization. The decline of regionalism did not mean that politics had been truly 'nationalized'. Apart from the vast areas of peasant hostility or indifference to the new state, the town hall in most cases continued to be the primary focus of political competition, and even class conflict took intensely provincial forms. Paradoxically, one could suggest that the limits of national integration minimized the occasions of regional conflict. Ironically, in the last forty years, the penetration of all parts of the nation by the mass media, the spread of a consumer culture, the threat to the autonomy of local cultures, and, above all, the massive South–North immigration have brought the regions of Italy into closer contact with each other, but have also created new tensions which help to explain the regionalist explosion of today.

Notes

1. The western provinces of Alessadria and Novara had been ceded to Piedmont in the first half of the eighteenth century, while the eastern provinces of Brescia and Bergamo were separated from the Veneto in 1815. See Vigezzi (1975: 268–9, 284), 'the reality of the region ended by being suspended in mid-air between the ancient reality of the State of Milan', and the whole of Northern Italy.

2. The Marche were even more fragmented; down to 1815, the relationship between the central government and the local communities was regulated by the agreements which the latter had separately concluded at the time of their submission to the Papacy. The 'March of Ancona' was a historic unit, but it did not coincide with the whole region, and Ancona's role as a regional capital was contested by Macerata. The northern and southern Marche had different histories and different dialects; and, interestingly enough, the political orientation of the region after 1860 split along the historic fault-line. The northern Marche shared the anti-clerical, republican and anarchist sympathies of the Romagna, whereas the south was a 'white' region where the influence of the Church remained strong (Anselmi 1987: xvii–xx).
3. For the reasons behind this decision, see Covino (1989: 508–12). Instead, Minghetti had contemplated incorporating Umbria in the Tuscan region (Lipparini 1942: Vol. 1, 228).
4. During the 1799 rising against the French occupation of Tuscany, 'the cries of *Evviva Maria* mingled with those for Ferdinand III (the deposed Grand Duke of the House of Lorraine) and for Gian Gastone (the last prince of the Medici dynasty, extinct for more than fifty years). Gian Gastone, indeed, received the greatest honours. . .' (Turi 1969: 255).
5. In the plains, landed property was heavily concentrated in a few hands, and the power of the large landlords was safeguarded by the provision that one-third of the members of the permanent deputation of the commune had to be chosen from among the highest third of the taxpayers. In 1859, Lombard representatives tried to consolidate this privileged status by introducing a requirement that mayors be chosen from among the six biggest taxpayers (Meriggi 1987: 66).
6. While the governors were to be appointed by the government, and to be dependent on the Ministry of the Interior, like the Prefects, the representative regional delegation proposed by Minghetti would have been elected indirectly from among the provincial councillors. The governor would have had his own staff of bureaucrats. The powers of the region would only have covered higher education, archives, academies and major public works (but not including railways or ports); however, there was a proviso that they could acquire extra powers by special legislation (Ragionieri 1967: 86).
7. For an excellent study of the different forms of patronage and mediation exercised by the leading notables of the Veneto, see Franzina (1990: 105–70); particularly interesting is his study of the Vicenza notable Fedele Lampertico, whose network extended into

every ministry. Franzina emphasizes that Lampertico avoided the use of direct pressure to obtain favours for his clients (115–16).

Bibliography

Anselmi, S. (1987), 'Introduzione', in S. Anselmi (ed.), *Le Marche (Storia d'Italia: Le Regioni dall'Unità a oggi)*, Turin, pp.xvii–xxx.

Bracco, F. and Irace, E. (1989), 'La memoria e l'immagine. Aspetti della cultura umbra tra otto e novecento', in R. Covino and G. Gallo (eds), *L'Umbria (Storia d'Italia: Le Regioni dall'Unità a oggi)*, Turin, pp.609–58.

Caracciolo, A. (1960), *Stato e società civile*, Turin.

Covino, R. (1989), 'Dall'Umbria verde all'Umbria rossa', in R. Covino and G. Gallo (eds), *L'Umbria (Storia d'Italia: Le Regioni dall'Unità a oggi)*, Turin, pp.507–605.

Covino, R. and Gallo, G. (1989), 'Le contraddizioni di un modello', in R. Covino and G. Gallo (eds), *L'Umbria (Storia d'Italia: Le Regioni dall'Unità a oggi)*, Turin, pp.75–133.

Davis, J.A. (1988), *Conflict and Control: Law and Order in Nineteenth-Century Italy*, London.

Franzina, E. (1990), *La transizione dolce*, Verona.

Grohmann, A. (1989), 'Caratteri ed equilibri tra centralità e marginalità', in R. Covino and G. Gallo (eds), *L'Umbria (Storia d'Italia: Le Regioni dall'Unità a oggi)*, Turin, pp.5–72.

Jacini, S. (1926), *Un conservatore rurale della nuova Italia*, Bari.

Lanaro, S. (1984), *Il Veneto (Storia d'Italia: Le Regioni dall'Unità a Oggi)*, Turin.

Lipparini, L. (1942), *Minghetti*, Vol. 1, Bologna.

Livorsi, F. (1988), 'Urbano Rattazzi', in *Il Parlamento italiano, 1861–1988: Vol. 1 1861–1865, L'Unificazione italiana da Cavour a La Marmora*, Milan.

Meriggi, M. (1987), *Il Regno Lombardo-Veneto*, Turin.

Pavone, C. (1964), *Amministrazione centrale e amministrazione periferica da Rattazzi à Ricasoli, 1859–1866*, Milan.

Ragionieri, E. (1967), *Politica e amministrazione nella storia dell'Italia unita*, Bari.

Raponi, N. (ed.), (1962), *Atti della Commissione Giulini per l'ordinamento temporaneo della Lombardia (1859)*, (Fondazione Italiana per la Storia Amministrativa, *Acta Italica*, Vol. 2), Milan.

Rossi, M. (1976), *Università e società*, Florence.

Salvestrini, A. (1965), *I moderati toscani e la classe dirigente italiana, (1859–1876)*, Florence.

—— (1967), *Il movimento antiunitario in Toscana, (1859–1866)*, Florence.

Saredo, G. (1861), *Marco Minghetti*, Turin.

Turi, G. (1969), *'Viva Maria'. La reazione alle riforme leopoldine, 1790–1799*, Florence.

Ullrich, H. (1975), 'Il declino del liberalismo lombardo nell'età giolittiana', *Archivio Storico Lombardo*, **10**, 1, pp.199–250.

Vigezzi, B. (1975), 'La Lombarda moderna e contemporanea: un problema di storia regionale', *Archivio Storico Lombardo*, **10**, 1, pp.262–96.

Zanni Rosiello, I. (1965), *L'Unificazione politica e amministrativa nelle 'Province dell'Emilia', (1859–1861)*, Milan.

–3–

Changing Perspectives on Italy's 'Southern Problem'

John A. Davis

The appearance of Italy's Northern League in the late 1980s and early 1990s once again put the present and past role of the South at the centre of political debate in Italy. If the context is new, the vocabulary is familiar. Nor is this surprising. Since Unification, the South has tended to be closer to the centre than the margins of Italian political life, and the 'Southern Problem' (*Questione Meridionale*) has frequently been seen as the most intractable issue facing the development of the Italian state and society.

The recent debate on the role of the South in the development of the Italian state and Italian society has tended to draw heavily and indeed rhetorically on a series of well-worn stereotypes that equate the South with forms of social and economic backwardness, delinquency, organized crime and political corruption. There is good reason to reflect, therefore, on the historical accuracy of these images, and indeed to look more closely at the assumptions that have equated the history of Southern Italy over the last century with the 'Southern Problem' (Bevilacqua 1980, 1993).

It does not do any harm to start by asking what is meant by the South or the '*Mezzogiorno*'. Do the terms refer to a region with clearly defined boundaries and characteristics, and if not, in what sense – if any – can the Southern Problem be considered historically and primarily a *regional* problem? To ask that question is at once to be aware that even in geographical terms the South is far from self-explanatory – and those uncertainties are not significantly reduced by alternative formulations like the *Mezzogiorno*, 'the South and the larger islands', which also fail to define where the boundaries that separate South from North fall: boundaries which, as every traveller to Italy knows, depend on how northerly your vantage point may be.

Nor can the South be defined easily in economic terms. Thanks to new research, the contours of the Southern economies and their development from the mid-nineteenth century to the present are becoming more visible. As a result, the physical and economic diversities that distinguished Apulia, Calabria, the Campania and Sicily, as well as the diversities that existed within each of these provinces or regions, have now been documented in ways that make it increasingly difficult to refer to the South as either an undifferentiated or a coherent economic region. (See, for example, the four volumes devoted to the South in Einaudi's history of the Italian regions, *Meridiana*, Bevilacqua 1985; Bevilacqua & Placanica 1985, etc.)

What about political and cultural identities? Down to 1860, the South was defined in terms that were essentially dynastic and territorial. Even Croce, who argued that the dynastic state had been the historical premise for the development of a deeper sense of national consciousness in the South, identified that consciousness not in regional terms but with a more abstract and generalized concept of the State. When Unification in 1860 brought the Bourbon state to an end this did not open the way for the emergence of a new 'regional' awareness. This was partly because the provinces were administrative constructs that coexisted uneasily with their historical or cultural counterparts. The classical Lucania with which many Southern intellectuals chose to identify, for example, bore little relationship to the realities of nineteenth-century Basilicata. The Southern provinces also lacked internal cohesion. The flourishing regional cultural centres of the eighteenth century that made the salons of the Abruzzi gentry an epicentre of the Southern Enlightenment, or the cultural magnetism that made Cosenza the 'Athens of the Sila', never established broader roots at a provincial level. Although the Southern provincial cities played an important role in the emergence of a new Southern middle class in the early nineteenth century, this did not translate into a strong sense of identity at the level of the province (for a recent discussion see Di Ciommo 1993).

Allowing for the few exceptions that prove every rule, regions have had weak roots in Italian history. States have historically been superimposed over different and consistently changing administrative regions, which in turn rarely coincide with historical regions. As Giovanni Levi has argued, the true historical locus of identity and loyalty in Italy has been more localized – the city, the village, the community. This is not to imply an inward-looking isolationism – from the earliest times individual towns, cities and communities were closely dependent on a web of ties that made them part of a wider civilization and political entity: the state, or more generically Christendom (hence the choice of Carlo Levi's title to describe the isolation of those who lived beyond Eboli) (Levi: 1979).

After Unification, the South was to be subject to even more strongly centrifugal economic, commercial and administrative forces. After the collapse of the Bourbon state, Naples was unhitched from what formerly (and perhaps only formally by the nineteenth century) had been its 'provinces', and the former provincial centres struck out to establish their autonomy and their own networks of commercial contacts. Bari and the Apulian ports reached out along the Adriatic towards Central and Northern Italy, Trieste, the Balkans and *Mitteleuropa*. Catania, Messina and Palermo, on the other hand, strengthened their commercial links with Northern Europe and above all with the rapidly expanding markets across the Atlantic in South America and the United States.

As a result, the South became increasingly fragmented and diversified in its outward orientations, as well as in its internal structures after 1860. Indeed, administrative and political integration into the new state tended to accelerate rather than reverse the process of fragmentation in ways that are well illustrated by recent studies of local administration in the South. Giuseppe Civile's recent monograph on Pignataro Maggiore in the Terra di Lavoro and Gabriella Gribaudi's reconstruction of the political anthropology of Eboli over a century and a half reveal how the dynamic of local politics remained firmly rooted within the locality and the community. The development of political alignments and networks within these communities involved constant exchanges with external systems of power and authority that required constant interaction with changing external intermediaries and representatives of the state (Civile 1990; Gribaudi 1990). But even in this context, the province was not a significant entity in the system of power in Liberal Italy, whose axis lay in the relationship between centre and locality (see especially Romanelli 1988 and *Meridina* 1988(2) & 1988(4)).

The lack of strong internal elements of economic, political or social cohesion in the South has frequently been cited to explain why attempts to create broader political or cultural movements, linked more generally but specifically to the South, have proved unsuccessful in both the nineteenth and the twentieth centuries. In the nineteenth century, for example, the South never became the home for a regional counter-Liberal political movement. Sanfedism might have played that role
have evolved towards a populist and clerical counter-revolu...o
movement with strong regional roots comparable to Span... tial
But despite Liberal fears, the Sanfedist tradition repe... nts at
materialize when it was most expected (Davis 199... nt hold
exceptions in the case of Sicily and Sardinia,
either a regional or wider level also failed
(Aymard & Giarrizzo 1987).

On the other hand, those political and cultural movements that did succeed in establishing strong and broad followings in the South were primarily supra-regional and even anti-regional in their outlook. Liberalism, nationalism and the doctrine of the State all bore a strong Southern imprint and found widespread support throughout the Southern regions. It is easy to forget the importance of not just Southerners (in one case Croce, in the other Alfredo Rocco), but also of the South in the formulation of these pan-Italianist movements. As Silvio Lanaro has recently pointed out, the North and Centre have by contrast been the intellectual homes of federalism, localism and strong resistance to the development of the State (Lanaro 1979, 1993; De Rosa 1984).

In the absence of clear geographical, economic or cultural boundaries, does it perhaps make more sense to view the *Mezzogiorno* not as something that really existed, but as a 'construct' or 'artefact', as a series of images and perceptions? This is a line of inquiry which has a pedigree that can be traced back as far as to the polemics that arose over the repression of brigandage in the South after Unification. The claim that the anarchy and disorder that Unification had unleashed in the South necessitated the abandonment of Cavour's programme of political decentralization and local autonomy was fiercely challenged by those who argued on the contrary that brigandage and the publicity devoted to it were little more than a pretext to suspend civil liberties and compromise many of the concessions to liberal principles that had been wrung from the Piedmontese monarchy.

Both Gramsci and Salvemini emphasized how the Southern Problem offered opportunities for depicting Southerners in terms of racial and biological discrimination that served to impress on the workers of the North that they shared no common interests with the primitive and half-savage labourers of the South. More recently, cultural historians like Asor Rosa have examined how these images of the South were constructed and how they played a part in identifying the traits and characteristics that the new Italian state and its cultural élites sought to establish as norms in the process of nation building (Asor Rosa 1976).

In similar terms, Daniel Pick has argued that in linking criminality to the biological and racial traits found predominantly amongst …utherners, the function of Lombroso's theories was to define through …sites the qualities and characteristics of respectability in the new …tate. John Dickie's recent rereading of the representation of the … Southerners in the forty years after Unification, in the light …id's *Orientalism*, develops a similar perspective. Through …of Southerners with forms of barbarism and violence …ot end with brigandage, Dickie claims that the South was transformed into an 'Otherness' against which the new Italian state and society sought to define itself (Pick 1986; Dickie 1992).

Images that identified the South with backwardness, barbarism, primitiveness, crime and violence amounted to more than ill-informed and prejudiced Northern perceptions. The messages they bore were more complex and, as Dickie rightly points out, writers from the South like Pasquale Turiello, Matilde Serao, Renato Fucini and Alfredo Niceforo, author of the notorious *Italia Barbara Contemporanea*, were prominent amongst those who played a critical role in formulating these images.

The function of these images of the South and of Southerners in the process of state formation in Italy invites comparison with Britain's Celtic Fringe, with the South in the United States or with much of rural and provincial France. But while the analysis of these images throws interesting light on the cultural history of state formation, it risks only partially deconstructing a perspective that views the South primarily through the eyes of the North and takes the dualism between North and South for granted.

That perspective and the dualism on which it is premised has been a central target of a lively revisionist historiography that has been taking shape over the last decade. Challenging the notion that the *Mezzogiorno* has been locked into a time-warp of economic and social immobilism for most of the life of the Italian state, a generation and more of Southern historians have been arguing that the South suffered from too much, rather than too little, economic change. The problem was not immobilism, but rather exposure to external and unpredictable forces of change that originated in external markets and in the international economy. The central drama of the South, it is argued, lay in the impact of exposure to the unpredictable forces of the international economy. It was this that determined what has been described as a process of 'Difficult Modernization' or alternatively 'Modernization without Growth', in which the forces of change proved more often disruptive than constructive and where economic change did not go hand-in-hand with economic growth (see Giarrizzo 1983; Salvemini 1984; Macry's Introduction in Macry & Villani 1990; Bevilacqua 1993).

While far from free of ambiguity themselves, the substitution of terms like 'difficult modernization' or 'modernization without growth' for 'backwardness' and 'under-development' brings fresh perspectives that often stand on their head what have commonly been taken as indicators of Southern 'backwardness' (Banti 1989a & b). For example, the *latifondo* – that quintessential symptom of the 'backwardness' of Southern agriculture in the nineteenth century – is now depicted not as a feudal relic, but as a relatively modern and rational system of production. Combining the production of high-value added crops (citrus fruits, olive oil, Mediterranean garden products) with more traditional extensive grazing and wheat cultivation, the rationale of the *latifondo* (it is argued) lay in its capacity to spread risks and respond to favourable and unfavourable market conditions: when export markets were poor, the estates could fall back on extensive production where capital inputs were low (Masella 1984; Petrusewicz 1989; Lupo 1990).

Another example of the ways in which the prevailing circumstances of economic uncertainty and exposure can be used to explain the rationality of Southern institutions can be found in Diego Gambetta's recent interpretation of *Mafia* as a surrogate for commercial trust. Setting the emergence of *Mafia* in the nineteenth century in the context of the extreme economic uncertainty that existed in western Sicily, Gambetta argues that in the absence of more settled channels of commerce and economic exchange, *Mafia* intermediaries were able to provide forms of protection and guarantees that were surrogates for commercial trust. *Mafia* was born, therefore, as an enterprise that supplied commodities – protection, guarantees – that were not available in either local markets or in local social institutions (Gambetta 1993).

The revisionist interpretations of the latifundist economy and of *Mafia* share the assumption that the peculiar features of economic and commercial instability in the South determined institutional development, forms of economic activity and behaviour. Does this then offer a new key to understanding the features that gave the South characteristics that were comparable throughout the region? Was it subordinate integration into international markets and the international economy that distinguished the Southern regions from the rest of Italy and accounted for their economic and social diversity?

The weakness of that argument is that these conditions were not peculiar to Southern Italy alone. Although Gambetta's analysis offers brilliant and original insights into the function of *Mafia*, his market-driven interpretation proves too general to explain why historically *Mafia* existed only in western Sicily and not in other parts of the South where similar economic, political and social conditions prevailed (Schneider 1976; Blok 1985; Tranfaglia 1991). More generally, the unique impact of commercial and economic uncertainty in the South is diluted by the fact that the same conditions were also common to much of the rest of Italy: indeed, the term 'difficult modernization' is applied to Italy as a whole as often as to the *Mezzogiorno* alone.

Any argument that rests solely on economics is likely to prove too blunt an instrument to tease out the peculiarities of the South. This has encouraged others to focus instead on social constraints on growth. Carlo Trigilia, for example, has recently re-examined Gramsci's insistence on the 'disaggregation' of society in the South, to argue that the failure to develop forms of horizontal social mobilization comparable to the trade union and cooperative movements in Northern Italy have been central barriers to economic growth and social change in the South. In the absence of alternative forms of collective organization, primary social institutions retained their primacy in ways that (apparently) inhibited the emergence of small-scale entrepreneurship and encouraged the persistence of clientelist politics (Trigilia 1988, 1992).

By switching the focus back to the internal, as opposed to the external obstacles to development, the debate on the 'social constraints' revives the earlier contrasts between endogenous and exogenous obstacles around which earlier debates on the Southern Problem revolved without reaching any clear conclusions. E. C. Banfield's less than happy concept of 'amoral familism' has found a new lease of life, while recently the American political scientist Robert Putnam has revived the old argument that the divergence between North and South is rooted in the absence of a civic tradition in the South and has tried to breathe new life into a thesis of cultural determinism that extends from the Middle Ages to the present (Putnam 1993).

Such arguments serve to reintroduce the concept of historical and structural dualisms been North and South, and not surprisingly have found enthusiastic supporters amongst the champions of the dualistic interpretation of Italian economic growth. Luciano Cafagna, for example, continues to insist on the reactionary and anti-modern mentalities of the Southern élites. Confronted by the inescapable realities of economic change, Cafagna argues, they consistently opted for defensive responses designed to limit as far as possible the impact of economic change, thereby ensuring that the South would experience a process of merely 'passive modernization' (Cafagna 1989 and see the earlier Sereni 1947).

The objections to these attempts to redefine the structural dualisms that separated North and South are easy to list. In the first place, little or no attempt is made to explain why these structures, mentalities or values remained unchanged over centuries, or indeed to map the extent to which they were present throughout the *Mezzogiorno* as a whole (assuming that we have some clear definition of what the *Mezzogiorno* was or is). More importantly, these contrasts pay little attention to the positive models against which the South is generally depicted as a negative. But the validity of the models of social and economic development in the North that underpin these contrasts is at least open to question. Although the systematic study of Italian entrepreneurship has been relatively recent, the work of Silvio Lanaro, Carlo Fiumian,

Maria Malatesta and Alberto Banti – to name but a few – has revealed the presence, in Lombardy, Emilia and the Veneto in the late nineteenth and early twentieth centuries, of forms of entrepreneurship and economic innovation that bore little resemblance to the models of balanced social and economic growth against which the South is deemed to have failed (Lanaro 1984; Banti 1989a & b; Malatesta 1989; Fumian 1990). A steadily growing body of research provides examples that suggest that capitalist development and 'modernization' in many parts of Northern Italy was as 'unregulated' or 'self-regulated' as in the South, and that neither the State nor collective social mobilization were significant intermediaries. Precisely those features that are often deemed peculiar to the South – the weakness of the state, the predominance of private over public power, the persistence of forms of paternalist social and economic organization, the juxtaposition of modern economic activity and 'traditional' social structures – can be found in those parts of Lombardy, Emilia and the Veneto that were leading Italy into the twentieth century. This is not to argue, of course, that there were no differences between North and South or that forms of social development were identical. It is rather to warn against easy generalization, and to emphasize the need to take more careful account of the historical specificities of each case.

Where then should the historical specificities of the South be located? There are some who would argue (or come close to arguing) that these specificities do not exist outside the political context of the integration of the South into the Italian state. This is not simply to revive the old thesis of the *Blocco Storico*, the reactionary alliance between Southern landlordism and Northern capital that both Marxist and liberal historians long held to be the cornerstone of Italian politics from the time of protectionism in the 1880s to the fall of Fascism – or perhaps later. But the concept of the *Blocco Storico* has been badly battered by the findings of new research on the development of political and economic interests in the South.

In the light of new research it is now clear that this thesis oversimplifies and distorts the nature of economic and political interests in the South. In the 1880s, for example, Southern landowners showed remarkably little enthusiasm for protective tariffs on agriculture, and it was well understood that protectionism would damage the South's most profitable commercial exports – wine, olive oil, citrus fruits – and make them vulnerable to reprisals (Cormio 1983; Masella 1984; Petrusewicz 1989; Lupo 1990).

Rather than open up a flaw line that set reactionary and progressive commercial interests in the South at odds, protectionism exposed the complex economic fabric of the South and the range of contrasting interests it embraced. If there was widespread agreement that state intervention was necessary to protect the particularly vulnerable economic interests of the South, there was inevitably little agreement over the form that this intervention should take.

This was really the central question in the debates on the Southern Problem that took shape after 1900 and culminated in the Parliamentary Inquiry into the Conditions of the Southern Peasants organized by Nitti in 1906. This inquiry's purpose (despite the title) was to decide what forms of tax concessions to the landowners would most effectively encourage economic growth in the wake of the mass emigration of the previous decade.

Nitti's proposals for major structural change, industrial development, incentivization of agriculture through tax concessions and closer ties with Northern capital found broad support amongst many commercial interests in Sicily, Campania and Apulia, but they also roused fears that the incursion of Northern capital – in the guise above all of the Commit – would destroy the autonomy of the Southern élites. The more conservative camp stood firm on liberal principles and fiercely denounced attempted incursions by the State – the first, as Manacorda showed long ago, being Crispi's attempt to reform the *latifondo* after the Sicilian *Fasci*. It was this reaction, as Salvatore Lupo's recent study of the Sicilian citrus trade documents very fully, that gave birth to the first attempts to establish a populist Sicilian regional movement. Salandra's agrarian programme offered an alternative for those wary of industrialism and the intentions of Northern capital (Manacorda 1972; Renda 1977; Barbagallo 1980; Barone 1983; Massafra 1988; Lupo 1990; Masella & Salvemini 1990).

These proposals and programmes reflected the lack of a clear sense of regional interest or identity. If that in turn reflected the variety of different economic interests present in the *Mezzogiorno*, it also revealed their relative weakness. In contrast to the image of a reactionary South flexing its muscle at the expense of the North, the findings of recent studies on Southern commercial and financial interests before and after the First World War indicate very clearly the relative inability of Southern interest groups to lobby effectively at the level of national politics (for a general account of the economy see Toniolo 1992).

One important example is that of the tariffs of 1889. Why did the Southerners vote for a measure that was damaging to their economic interests? The answer is as a trade-off for the shelving of a programme of tax reform which would have abolished the privileges the South received in 1861. Why was one interest traded for another? Because the fiscal question created greater unanimity than the tariff question. If that is one example of the ways in which the South was integrated into a system of political exchanges that traded off one set of interests for others, there are many others. Salvatore Lupo's recent study of the Sicilian citrus trade has, for example, shown how in the 1920s and 1930s the interests of first Southern commercial exporters and then the Southern landowners more generally were ruinously subordinated to the needs of Fascist economic policy (which traded Sicilian lemons with Hitler for coal and steel). There is no better example of the consequences of this vulnerability than the attempt by the Sicilian landowners to stage a strike against the Fascist internal colonization policies in 1940 (see especially Lupo 1990).

Taking those arguments forward into the post-Second World War era to embrace the failure to implement the programmes that lay behind the creation of the *Cassa per il Mezzogiorno*, Piero Bevilacqua depicts the South as a region whose particular needs have been acknowledged but never adequately protected by the Italian state, but to which it has, on the other hand, contributed since Unification a limitless supply of labour, skills and talent (Bevilacqua 1993). Rightly locating the evolution of the Southern Problem in the context of the Italian state, Bevilacqua's argument nevertheless comes close to denying that there have been any forces at work in the South that have themselves contributed to the aggregate differentials in terms of employment, per capita income and productivity, comparative levels of welfare expenditure and social facilities or the diffusion of organized crime that constitute the empirical realities of the Southern Problem today (Barbagallo 1989, 1990).

It is clear from the post-Second World War experience of the South that these issues cannot be related simply to the absence of economic and social change. They have to be seen in terms of political programmes, political negotiations and the terms of political exchange that have determined the fortunes of the South. But if all or most of these relationships have been essentially exploitative, the question that still has to be answered is: why has the South (or its composite parts if there is no single *Mezzogiorno*) consistently and repeatedly left itself exposed to exploitation?

At this point the discussion has to refocus on the formation and behaviour of the Southern élites. If new research on the development of economic and political interests in the South from the late nineteenth century to the present has made it necessary to modify the stereotypes of the *Blocco Storico* and to cast off the abstract contrasts between Southern and Northern capitalism found in much of the earlier literature, it has also repeatedly underscored the failure of the Southern élites to establish greater autonomy (Barbagallo 1990; D'Antone 1990; Frascani 1990; Lupo 1990; Rienzo 1996 are all significant in this respect). Here the contrast with the North is more striking, and in comparison with the aggressively autonomous entrepreneurs of Emilia and the Veneto their Southern counterparts remained more closely dependent on the state and public administration.

Why? Partly, as we have seen, because the vulnerability of the Southern economies made them more dependent on state intervention. Partly, too, because in contrast to Northern and Central Italy, the bureaucratic state was an older historical reality in the South whose importance grew in the nineteenth and twentieth century in direct proportion to the failure to develop more robust and spontaneous forms of economic growth. The point is well and subtly made in Paolo Macry's study of the changing fortunes of five Neapolitan patrician families. While demonstrating again that the South did experience profound and far-reaching economic change in the nineteenth century, Macry's sensitive analysis demonstrates that the central issue in the South was not the persistence of the *ancien régime* but the absence of any clearly delineated new social forces to take the place of the old (Macry 1988b).

If this absence, together with the difficulties that hedged around the emergence of more dynamic and spontaneous forms of economic development, encouraged reliance on the State as provider and protector, it in turn reinforced tendencies that were already strongly present in the South. Very often the debate on the Southern Problem has hinged around the premise that the State was in some sense absent in the *Mezzogiorno*. In reality, that case could probably be made much better for many parts of Northern Italy (see especially Lanaro 1984), and it should always be remembered that the polemic against the incursions of the bureaucratic State that gave force to Stefano Jacini's famous defence of the '*paese reale*' against the '*paese legale*' were quintessentially Northern in origin.

What distinguished the South was not an accident of geography or physical terrain, foreign occupation or whatever, but the historical evolution of the State in forms quite different from those in Central and Northern Italy (Barbagallo 1989, 1990). The reasons for this do not lie in the nature of the dynastic State in the South, which evolved with much greater difficulty towards a centralized bureaucratic State in the eighteenth and nineteenth centuries than its Piedmontese and Austrian counterparts, nor in any supposed lack of civic tradition. They are to be found in the precocious (again the comparison is with the North) collapse of paternalism and deference in the South. It was the social tensions and conflicts that reached greater levels of intensity in the mainland South and in Sicily in the first half of the nineteenth century that drove the propertied classes to seek the protection of the State, and wherever possible to bring public authority into the sphere of private power. No matter how willing they were to resort also to direct and even violent methods of control, the élites in many parts of Calabria, Sicily and Apulia relied on the State in ways that their Tuscan, Piedmontese or Emilian counterparts did not – or at least, not until much later.

If that blurred distinctions between public and private authority in many parts of Southern Italy, it also established a negotiating position which successive governments were prepared to exploit (Aliberti 1987; Pezzino 1987; Davis 1994a & b). That process is evident in the most recent research on the origins of the *Mafia*. Paolo Pezzino and Salvatore Lupo offer important evidence to show how the representatives of a weak state found themselves confronted in western Sicily by fiercely independent élites. In an attempt to establish their own political and administrative powers, they proved only too willing to enter into alliances with organized crime (Pezzino 1987, 1990, 1993b; Lupo 1993). It is also evident in more general terms in Gabriella Gribaudi's description of the ways in which successive governments of Liberal Italy sought to perpetuate factional divisions within Southern communities as a means to assert and increase their own power (Gribaudi 1990).

It is increasingly evident from recent research that many of the stereotypes that form part of the currency of political debate in Italy today derive from the vocabulary of the Southern Problem that has been formulated in ways that are frequently anachronistic and often inaccurate or misleading. As well as drawing attention to the historical specificities of time and place within which the Southern Problem has taken shape, critical reconsideration of the South as a physical or economic area throws into sharper focus the essentially political parameters of the Southern Problem, its origins and changing forms in a century and more in the life of the Italian state. No matter how pressing the problems currently posed by these regions – and their gravity should never be underestimated – the Southern Problem bears very firmly the imprint: 'Made in Italy'.

Bibliography

Aliberti, G. (1987), *Potere e società locale nel Mezzogiorno dell'800*, Bari.

Asor Rosa, A. (1976), 'La Cultura', *Storia d'Italia*, Vol. 4, Turin.

Aymard, M. and Giarrizzo, G. (eds), (1987), *La Sicilia* (*Storia d'Italia. Le Regioni dall'Unità a oggi)*, Turin.

Banti, A.M. (1989a), 'Gli imprenditori meridionali: razionalità e contesto', *Meridiana*, 1989, **6**, pp.63–89.

—— (1989b), *Terra e denaro; Una borghesia padana dell'ottocento*, Venice.

Barbagallo, F. (1990), 'Il Mezzogiorno come problema attuale', *Studi Storici*, **31**, pp.587–9.

—— (1989), 'Potere economico e economia assistita nel mezzogiorno repubblicano', *Studi Storici*, **30**, 1, pp.43–52.

—— (1980), *Stato, Parlamento e lotte politico-sociali nel Mezzogiorno 1900–1914*, Naples.

Barone, G. (1983), 'Stato, capitale finanziario e Mezzogiorno', in G. Giarrizzo (ed.), *La Modernizzazione Difficile: Città e campagne nel Mezzogiorno dall'età giolittiana al fascismo*, Bari, pp.27–79.

Bevilacqua, P. (1988), 'Acque e bonifiche nel Mezzogiorno nella prima metà dell'Ottocento', in A. Massafra (ed.), *Il Mezzogiorno Pre-Unitario: Economia, Società e Istituzioni*, Bari, pp.337–62.

—— (1993), *Breve storia del Mezzogiorno tra fascismo e dopoguerra*, Rome.

—— (1980), *Le campagne del Mezzogiorno tra fascismo e dopoguerra*, Turin.

—— (1985) 'Uomini, terre, economie', in P. Bevilacqua and A. Placanica (eds), *La Calabria (Storia d'Italia. Storia delle Regioni dall'Unità a oggi)*, Turin, pp.117–337.

Bevilacqua, P. and Placanica, A. (eds), (1985), *La Calabria (Storia d'Italia. Storia delle Regioni dall'Unità a oggi*), Turin.

Blok, A. (1985), *The Mafia of a Sicilian Village*, Oxford.

Cafagna, L. (1989), *Dualismo e sviluppo nella storia d'Italia*, Venice.

Civile, G. (1990), *Il comune rustico: Storia sociale di un paese del Mezzogiorno nell'800*, Bologna.

Cormio, A. (1983), 'Le campagne pugliesi nella fase di "transizione" 1880–1914', in G. Giarrizzo (ed.), *La modernizzazione difficile: Città e campagne nel Mezzogiorno dall'età giolittiana al fascismo*, Bari, 1983, pp.147–210.

D'Antone, Leandra (1990), *Scienze e governo del territorio. Medici, ingegneri, agronomi e urbanisti nel Tavoliere di Puglia (1865–1965)*, Milan.

Davis, J.A. (1994a), 'Changing contours of public and private in the 19th century Mezzogiorno', in A. Massafra and P. Macry (eds), *Studi in onore di Pasquale Villani*, Naples, pp.691–708.

—— (1994b), 'Remapping Italy's Path to the 20th Century', *Journal of Modern History*, **66**, pp.291–330.

—— (1991), '1799: the Santafede and the crisis of the Ancien Regime in Southern Italy', in J.A. Davis and P. Ginsborg (eds), *Society and Politics in the Age of the Risorgimento*, Cambridge, pp.1–25.

De Rosa, L. (1984), 'Economics and nationalism in Italy (1861–1914)',

Journal of European Economic History, **3**, pp.537–74.

Dickie, J. (1992), 'A world at war; the Italian army and brigandage', *History Workshop Journal*, **33**, pp.1–24.

Di Ciommo, E. (1993), *La nazione possibile: Mezzogiorno e questione nazionale nel 1848*, Milan.

Frascani, P. (1990), 'Mercato e commercio a Napoli dopo l'Unità', in P. Macry and P. Villani (eds), *La Campania (Storia d'Italia. Le Regioni dall'Unità a oggi),* Turin, pp.185–209.

Fumian, C. (1990), *La città del lavoro. Un utopia agroindustriale nel Veneto contemporaneo*, Venice.

—— (1984), 'Proprietari, imprenditori, agronomi', in S. Lanaro (ed.), *Il Veneto (Storia d'Italia: Le Regioni dall'Unità a oggi)*, Turin, pp.99–164.

Gambetta, D. (1993), *The Sicilian Mafia: The Business of Private Protection*, Cambridge.

G. Giarrizzo (ed.), (1983), *La modernizzazione difficile: Città e campagne nel Mezzogiorno dall'età giolittiana al fascismo*, Bari.

Gribaudi, G. (1990), *A Eboli; Il mondo meridionale in cent'anni di trasformazioni*, Venice.

Iachello, E. and Signorelli, A. (1987), 'Borghesie urbane nell'ottocento', in M. Ayamard and G. Giarrizzo (eds), *La Sicilia (Storia d'Italia. Le Regioni dall'Unità a oggi)*, Turin, pp.89–155.

Lanaro, S. (1984), 'Il Veneto: Genealogia di un modello', *Il Veneto (Storia d'Italia. Le Regioni dall'Unità a oggi)*, Turin, pp.5–98.

—— (1993), 'Le élites settentrionale', in *La Questione Settentrionale*, special issue of *Meridiana*, **16**, January, pp.9–40.

—— (1979), *Nazione e lavoro. Saggio sulla cultura della borghesia in Italia 1870–1925*, Venice.

Levi, Giovanni (1979), 'Regioni e cultura delle classi popolari', *Quaderni Storici*, **15**, 2, pp.720–31.

Lupo, S. (1990), *Il giardino degli aranci: il mondo degli agrumi nella storia del Mezzogiorno*, Venice.

—— (1993), *Storia della Mafia dalle origini ai nostri giorni*, Rome.

Macry, P. (1988a), 'Le élites urbane: stratificazioni e mobilità sociale, le forme del potere locale e la cultura dei ceti emergenti', in A. Massafra (ed.), *Il Mezzogiorno pre-unitario: Economia, società e istituzioni*, Bari, pp.799–820.

—— (1988b), *Ottocento: Famiglia, élites e patrimoni a Napoli*, Turin.

Macry, P. and Romanelli, R. (eds), (1984), 'Borghesie urbane nell'ottocento', *Quaderni Storici*, **56**.

Macry, P. and Villani, P. (eds), (1990), *La Campania (Storia d'Italia: Le Regioni dall'Unità a oggi)*, Turin.

Malatesta, M. (1989), *I signori della terra. L'organizzazione degli interessi agrari padani (1860–1914)*, Milan.

Manacorda, G. (1972), 'Crispi e la legge agraria per la Sicilia', *Archivio Storico per la Sicilia Orientale*, pp.9–95.

Masella, L. (1984), *Proprietà e politica agraria in Italia 1861–1914*, Naples.

Masella, L. (1983), 'Élites politiche e potere urbano nel Mezzogiorno dall'età giolittiana all'avvento del fascismo', in G. Giarrizzo (ed.), *La modernizzazione difficile: Città e campagne nel Mezzogiorno dall'età giolittiana al fascismo*, Bari, pp.92–116.

Masella, L. and Salvemini, B. (eds), (1990), *La Puglia (Storia d'Italia: Le Regioni dall'Unità a oggi)*, Turin.

Massafra, A. (cd.), (1988), *Il Mezzogiorno pre-unitario: Economia, società e istituzioni*, Bari.

Meridiana (1988), 'Circuiti Politici', – articles by S. Lupo, L. Masella, L. Musella, **2**, January.

—— (1988), 'Poteri Locali', – articles by R. Romanelli, P. Pezzino, G. Civile, M. Cammelli, **4**, September.

Petrusewicz, M. (1989), *Latifondo: Economia morale e vita materiale in una periferia dell'Ottocento*, Venice.

Pezzino, P. (1993a), *Il paradiso abitato dai diavoli: Società, élites, istituzioni nel Mezzogiorno contemporaneo*, Milan.

—— (1993b), *La congiura dei pugnalatori: Un caso politico-giudiziario alle origini della Mafia*, Venice.

—— (1987), 'Mezzogiorno e potere locale', *Rivista di Storia Contemporanea*, **4**.

—— (1990), *Una certa recipocità di favori. Mafia e modernizzazione violenta nella Sicilia post-unitaria*, Milan.

Pick, D. (1986), 'The faces of anarchy: Lombroso and the politics of criminal science in post-Unification Italy', *History Workshop*, 21, pp.60–86.

Putnam, R. D. (1993), *Making Democracy Work. Civic Traditions in Modern Italy*, Princeton, N.J.

Renda, F. (1977), *I Fasci Siciliani*, Turin.

Rienzo, G. (1996), 'L'Esorilio della Banca di Calabria nel tessuto economico mapoletana, Il percorso di un'oligarchia finanziaria in età liberale', *Società e Storia*, **69**, 1, pp.71–93.

Romanelli, R. (1988), *Il commando impossibile. Stato e società nell'Italia liberale*, Bologna.

Salvemini, B. (1984), 'Note sul concetto di ottocento meridionale', *Società e Storia*, **26**, pp.917–45.

Schneider, J. and P. (1976), *Culture and Political Economy in Western Sicily*, New York.

Sereni, E. (1947), *Il capitalismo nelle campagne 1860–1900*, Turin.

Toniolo, G. (1992), *An Economic History of Liberal Italy*, London.
Tranfaglia, N. (1991), *La Mafia come metodo*, Bari.
Trigilia, C. (1988), 'Le condizioni non-economiche dello sviluppo: problemi di ricerca sul Mezzogiorno di oggi', *Meridiana*, **2**, January, pp.167–87.
—— (1992), *Sviluppo senza autonomia*, Bologna.

–4–

Linguistic Variety in Italy

Anna Laura Lepschy, Giulio Lepschy and *Miriam Voghera*

Introduction

The title of this volume is *Italian Regionalism*; we could accordingly have discussed regionalism from the viewpoint of language, trying to identify (a) the connection between regionalism and linguistic variation (i.e., how far dialect fragmentation has contributed to, and in turn has been encouraged by, political and cultural differences between regions), and (b) the question of the correspondence, or lack of it, between regional and dialect boundaries, and in particular the presence of dialect entities which may be larger or smaller than individual regions.

But, on reflection, we decided that it was more helpful, for the readers of this book, if we took a step back, and offered a brief account of the linguistic situation in Italy and its remarkable variety. In the following sections of this chapter we shall look at three aspects of our theme: the background to Italy's linguistic variety in a historical perspective, the sociolinguistic situation of modern Italy, and language policy and linguistic legislation.

A Historical Perspective

It may be useful to clarify some of the basic notions we are going to use, such as those of national language, dialects and linguistic minorities. Italian is assumed to be Italy's national language. It originates as a written language based on the literary Florentine of the fourteenth century, and codified at the beginning of the sixteenth century, through discussions on the *questione della lingua*. The line which prevailed (against the upholders of both modern Tuscan and of a supra-regional, but still Tuscan-based, *cortegiana* variety) was that of the Venetian humanist Pietro Bembo: the literary language had to be based on the imitation of the great fourteenth-century writers, Boccaccio for prose and Petrarch for poetry. This archaizing, puristic view was adopted by the *Accademia della Crusca* and inspired its famous dictionary, which with its authority was to mark the development of Italian literature for many years to come, notwithstanding the criticisms of some modern-minded, progressive intellectuals (like the group around the periodical *Il Caffè* in the eighteenth century) and the attempt on the part of Italy's most important nineteenth-century novelist, Alessandro Manzoni, to abandon this archaic literary model in favour of modern, living, Florentine.

Literary Italian had been adopted as a written language, but the vast majority of Italians until recent years were in fact illiterate. Their mother tongues were Italy's local dialects. These dialects are in effect separate Romance languages and they can differ from each other as much as French differs from Spanish. These Italian dialects are not derived from Italian, nor are they varieties or adaptations of the national language. On the contrary, it is Italian which is based on one of the dialects (i.e., Florentine), or rather, on the standardization of its literary variety of the fourteenth century. But Turinese, Milanese, Venetian, Bolognese, Florentine, Neapolitan, Palermitano, etc. are all 'sister' languages, derived from spoken Latin. They differ from each other in phonology, grammar and lexis.

It may be useful to provide some examples, in order to give an idea of the nature of these differences. The outcome of Latin *dominicam (diem)*, 'Sunday', is *domenica* in Florentine, *domenega* in Venetian, *dmandga* in Bolognese, *rummeneca* in Neapolitan, *duminica* in Palermitano. As well as having different phonological developments, words may have different origins altogether: the word for 'fork' is in Florentine *forchetta*, a form derived from the Latin *furca*, but in Venetian it is *piron*, apparently of Greek origin (see modern Greek *pirouni*). The word for 'chair' is in Florentine *sedia* (or *seggiola*), related to Latin *sedere* 'to sit', but in Venetian it is *carega*, from the Greek *kathédra*, whence Latin *cathedra* (this is also the etymology of French *chaire, chaise* and its English *chair*). There are basic differences in syntax: for the Italian *sono malato*, we find Sicilian *malatu sugnu*; for *non capisco*, Piedmontese *capissu nen*; for *la si è presa*, Venetian *se la ga ciapada*.

We said that these dialects are separate Romance languages. But it should be understood that, from a strictly linguistic viewpoint, there is no difference between a language and a dialect. The distinction is not linguistic, but cultural, social and political. According to a jocular, but not inept definition, often quoted in linguistics textbooks, a language is a dialect which has an army and a navy: a dialect which is used officially by a state is called a language. The word and the notion of a 'dialect' seems to have been introduced into modern European culture by Italian humanists (see Alinei 1981; Trovato 1984) who took it from the Greek, where it designated accepted varieties of the literary language. In the Latin tradition the concept did not have immediate relevance, since the emphasis was on linguistic unity rather than diversity. But when the term was taken up in Italy, between the fifteenth and sixteenth century, it added to its meaning a hierarchical value, and it came to designate an idiom subordinated to a more prestigious one. When we said, above, that Italian was itself based on a dialect (i.e., the literary variety of early Florentine) we were of course using the term 'dialect' in an anachronistic way. The Florentine of Dante, the Milanese of Bonvesin da la Riva, or the Sicilian of Stefano Protonotaro in the thirteenth century are not properly designated by the term 'dialect', since they are not subordinated to a superior standard. The choice was, at the time, between the vernacular and Latin, not between dialect and Italian (even though Dante aimed at an 'illustrious', rather than parochial, kind of vernacular). We can legitimately talk of works written in Italian dialects from the moment in which these can be opposed to a supra-regional standard, i.e., from the beginning of the sixteenth century.

It is generally assumed that in Italy, at least since the Renaissance, a condition of *disglossia* (rather than *bilingualism*) prevailed, i.e., that a 'High' and 'Low' variety were available: literary Italian, used almost exclusively in writing, being the High Variety; and a non-literary variety, and the local dialects, used in speech, being the Low one. This requires some qualification. On the one hand many dialects have a long-standing, rich and sophisticated literary tradition, in many cases going back to the Middle Ages; but dialect literature proper presupposes, as we have seen, the ability to write in Italian. That is, it is not opposed to, but part of Italian literature. One should not forget that what we call Italian literature finds expression, up to the sixteenth century, mainly in two languages, Latin and vernacular, and from the beginning of the sixteenth century, a third medium is added – dialect. 'Dialect literature' is of course not the same as 'popular literature' (see Jones 1990), and normally belongs to a sophisticated level of elaborate, self-conscious 'high' culture, rather than to spontaneous 'popular' culture. On the other hand the written language used for everyday correspondence, for business and administration, was not literary Italian of the Bembian mould, but a local *koiné*, with a heavy dialect colouring. (*Koiné* is a term derived from the Greek *koiné diálektos*, i.e., the 'common dialect', based on Attic, which during the Hellenistic period came to replace classical Greek dialects.) In Italy during the fourteenth and fifteenth centuries, written languages or *koinaí* based on Tuscan developed, owing to the prestige of *Trecento* Tuscan literature and culture, but with strong dialectal colouring. A clear example is offered by Boiardo's *Orlando innamorato* (or *Innamoramento d'Orlando*), written in a Northern, Padana *koiné*, in contrast with Ariosto's *Orlando furioso*, which in its three editions came progressively nearer to the ideal represented by Bembo's norm (see Lepschy 1993).

Dialects can differ so much from each other as to be reciprocally unintelligible to their users. How many different dialects are spoken in Italy? The question is problematic, and not easier than one concerning the number of languages in the world. Modern handbooks suggest figures, for the languages in the world, between 3,000 (Décsy 1986–88) and 6,000 (Grimes 1988), and some estimates reach even higher figures. This oscillation may give an idea of the difficulties involved. For Italy it is relatively easy to identify about fifteen main dialect groups, clearly different from each other, and roughly corresponding to the traditional subdivisions into regions. But it is clear that often there are noticeable differences between neighbouring towns, and even within the same town. Dante observed this at the beginning of the fourteenth century in his *De vulgari eloquentia* (I, IX, 4), noting that in Bologna the inhabitants of a central district of the town (Strada Maggiore) speak differently from those of the outskirts (Borgo San Felice). Similarly we can observe today that the dialect of Venice is different not only from that of Padua, Vicenza, etc., but also from that of nearby Chioggia (remember the use made of this difference in Goldoni's *Baruffe Chiozzotte*), from that of the Lagoon islands, like Burano and Torcello; it even differs, however marginally, from one *sestiere* to another. A further complication is introduced by the distinction between regions, like the Veneto, in which speakers can use a regional dialect as well as a local one, and regions, like Emilia-Romagna, in which only the local dialect and not the regional variety is available. John Trumper (1977: 265) has identified the former situation as 'macrodiglossia', and the latter as 'microdiglossia', and has discussed their different implications for the ability (greater in the former than in the latter case) of the dialects to survive in the face of pressure from the national language.

Usually the question of the dialects is treated separately from that of the *linguistic minorities*. These are enclaves of speakers of foreign languages, often established in Italy for many centuries. From current literature the following list emerges, with the estimated (and very hypothetical) number of speakers in brackets:

- small historic 'relics', often going back to the fifteenth and sixteenth centuries: Greek (30,000) and Albanian (100,000) in several villages in Southern Italy; Catalan (15,000) in Alghero; German (13,000) in small communities in Piedmont and in the Veneto; Croat (3,000) in the Molise; Occitanic and Franco-Provençal in small colonies in Southern Italy;

- stronger groups, adjacent to bordering foreign countries: German (280,000) in South Tyrol; Occitanic and Franco-Provençal (115,000) in Piedmont; Slovene (53,000) in the Veneto;
- in the classification of the Romance languages sometimes Friulian (625,000), Dolomite Ladin (50,000) (both grouped together with the dialects of the Swiss Canton of Grisons, as Rheto-Romance), and Sard (estimates vary between 160,000 and 1,200,000) are associated with the other Italian dialects, and sometimes listed as separate Romance varieties. Within these communities there is however a lively feeling for their own linguistic individuality, often linked to the demand that their idiom be recognized as a 'language' rather than a 'dialect';
- some surveys refer also to Romany (16,000), Judeo-Italian, and Italian sign-language used by people with hearing and speech impediments.

There is also a large group of recent immigrants (estimated to be about 1,000,000), mostly from North and Central Africa. It is difficult to evaluate how far these will become part of the permanent population, and whether they will preserve their original languages.

The Linguistic Situation of Modern Italy

The attempt to establish how many people use Italian and how many use dialect poses considerable difficulties. Tullio De Mauro (1976), in his ground-breaking volume *Storia linguistica dell'Italia unita*, valiantly marshalled evidence for the years of Unification. He used mostly statistics for literacy, which gives an 80 per cent illiteracy rate for 1861. However, these statistics are difficult to translate in term of familiarity with the national language. Only since 1951 do statistical data distinguish between 'literates' and 'semiliterates'. The 20 per cent described as 'literate' in 1861 apparently included also the 'semiliterate', i.e., those who could only read and not write, and those who could neither read nor properly write, but only trace (or perhaps 'draw') their signature. This would have been clearly insufficient to guarantee to a dialect speaker a command of the national language. De Mauro correctly distinguishes between the situation of Tuscany and Rome on the one hand, and the rest of Italy on the other. In Tuscany and Rome the mother tongue was sufficiently similar to Italian to allow us to assume that people classified as literate were in fact able to communicate in the national language. This provides us with 400,000 Tuscan and 70,000 Roman literates. For the other parts of Italy however, in which the mother tongue differed more sharply from Italian, De Mauro suggests that familiarity with the national language can only be assumed on the basis of post-elementary education. This was provided only to about 0.8 per cent of the population, i.e., outside Tuscany and Rome, 160,000 people out of 20,000,000. The total number of Italophones is therefore calculated at 630,000 out of a population of 25,000,000 which is about 2.5 per cent.

The figure is particularly striking, De Mauro points out, as it is just a little higher than the official figure for '*alloglotti*', i.e., speakers of foreign languages within the boundaries of the Italian state after the First World War. An eminent historian of the Italian language, and specialist of Old Tuscan, Arrigo Castellani (1982), was so disturbed by these conclusions that he re-examined all the evidence in the hope of reaching a higher figure, but he was unable to go beyond a maximum of about 10 per cent. This then seems to be the order of magnitude we have to accept for the people able to use Italian at the moment of unification: between 2.5 and 10 per cent. It is clearly difficult to overestimate the social and political implications of a state of affairs in which over 90 per cent of the population of a country are not only illiterate, but also unable to communicate in the official language of the state.

The situation gradually improved after Unification. Literacy has now reached Northern European standards; but the crucial factor for this newly generalized familiarity with the national language seems to have been, even more than education, the spread of television, which has guaranteed constant contact with spoken Italian, and therefore detracted from the traditional importance of literacy and schooling as the main way of access to the national language.

We can form an idea of the relative weight of Italian and dialect over the last twenty years from the following data based on Doxa polls (Doxa 1982, 1988, 1992). We have to keep in mind, however, the small size of the samples considered (a few thousand people at best), and the nature of the questionnaires employed, which appeal to self-evaluation and not to an objective observation of linguistic behaviour. There are also interesting variations according to age, sex, region, size of conurbation: the figures for Italian are higher for younger than for old people, for females than for males, for the Centre and North-West than for the South and North-East, for large than for small towns.

These data can be looked at from different viewpoints. They obviously show a fall in the use of dialect and a rise in the use of Italian.

Table 4.1.

Usage in the family	*1974*	*1982*	*1988*	*1991*
dialect with everyone	51%	47%	40%	36%
Italian with everyone	25%	29%	34%	34%
Usage with friends and colleagues				
only or mainly dialect	42%	36%	33%	23%
only or mainly Italian	36%	42%	47%	48%

But what seems to be particularly noticeable, in contrast with the general assumptions and expectations, is that the curve is not steeper. It is striking, and perhaps surprising for some observers, that the latest data, for 1991, give less than half of the population using only or mainly Italian with friends and colleagues, and that the language exclusively used at home is, for more people, dialect (36 per cent) rather than Italian (34 per cent). If we compare the present situation with that of the years of Unification, the main difference seems to be that, with reference to the range available to individual communities, Italy is now a largely bilingual country, whereas before it was effectively a monolingual one, consisting of dialect speakers.

If we look at the progress of Italian, we have to also ask: what sort of Italian? The answer is that Italian is not a monolithic, inflexible language adhering to unitary norms. It is instead a supple medium, adaptable to different sets of circumstances and standards. On the one hand, the spread of Italian as a spoken language has given rise to regional varieties. On the other, during the last decades the balance between colloquial and literary has shifted in favour of the former (see Sabatini 1985), making it more generally accepted, also in writing, words and structures which originate in regional and/or spoken usage, which in the past would have been frowned upon if they appeared in written texts. The outcome has, in our opinion, reduced tolerance towards all-too-widespread pompous, bombastic rhetoric, and favoured the development of clearer, simpler, and more spontaneous linguistic usage. Inevitably, however, the wide diffusion of the national language, now employed by larger sections of the population than ever before, has brought with it a rise in the number of unskilled users, who have an imperfect command of certain spelling and grammatical rules, particularly in the domain of the written language. We believe that these are teething troubles, which will be cured by better educational provisions, and not by short-sighted complaints about corruption of language and debasement of standards.

Language Policy

As far as linguistic legislation is concerned, we can identify three distinct periods.

Between 1861 and 1918 unitary assumptions prevailed. Italian was considered to be the national language, and dialects were generally disregarded. The Piedmontese law which authorized the use of French in the Valle d'Aosta was abrogated or became obsolete. In education there were some inconsequential attempts to enforce the Manzonian view of Florentine usage as the standard to be upheld; grammars were produced and officially encouraged which quaintly presented Florentine expressions as preferable or alternative to Italian ones: for instance, *core* for *cuore*, *si parlava* for *parlavamo* (while forms like *continuiamo* were excluded altogether, in favour of *si continua*), *verrai anche te* for *verrai anche tu*, *anderò* for *andrò*, *la era molto pallida* for *era molto pallida*, etc. (Lepschy & Raponi 1988). There were also some attempts, on the part of the most enlightened educationalists, to take into account that dialects were the mother tongue of most children, and could therefore be exploited for a more effective teaching of Italian.

In the period 1918–45 the authorities tried to introduce forced assimilation of linguistic minorities, including the Italianization of placenames and surnames. The regulations concerning school-teaching were particularly inept, in as far as they imposed the use of Italian also in schools for children who were German or Slovene speaking. The Fascist attitude tried to impose, even though inconsistently and halfheartedly, a measure of artificial linguistic unification, sweeping under the carpet the fact that most people, in Italy, normally communicated in dialect. The regime attempted to suppress by law the use of foreign words in Italian, and to introduce in their place, through the farcical deliberations of the *Accademia d'Italia*, autarchic Italian substitutes (Raffaelli 1983; Klein 1986).

After 1945 the Republic's Constitution adopted a pluralist attitude. Article 6 of the Constitution reads: 'The Republic protects linguistic minorities with the appropriate laws.' The preliminary discussions indicate that this was a deliberate statement of principle and not a norm introduced to obey international obligations. The wording is due to an amendment by T. Codignola which mentioned 'minoranze etnico-linguistiche'. Little was subsequently done, however, to enforce this article in practice.

Two different models were followed for the protection of 'strong' minorities, i.e., those which associate their language with that of a neighbouring foreign country (Pizzorusso 1976; Stipo 1992). One is the model of *bilingualism*, adopted for the Valle d'Aosta, which assumes all citizens must know both the majority and the minority language. Everyone is expected to attend the same kind of school, in which both languages are studied, for the same number of hours, and they alternate as mediums for teaching the other subjects. Either language may be used in official documents, without need of translation. This solution is clearly more civilized and favours integration, but in the long run appears to offer only a weak safeguard to the minority language. The other model is that of *linguistic separation*, or apartheid, adopted for German in South Tyrol and for Slovene in Friuli-Venezia Giulia; members of each group are not expected to know the language of the other group. There are separate schools, where the minority language is the medium of instruction, and the *other* language is studied as a second language. In public offices and in official texts individuals can expect their language to be used; in dealings between the two communities bilingual texts (or translations) are to be used. This model offers a strong safeguard to the minority language, but does not guarantee that its speakers are also capable of using the majority (national) language (which may, like Italian in South Tyrol, be the minority language in the relevant region). It is also worth remembering that the language which is thus accorded protection, in the Valle d'Aosta and in South Tyrol, is not the mother tongue (Occitanic and Franco-Provençal patois, and a Bavarian-type dialect, respectively), but standard French and standard Italian.

Many discussions (see for instance Bolelli 1992; Simone 1992) have been occasioned by a bill, *Norme in materia di tutela delle minoranze linguistiche – Proposta di legge N.612 (Norme 1992)*, approved by the Chamber of Deputies on 20 November 1991, but not by the Senate (Parliament was subsequently dissolved). The bill introduced a measure of protection for the 'weak' linguistic minorities, which are not supported by foreign governments. The law would allow these minority languages to be used in schools, in certain public contexts, in local radio and television broadcasts, etc. An element of confusion was however introduced by the mention in the bill of Sard and Friulian. This provoked a series of outbursts in the press, reacting to the implication that if the bill applied to Sard and Friulian, it would also apply, for instance, to Lombard and Venetian, and therefore encourage some of the *Leghe*'s more extreme positions in favour of adopting the dialects as official languages of the regions. This would indeed be an anachronistic and objectionable project, but according to De Mauro (1992), who appears to be the intellectual driving force behind the proposal, it is not what the bill is about.

It seems to us that more liberalism and less *dirigisme* in linguistic matters can only be a good thing, and that small communities ought to be assisted if they wish to preserve their traditions, including linguistic ones. On the other hand it appears that more information is needed (even though it was not the function of the bill to provide it) about the actual consistency, or obsolescence, of these linguistic communities, and about the difficulties which may be caused by the lack of standardization, of adequate study aids, classroom materials, trained teachers, etc. It is however interesting to observe that these difficulties seem to have fuelled resentment against the bill, rather than against the political, cultural and educational establishment which over the years, through its sins of omission and commission, has contributed to making these problems intractable, and has even failed to collect the information necessary for a dispassionate assessment of the situation.

Further Reading

For 'A Historical Perspective': Bruni 1992; C.E.C. 1986; Holtus *et al.* 1988; Jones 1990; Lepschy & Lepschy 1988; Serianni & Trifone 1993; Simone & Vignuzzi 1977; Stussi 1993.

For 'The Linguistic Situation of Modern Italy': Berruto 1987; De Mauro 1976; Holtus & Radtke 1985; Lepschy & Lepschy 1992; Lepschy & Raponi 1988; Mioni & Cortelazzo 1992; Sabatini 1985.

For 'Language Policy': Bolelli 1992; Catricalà 1991; De Mauro 1992; Klein 1986; Pizzorusso 1976, 1993; Raffaelli 1983; Simone 1992, Stipo 1992; Zanghi 1992.

Bibliography

Alinei, M. (1981), '"Dialetto": un concetto rinascimentale fiorentino', *Quaderni di Semantica*, **2**, pp.147–73 (also in Alinei 1984: 169–99).

Alinei, M. (1984), *Lingua e dialetti: struttura, storia e geografia*, Bologna.

Berruto, G. (1987), *Sociolinguistica dell'italiano contemporaneo*, Rome.

Bolelli, T. (1992), 'Le minoranze linguistiche in Italia', *Atti della Accademia Nazionale dei Lincei. Classe di scienze morali, storiche e filologiche, Rendiconti*, **IX**, III, 1992, pp.1–8.

Bruni, F. (ed.), (1992), *L'italiano nelle regioni. Lingua nazionale e identità regionali*, Turin.

Castellani, A. (1982), 'Quanti erano gl'italofoni nel 1861?', *Studi Linguistici Italiani*, **8**, pp.3–26.
Catricalà, M. (1991), *Le grammatiche scolastiche dell'italiano edite dal 1860 al 1918*, Florence.
C.E.C. (1986), *Linguistic Minorities in Countries Belonging to the European Community*. Summary Report Prepared by the Istituto della Enciclopedia Italiana, Luxembourg.
De Mauro, T. (1976), *Storia linguistica dell'Italia unita*, Bari (1st ed. 1963).
De Mauro, T. (1992), 'Una legge per le lingue', *La Rivista dei Libri*, Sept., pp.12–14; Oct., pp.11–13.
Décsy, G. (1986–8), *Statistical Report on the Languages of the World as of 1985*, 5 vols, Bloomington.
Doxa (1982), 'I dialetti', *Bollettino*, **XXXVI**, 10, 22 June, pp.61–7.
—— (1988), 'Parlare in dialetto', *Bollettino*, **XLII**, 6–7, 27 April, pp.55–62.
—— (1992) , 'Parlare in dialetto', *Bollettino*, **XLVI**, 9–10, 3 July, pp.77–92.
Grimes, B. (ed.), (1988), *Ethnologue. Languages of the World*, Eleventh ed., Dallas (1st ed. 1951).
Holtus, G., Metzeltin, M. and Schmitt, C. (eds), (1988), *Lexikon der Romanistischen Linguistik. Band IV: Italienisch, Korsisch, Sardisch*, Tübingen.
Holtus, G. and Radtke, E. (eds), (1985), *Gesprochenes Italienisch in Geschichte und Gegenwart*, Tübingen.
Jones, V.R. (1990), 'Dialect Literature and Popular Literature', *Italian Studies*, **45**, pp.103–17.
Klein, G. (1986), *La politica linguistica del fascismo*, Bologna.
Lepschy, A.L. (1993), 'The Language of Sanudo's *Diarii*', in D.S. Chambers *et al.* (eds), *Culture and Society in Renaissance Venice. Essays in Honour of John Hale*, London, pp.199–212.
—— and Lepschy, G. (1992), 'La situazione dell'italiano', in A.M. Mioni and M.A. Cortelazzo (eds), *La linguistica italiana degli anni 1976–1986*, Rome, pp.27–37.
—— and Lepschy, G. (1988), *The Italian Language Today*, London (1st ed. London, 1977).
Lepschy, G. (1989), *Nuovi saggi di linguistica italiana*, Bologna.
Lepschy, G. and Raponi, L. (1988), 'Il movimento della norma nell'italiano contemporaneo', *Comunità*, **189–90**, pp.364–79 (also in Lepschy 1989: 9–24).
Mioni, A.M. and Cortelazzo, M.A. (eds), (1992), *La linguistica italiana degli anni 1976–1986*, Rome.
'*Norme in materia di tutela delle minoranze linguistiche*' (1992), *Atti*

Parlamentari, Camera dei Deputati, X Legislatura, Testo della proposta di legge N.612. (Reproduced also in *Italiano & Oltre*, **VII**, 1, pp.41–3).

Pizzorusso, A. (1993), *Minoranze e maggioranze*, Turin.

—— (1976), 'Minoranze etnico-linguistiche', in *Enciclopedia del diritto*, **XXVI**, Milan, pp.527–58.

Raffaelli, S. (1983), *Le parole proibite*, Bologna.

Sabatini, F. (1985), 'L'"italiano dell'uso medio": una realtà tra le varietà linguistiche italiane', in G. Holtus and E. Radtke (eds), *Gesprochenes Italienisch in Geschichte und Gegenwart*, Tübingen, pp.154–84.

Serianni, L. and Trifone, P. (eds), (1993), *Storia della lingua italiana*, Vol. 1, Turin.

Simone, R. (1992), 'Minoranze in minoranza', *Italiano & Oltre*, **VII**, 1, pp.3–4.

Simone, R. and Vignuzzi, U. (eds), (1977), *Problemi della ricostruzione linguistica*, Rome.

Stipo, S. (1992), 'Minoranze etnico-linguistiche. I) Diritto pubblico', in *Enciclopedia giuridica*, Rome, pp.1–12.

Stussi, A. (1993), *Lingua, dialetto e letteratura*, Turin.

Trovato, P. (1984), 'Dialetto e sinonimi ("idioma", "proprietà", "lingua") nella terminologia linguistica quattro e cinquecentesca', *Rivista di Letteratura Italiana*, **2**, pp.205–36.

Trumper, J. (1977), 'Ricostruzione nell'Italia settentrionale: sistemi consonantici. Considerazioni sociolinguistiche nella diacronia', in R. Simone and U. Vignuzzi (eds), *Problemi della ricostruzione linguistica*, Rome, pp.259–310.

Zanghi, C. (1992), 'Minoranze etnico-linguistiche. II) Diritto internazionale', in *Enciclopedia giuridica*, Rome, pp.1–6.

–5–

Sardinia: Cheese and Modernization

Martin Clark

My aim in this chapter is not so much to discuss the Sardinian regionalist movements or the workings of Sardinian 'autonomy', as to argue that Sardinian regionalism can best be understood within the context of the long historic struggle, fought out since the eighteenth century, over the issue of Sardinian 'backwardness' and over how to 'modernize' the island's economy and society. Apart from a brief occupation of Sicily, Sardinia was the first part of the South to be taken over by Piedmont, in 1720. It did not take the Piedmontese long in the 1720s to discover that Sardinia was irredeemably 'backward', i.e., could contribute little to Piedmontese coffers, just as they soon realized after 1860 just what they had acquired in the rest of Southern Italy. Nor could the Piedmontese change Sardinian laws, customs or taxes – including, it was assumed, the fiscal system, whereby Spanish feudal grandees retained jurisdiction and revenues – for these were all guaranteed by the Treaty of London in 1718.

The Piedmontese saw Sardinia as an 'Ireland', remote and useless, and furthermore infested with malaria and bandits. Soon the Piedmontese located the sources of the problem – feudalism, of course, but also the persistence of the pastoral 'model' of society. Sardinia became regarded as an island of independent, indeed bloody-minded, shepherds, accompanying their transhumant flocks that trampled over any crops, living by their own violent codes (vendetta, banditry, etc.) and always resisting civilizing influences from outside. By the 1760s the Piedmontese were proposing – and, from the early nineteenth century, imposing – an alternative, 'modernizing', 'European' model of a settled peasantry, peacefully farming family plots on irrigated lands. This model, proposed by Fr Gemelli and other enlightened reformers in the eighteenth century (Gemelli 1776; Bulferetti 1967) and by the Liberal economist Baudi di Vesme in 1848 ('Pasturage is incompatible with agriculture; one or the other will have to go; there can be no doubt of the choice' (Bulferetti 1967: 83)), was implemented by the abolition of feudal usages in the 1830s, and continued by Fascist improvement schemes and Christian Democrat land reforms in this century, the Christian Democrats compounding matters by adding an industrialization drive as well. The point, however, is that nearly all these schemes were thought up by outsiders. 'Modernization' has been imposed on Sardinia from outside, usually by 'Northerners' who knew little about the island and assumed it could be turned into something like the Po Valley or Piedmont.

Sardinian responses to this modernization programme have varied greatly. In the eighteenth century few Sardinians took much notice, except for Cossu, the official 'censor' for agriculture, who was an enthusiastic advocate of the new enlightened ideas – too enthusiastic, for Turin disapproved strongly when he sent out leaflets about the new agricultural methods in Sard! (Persuading people to use Italian was a serious issue in eighteenth-century Sardinia, and often solemnly discussed by Piedmontese officials, writing in French.) But at that time the Piedmontese government was not really serious about reforms anyway; it was certainly not willing to tackle the island's feudal system, partly because most of the feudal barons were Spaniards, backed by the Court at Madrid. Indeed, for that reason in the 1790s Piedmontese rule and feudalism became associated in the popular mind, both being detested by the more radical, French-influenced urban élite in Cagliari, and by rural rebels in the North. In 1794 all the Piedmontese officials on the island, including the Viceroy, were expelled from the island, and there was a brief – and soon unsuccessful – effort to ensure that all government posts in Sardinia were reserved to Sardinians. 'Autonomy', at this time, meant essentially control of jobs, especially jobs for lawyers in Cagliari; it also meant anti-Piedmontism, meaning a dislike of carpetbagging incomers with or without fancy new ideas. It did not, as yet, mean 'home rule', partly because the Sardinians had that already: until 1847 Sardinia was a separate kingdom, with its own laws and customs, which happened to be ruled by the House of Savoy; its position was similar to that of Scotland between 1603 and 1707.

In the early nineteenth century Carlo Felice (who was Viceroy himself for many years, who liked Sardinians, and who gave them jobs in Turin as well as in Sardinia) and Carlo Alberto began seriously to undertake 'modernization', particularly of land tenure. The essential strategy was privatization, selling off the communal, feudal and ecclesiastical lands to new private farmers. The decree on enclosures in 1820, and the abolition of feudalism in the 1830s, together with later measures on church lands and woodland, certainly transferred land to private farmers: over half the usable land was privately owned by 1849, and over half the rural population owned some land by 1860. However, 'modernization' was by no means a success. The holdings were often too small, and too scattered, to be useful; and it was often the *prinzipales*, a somewhat dubious class of kulaks who controlled the local council, who secured the best land. The shepherds, of course, lost their common grazings, especially on the good low-lying land. Moreover, the old feudal owners had been compensated in cash, raised by new local taxes. Taxes went up by 2 1/2 times between 1850 and 1870, and became a crushing burden on the new landowners: from 1870 to 1894 50,000 landholdings were confiscated by the Treasury to pay tax arrears. As for agriculture, the new owners often could not practise it – they could afford neither machinery, nor irrigation, nor 'insurance'. In practice they soon began to let out the land to shepherds for rent, as their feudal predecessors had done, and the amount of land under pasture probably went up, not down. So the 'modernizing' reform essentially failed. Its main result was a great deal more rural mayhem: riots (as at Nuoro in 1832), murders of new landowners or mayors, banditry and so forth. Privatization of woodland was an environmental disaster as well, particularly as it coincided with a big surge in demand for wood (for railway sleepers and for mining pit-props); it all led to rapid deforestation and consequent soil erosion and droughts. Confident mainland Liberals had assumed that land reforms would create a respectable rural peasantry, perhaps in time even a gentry; in the short term, however, it exacerbated the age-old conflict between shepherds and settled farmers, and it created great rural distress and conflict, persisting over many decades. Still, it did mean that in Sardinia – unlike Sicily and most of the mainland South – there was no big landowning élite. Rural areas were dominated by the *prinzipales* on local councils, who were often flockowners rather than agriculturalists, and by local doctors, priests, etc.

In the towns, however, there did exist by the 1840s an educated urban élite, imbued with liberal ideas and enthusiastic for modernization; an élite that often held state posts – as judges, army officers, etc. – and wanted Sardinia to have the same status as the mainland. This group was typified by the career of Giuseppe Manno, a Sardinian who started his career as Carlo Felice's secretary, held many important bureaucratic posts in Turin, and wrote the first major history of modern Sardinia (Manno 1842). Manno was indeed typical of the new Sard Establishment: Liberal, modernizing, royalist and '*piemontizzato*', he played the Sardinian card on occasions when it was useful, while in fact rejecting any Sardinian claim to 'autonomy'.

The 'fusion' – political union – of Sardinia with the mainland territories in 1847 owed much to this group of intellectuals, and was also, of course, part of the confident process of 'modernization'. It was pushed through hastily in the autumn of 1847 by a Sardinian (especially

Cagliaritan) élite that wanted to share in the benefits of the liberal reforms promised by Carlo Alberto to his mainland subjects – a free press, freedom of association, elected local government, etc. The Cagliari and Sassari merchants also hoped to have access to the newly-formed Italian Customs League. New landowners, badly needing protection for their estates, hoped to secure Piedmontese *carabinieri*; students hoped there might be more chance of a job on the Continent. In short, the usual 'parcel of rogues in a nation', selling out their birthright for a mess of pottage (or for 'modernization'). Sardinia lost its ancient Constitution and became simply part of Piedmont. Of course, at popular level there was the usual confusion, and suspicion of the Piedmontese died hard. The slogan 'Long live the Italic League and the new reforms; death to the Jesuits and to the Piedmontese; fellow-citizens, here is the long-awaited moment of Sardinian rebirth' was found hanging on the Torre dell' Elefante at Cagliari (Cao 1928: 53; and for 1848 see Sorgia 1968).

But the pro-'fusion' enthusiasm of late 1847 did not last long; another Sardinian historian thirty years later, Giovanni Siotto Pintor, was to write of those days, 'We were all, with few exceptions, possessed by a collective madness. . .confusing politics with the economic state of the country' (Siotto Pintor 1877: 518). Like agricultural 'modernization', 'fusion', too, turned out disappointingly. One problem was that Sardinian grain could now be exported freely to the mainland, where the price was higher, leaving the Sardinians to starve. Rioting soon began again, and General Alberto La Marmora had to be sent back hastily as *commissario straordinario* to restore order – an episode that the Sardinians have never forgiven him. By the mid-1850s Cavour had become deeply unpopular in Sardinia, as news of his sale of Sardinian assets – forests, mining concessions – became known; and rioting had once again become endemic even in the more civilized parts of the island.

Thus 'Piedmontization', i.e., modernization, including annexation, was not a success. Its failure lay the bases for what I now identify as the three major types of 'autonomy' movements in later years. Firstly, 'autonomy' could mean simply 'resistance' to modernization, to 'colonialism', to invasion, to transformation of old-established values. The popular rioting of the mid-century, and much of the rural unrest in pastoral areas, comes into this category. It was certainly anti-Piedmontese, and it was certainly attempting to resist enforced 'modernization'. It aimed at restoration of '*su connottu*' ('*lo conosciuto*' 'the known') at local level, as the rioters demanded at Nuoro in 1868: for grazing land, for rights to gather firewood, for cheap bread, against the new taxes and so forth. These riots were not successful. Many of the rioters were shepherds, who could safely be ignored as anachronistic or worse (i.e. as bandits), who had little support outside their own villages, and who of course had no vote. Furthermore, their demand for 'autonomy' was localistic; they had no concept of united Sardinian action against outsiders, and no political support: indeed, they got little sympathy even from democratic or Mazzinian politicians, who also thought shepherd society was doomed. The leading Sardinian democrat of the day, Giorgio Asproni, was all in favour of privatizing communal land, denounced the '*su connottu*' riots very firmly, and in his diary took it for granted that the local clergy was to blame: 'It seems that the priests were the instigators, and I would think Canon Manca in particular: a man of barbarous, pastoral instincts'(Asproni 1974–83, V:77). Shepherd society certainly 'resisted' modernization, and did so with increasing success in the 1880s as more settled farmers went bankrupt and more land therefore became available for grazing, but it did not do so in the name of any Sardinian political 'autonomy'.

But the second type of 'autonomy' movement did. Early in 1848 – virtually immediately after 'fusion' – Federico Fanu issued a pamphlet saying a Sardinian parliament was essential; uniform legislation passed in Turin would be a disaster for the island (Fenu 1848). Once disillusionment with Cavourian Liberalism set in, this became a relatively common theme among pamphleteers. 'Modernization' must not come to mean 'dependence', and therefore 'exploitation'; the remedy was 'autonomy', to slow down or mitigate the 'modernization from outside' process, to protect pasturage and to protect Sardinian interests; ideally to implement an alternative, 'Sardinian' model of development. However, these pamphleteers, however distinguished – they included Giovan Battista Tuveri and Giovanni Siotto Pintor – had little political support nor economic plausibility, and for a long time no one took much notice.

The third type of 'autonomy' demand welcomed the orthodox, liberal version of 'modernization', had no wish to slow it down (on the contrary!), but wished it to be under Sardinian control, and to be for Sardinian benefit. Probably Asproni should be counted in this group, at least by the 1860s; certainly it was the only form of 'autonomy' that had some political influence, mainly because other Southern politicians, from other regions, shared this view. Hence the eleven Sardinian deputies after 1860, too few by themselves to have any effect, could form alliances with others to secure their aims: Sardinian 'autonomy' could become part of 'the Southern question'. With the Sardinian politician Francesco Cocco Ortu at the Ministry of Agriculture later in the nineteenth century this concept of 'autonomy' became really influential. 'Autonomy' in this sense was (and is) essentially economic: it was (and is) a demand for resources to be placed in Sardinian hands. The central State should provide the finance for public works; local politicians should distribute it. This strand of 'autonomy', first prominent in the debates about railway construction in the 1860s and 1870s, has, of course, become the dominant theme since 1897 (the date of the first 'special law' for Sardinia, and the beginning of a new age of patronage politics), and is still very evident today. It relies, of course, entirely on the wealth and goodwill of the central State. It is therefore essentially ambiguous: Sardinian politicians have commonly used the rhetoric of 'autonomy' in order to boost claims for greater Sardinian control over central resources – to be devoted to 'modernization'.

Despite all the talk of 'autonomy', the last thing this third group has ever wanted was to rely on Sardinia's own resources (which have, therefore, always been portrayed as very poor: Nitti found that wealth per head was 856 lire in 1901–3, the lowest in Italy – even Calabria had 1186) (Nitti 1905: 62). Perhaps the finest expression of all this was the congress of the island's entire political establishment, held in 1914 to plead for more government subsidies for Sardinia; it took place in Castel Sant'Angelo, Rome! However, it must be said that central state subsidies were not munificent before the First World War, partly because many schemes collapsed when the municipalities could not afford to pay their own share. Of 185 million lire of government money spent on land improvement/reclamation schemes between 1886 and 1910, only 3.5 million were spent in Sardinia. And Sardinia was particularly badly hit by the 'Tariff War' with France after 1887, which wrecked the economy of the north of the island. Hence the two other major interpretations of 'autonomy' both revived in the 1880s. 'Resistance' became widespread, with much banditry (and repression thereof) in the pastoral areas. This banditry attracted much mainland attention, for the first time; it was in the 1890s that Niceforo and Sergi formulated their anthropological views of Sardinian degeneracy (Niceforo 1897, 1898; Sergi 1907), and it was in the 1890s, too, that we see attempts to romanticize the bandit, to portray him as an admirable figure, the archetypal Sardinian 'resister', clinging to his traditional way of life and contemptuous of bourgeois conformity. These efforts by both detractors and admirers led to the ludicrous equation 'shepherd = bandit = Sardinian', a view that still bedevils serious study of the island.

Perhaps more significantly, the second type of 'autonomy' programme became far more plausible. Some Sardinians began to notice that an alternative model of 'modernization' had emerged, or rather survived. Pasturage flourished from the 1870s onwards, thanks to the French market; the grain crisis of the 1880s made more land available to shepherds. Despite the 'Tariff War', shepherds continued to do relatively well thereafter, because of cheese. *Pecorino* cheese, made from Sardinian ewes' milk, became a renowned delicacy, particularly in the USA. The number of sheep doubled from 1881 to 1908; cheese-making plants grew up all over the island. The *prinzipales* prospered, but from sheep, not agriculture. For half a century governments had been attacking pasturage in the name of settled agriculture; yet hill dwellers still drove their sheep where they always had, and pasture flourished where agriculture did not. It all meant, obviously, that Sardinians could manage their own affairs better than Rome could; perhaps Italy was an obstacle to real 'modernization'? This argument was strengthened by the 'free trade' agitations of the 1890s. Todde, following an idea of Asproni, urged that all Sardinia be declared a 'free port' in the Mediterranean, and Deffenu in 1914 repeated the demand with greater fervour (Todde 1895; Deffenu 1976). The Home Rule movement in Ireland, and the Sicilian civil commissioner, were other obvious influences. The point is that there was a nascent, intellectual demand for an alternative model of modernization before 1914, although it usually stopped short of overtly political demands.

Incidentally, even the island's notorious poverty could, on this last interpretation, be disputed. Sardinia was, after all, an underpopulated island (less than 800,000 inhabitants in 1901), full of wildlife and easily accessible game, where most families owned land, made their own bread and wine and were largely self-sufficient; they may have seemed poor according to the calculations of the Dismal Science, but that is not the impression given by many travellers' tales (on the contrary – Tyndale in the 1840s was greeted with excessive feasts wherever he went (Tyndale 1849)), nor by the very low emigration figures (only 8,000 a year even at the peak in 1911–14).

At any rate, the 'autonomy' debate was transformed by the First World War. Pasturage flourished in the war, for land reverted to pasture in the absence of peasant farmers; shepherds were called up too, of course, but their job could be done by boys. Moreover, there was a huge army demand for leather, wool and meat. The 'pastoral route' to Sardinian modernization was therefore reinforced. Moreover, practically all the able-bodied males (almost 100,000) were called up, most of them serving in 'regional' regiments of the 'Sassari Brigade'. The brigade – thanks to the High Command's propaganda about the 'intrepid Sardinians' – soon became legendary for courage and disciplined heroism. It had, after all, been set up because the Sardinians were thought to be 'different': the racial theories of Niceforo taught that Sardinians were violent barbarians, and violent barbarians were just what the army wanted. The point, however, is that Sardinian peasants and shepherds fought the war together, in one of the very rare regional units of the Italian army; they were meeting and sharing immense danger with Sardinians from other parts of the island. Many of the junior officers were also Sardinians, learning far more about the people and customs of their own island than they would ever otherwise have done; the archetypal product of this experience was Emilio Lussu. The Brigade was, more than most armies, the school of the nation. It bred a community, with fierce loyalties and fierce resentments. The loyalties, of course, were not only to Sardinia, at least in the case of the officers; patriotic 'Italianist' rhetoric was very important for them. The resentments were against the *imboscati* (shirkers), and against the old time-serving Liberal cliques of politicians. The new officer-heroes, enjoying much popular support, were almost bound to seek to replace the 'neutralist' Giolittian Liberals as political leaders in Sardinia; and, having done so, to seek a large measure of 'home rule'.

Moreover, the war also boosted the Sardinian claim to special treatment, i.e. for more resources from the central State. At last the Sardinians could plausibly claim to be 'special', in a non-pejorative sense. In 1918 Orlando as Prime Minister acknowledged this: 'Italy has contracted a huge debt of gratitude towards the noble island; it has a duty to pay this debt, and will do so' (quoted in Brigaglia 1986, I:3). The agenda of Sardinian politics for the next few years, perhaps for the next few decades, was concerned with how this debt should be paid – and who to.

The post-war ex-servicemen's movement in Sardinia, which in 1921 became the Sardinian Party of Action, may therefore be regarded as representing a happy fusion of the second and third major 'types' of autonomy movement that I have tried to identify. The second, inasmuch as it called for some (rather vague) degree of political autonomy, based on Sardinian control of Sardinian resources; and inasmuch as it spoke for the shepherds, overtly adopted the 'pastoral model', and founded co-operatives all over the island to give shepherds a decent price for their milk, and to make and market *pecorino*. But it also adopted the third type, with its 'Italianist' rhetoric inherited from the war, and its claim to 'reward' from central government. For some years it managed to combine these two approaches, particularly after 1923 when, after a split that left Lussu and his followers isolated, most of the party's leaders, led by Paolo Pili, merged the Sardinian Party of Action into the tiny Fascist party in Sardinia. They then took over the running of the island from the old Liberals, and secured Sardinia's reward from a grateful Mussolini – a Mussolini who remarked that if he were not *romagnolo*, he would wish to be a Sardinian. The reward was a '*miliardo*', a billion lire, to be spent over ten years on public works and land reclamation. This was real 'autonomy' – Sardinians (or *sardo-fascisti*) running Sardinia, and along different lines from the mainland – but of course it could not be recognized or talked about openly during the Fascist regime, and in any case it did not last. Pili's 'pastoral model' was in direct conflict with the Fascist government's 'battle for grain' (and also, more importantly, with the revaluation of the lira to *quota novanta* (90 lire to the £ sterling) which wrecked the prospects of cheese exporters), and the contrast was too obvious to be acceptable for long in Rome. Pili was sacked, and after 1928 the mainland Fascists imposed a much more orthodox, traditional 'model' of rural modernization: land reclamation/drainage, irrigation, settling of peasants (often from the Veneto) on reclaimed land, in suitably named localities – Mussolinia (now Arborea), Fertilia, etc. During the rest of the Fascist regime, there was no more 'autonomy' movement in any of the senses I have used, except the first: when the inevitable 'resistance' reappeared in the pastoral areas, it was simply suppressed as 'banditry'.

Sardinia was relatively unaffected by the Second World War, and also had no experience of civil war and Resistance after 1943. This time, therefore, there was no new élite emerging from victory, and no traumatic common experiences binding together the people and its leaders. Instead, the old party leaders – advocates and professors all – re-emerged from the shadows, happy to have a role in the Consultative Council that advised the High Commissioner, a Sardinian Air Force general named Pietro Pinna, who in effect ran the island from late 1943 until 1949.

For the first two years of this period Sardinia was virtually cut off, and really was 'autonomous'. But few Sardinian politicians welcomed this. They all – including the anti-Fascist rump of the Sardinian Party of Action (PSd'Az), led by Lussu – belonged to mainland parties, and relied heavily on their contacts on the mainland. Lussu himself was by this time a 'federalist', but he was also a minister in Rome in 1945–6 and in any case was, as always, an isolated figure. The PSd'Az was reasonably large and it, too, called for a 'federal' system, but it was tarnished by its long association with Fascism, and lacked the automatic support of ex-servicemen's associations that had given it its strength after 1918. Liberals, Socialists and Communists tended to favour a unitary, centralized State, the Left because it did not want Sardinia to miss out on the forthcoming revolution. Eventually the Communist leader Togliatti imposed acceptance of 'autonomy' on a very reluctant Sardinian party, and even then the Sardinian Communists adopted a novel interpretation of the word: 'autonomy' meant 'the end of exploitation of our economic resources by the State and Northern capitalists, but also by Sardinian agrarian castes' (Sanna 1978: 132). In other words, it was to mean 'regionalization' (mini-nationalization) of industry and big landed estates.

Only the Christian Democrats (DC) under Antonio Segni adopted an 'autonomy' programme with any enthusiasm, and they adopted the third interpretation of the word. The DC was the heir of Fascist agrarian policies, and was winning the peasant vote on the plains; it favoured land reform and agricultural subsidies, and thought pasturage was obsolete, just as nineteenth-century Liberals had done. The DC stood for special laws, but with regional distribution of the patronage. This formula was successful, not because of any real Sardinian pressure but because of the DC strength nationally, and because of Sicily and other outlying regions. Sardinia in 1948 became an 'autonomous' region against the wishes of most of its elderly political class, and in the virtually total absence of any 'nationalist' agitation or concern over '*sardità*'. The Christian Democrats held out the prospect of capital investment and development projects: that was all. The PSd'Az, which Lussu soon left, became simply a minor ally of the DC.

Why were the leading Sardinian politicians, of all parties, so reluctant to demand more 'independent' powers? They were markedly more reluctant, for example, than their counterparts in Sicily, where a serious separatist movement flourished for several years. Part of the answer is that they were elderly men, cut off from political activity for twenty years, and out of touch with the world elsewhere. But perhaps the more fundamental answer had been suggested by Antonio Gramsci almost two decades earlier. In Sicily, he had argued, the large landowners were economically, politically and culturally powerful, and had major interests to defend against Rome; in Sardinia such people barely existed, and were certainly not in any position to lead a political movement. 'The class of large landowners is very small, carries out no functions and lacks the ancient traditions of the mainland South'(Gramsci 1966: 153). Instead, the local rulers were members of a dependent middle class, largely created by the 'colonial' power, a class that relied on state jobs and state subsidies.

This was still true in 1945. Sardinia still had almost no established landowning, commercial or managerial élite of her own. She had her semi-literate *prinzipales* in the countryside, and her lawyers and state officials in the towns. The *prinzipales* had little prestige even within their own villages, and few contacts with their counterparts elsewhere; immersed in dubious land deals and parish-pump politics, they conspicuously lacked any sense of *sardità*. And the urban élite had been absorbed into the existing system – they drew their status, income and values from state institutions. In any case, neither group could have mobilized peasants, shepherds, miners and artisans in defence of 'Sardinian' interests, even if they had wanted to. Only for a few years after the First World War had this been possible, by leaders who had proved themselves in the shared dangers of war – and most of these people had been happy to accept what soon turned out to be a subordinate role under Fascism after 1928. No comparable group of new leaders existed after 1945. Nor could illiterate shepherds and peasants, or barely literate miners and artisans, be effective on their own: they could, and did, 'resist' (sometimes still by riot, more often by occupying land, or going on strike), but they did so to protect local jobs, or to defend *su connottu*. Sardinia had no potential 'national' leaders, and no 'national' intellectuals. She had merely a legacy of demanding an ill-defined 'autonomy', a demand that was easily bought off by public works.

In 1945–46 the Sicilians drew up their own regional *Statuto*, giving themselves exclusive legislative powers on a wide range of issues. In May 1946 they persuaded the De Gasperi government to approve it by decree, even before the national Constituent Assembly had been elected. The Sardinian Consultative Council could have had the same text extended to Sardinia, if its members had so wished. But it proudly and unanimously rejected this proposal. Why? The best explanation is Lussu's: '. . .partly because of a romantic rejection of autonomy being granted by royal decree, partly because of a feeling that the Sardinian *Statuto* should be drafted by Sardinians, not taken from Sicily, and above all, in order to have time to draft their own *Statuto* properly, with adequate discussion and reflection' (Lussu 1947). The fact remained that the elderly Sardinian ruling class had been offered real 'autonomy'; and they had all – including the PSd'Az – rejected it.

After June 1946 two bodies were active in deciding Sardinia's future. In Rome, the Constituent Assembly contained fourteen Sardinian members, including the most able party leaders – Lussu, Segni, Spano, Laconi, Mastino and Mannironi – and was drafting a new Constitution which would include general provisions for regional government. In Cagliari, the Sardinian Consultative Council, reconstituted to reflect party strengths as shown in the Constituent Assembly elections in Sardinia (where the DC won 41 per cent of the vote and the PSd'Az almost 15 per cent), was drafting its own regional *Statuto*. It set up two groups of a Special Commission to Study the Regional Constitution, to do the work, but there was little inter-party collaboration on it. Only the PSd'Az and the DC drafted versions of a regional *Statuto* for the Consultative Council to discuss; the other parties were all suspicious or hostile to the whole idea. Eventually, after much delay and compromise, a draft was approved on 29 April 1947 by the whole Consultative

Council. It was basically the DC scheme for limited legislative autonomy, with no 'exclusive' legislative competence on major economic issues, and no control over education or cultural life (Contini 1971).

But would the Constituent Assembly approve the Sardinian Consultative Council's text? On 21 July 1947 Lussu urged them to do so (although he himself regarded it as 'absolutely inadequate'), and cited the Sicilian precedent; the Communist leader Togliatti supported him. But the Constituent Assembly, by now politically split, decided merely to examine the Sardinian text as a basis for its own. In practice, the Assembly's sub-commission for the *Statuti* drew up a more moderate scheme, limiting the legislative and – especially – financial powers of the Sardinian Regional Council and of the President of the Sardinian Executive. For example, the Regional Council's power to suspend the application of national laws in Sardinia, 'when they are obviously damaging to the Region', was reduced to a mere 'power' to request the national government to suspend the law (Article 64 of the Sardinian draft, Article 51 of the *Statuto)*. The sub-commission's scheme was rushed through the whole Assembly on 28 and 29 January 1948, just before the final deadline. So the eventual text of the Sardinian *Statuto* (Constitutional Law, 26 Feb. 1948, n.3) was not drawn up by Sardinians after all, nor even by Sicilians. 'Regional autonomy' was granted, at the last minute, by bored mainland politicians anxious by then to minimize any possible concessions to the political Left. And, as it was a 'constitutional law' of the Italian Parliament, it proved extremely difficult to change later – an issue that is still important today.

The *Statuto*, as eventually passed, provided that the Sardinian Council had legislative powers on certain matters, listed in Article 3: agriculture and forestry, tourism, artisan and craft support, regional public works, minor land improvement schemes, and allocation of the State's rights over public waters, mines, saltpans, etc. However, Sardinian laws on these matters had to respect not only the Italian Constitution and international treaties, but also 'the fundamental norms of the economic and social reforms of the Republic' – major national legislation on these topics. They also had to respect the 'national interest' – and the national Parliament in Rome would decide what this was (Article 127 of the Italian Constitution). So the region's legislative powers, although sometimes called 'primary', were clearly not 'exclusive' powers such as Sicily (in principle) enjoyed.

The Sardinian Council could also legislate 'concurrently' with the Italian Parliament on other topics, listed in Article 4: industry, commerce, mines and saltpans, major land improvement, public health, regional credit, welfare, etc. Such legislation had to be within 'the principles laid down by the laws of the State'. Furthermore, the Council could also (Article 5) issue 'supplementary and implementary norms', adapting state laws to Sardinian circumstances, on education, labour, welfare and insurance, antiquities and fine art. Thus the Sardinian Council had three types of legislative power, depending on the subject matter concerned. But all of them could be superseded by national law. And the third type, which included education, was hardly 'autonomous' at all.

The region was also formally given administrative functions, on the first two types of issue, as well as being expected to carry out 'delegated' administrative tasks for the central authorities. In practice, many of these administrative powers – and officials – were transferred to Sardinia very slowly, partially and reluctantly, if at all, and this fact made much 'autonomous' regional legislation, e.g. the Sardinian laws on fishing, impossible to police. To take another example, the Sardinian Council soon found that any laws it passed on town planning (an Article 3 topic) not only had to conform to the existing state law of 1942, but any actual proposals had to be approved by the Ministry of Public Works and the Public Works Agency.

Altogether, it was not too impressive a degree of legislative, or even administrative, 'autonomy'. Some important issues were conspicuously absent, e.g. any reference to the Sard language. But the new system suited the Sardinian élite. In particular, Article 13 suited them: 'The State, with the co-operation of the Region, provides for a comprehensive plan to encourage the economic and social rebirth of the Island.' Here was an explicit promise of major capital investment from the mainland: new 'special laws', the constant goal of Sardinian politicans since the nineteenth century. No other region in Italy included such a promise in its very Constitution. For the next thirty years or more, Sardinian politics was to resolve around this modernization plan. So 'autonomy', in Sardinia, did not mean self-government; it meant a claim to material concessions, and a claim to 'modernization'. The rhetoric of 'autonomy' was useful on the island, in uniting Sardinians behind such claims; it was even more useful in negotiating with Rome. But it was used to disguise a real dependence. In practice it would be the State, not the region, that drew up the plan and decided the priorities.

The 'modernization', as usual, was essentially of settled agriculture. The DC dominated both in Rome and Cagliari; the party subsidized peasants and organized co-operatives, staffed the land reform boards and distributed welfare, controlled rural credit and organized markets. The money – 98 per cent of the region's income in 1960 – came from Rome, and much of it was used to reward clients on the island, rather than for any genuine modernization. Even so, Sardinia had her land reform too, like other areas of the South: ETFAS (*Ente per la Trasformazione Fondiaria e Agraria in Sardegna*) expropriated 45,000 ha, and took over the old Fascist improvement areas as well, continuing the old Fascist improvement policy. But it was not really a success. A few thousand peasant families got land, but this simply accentuated Sardinia's real land tenure problem – excessive fragmentation – and of course the shepherds got nothing at all. The one real 'modernizing' success in these years was the elimination of malaria between 1946 and 1952, by heavy spraying with DDT; it was one of the great triumphs of the pesticide industry. Done largely by American technical staff and financed by the Rockefeller Foundation, it owed nothing to 'autonomy', in any sense of the word (Logan 1953).

Yet it is striking that agriculture did not really succeed, despite all the subsidies and political support. In the 1960s, perhaps 200,000 ha of land went out of agricultural production, half of it cereals; cereals covered only 75,000 ha by 1975, compared with 190,000 ha in 1946. Some specialist crops, like artichokes, expanded, but none the less Sardinia imported most of her fruit and vegetables. She also began to export her rural people: 280,000 people left the land in the 1960s, and 150,000 of them (10 per cent of the island's total population) went forth of the island; a third of the jobs in agriculture were lost in a decade. Peasants with fragmented small plots were giving up, and leaving the land. The land began to revert to pasture. As agriculture declined, sheep began to prosper: there were 2.1 million sheep in 1970, over 3 million by 1980, and *pecorino* was still selling well world-wide. Here was a rich, and for Establishment politicians deeply embarrassing, irony. Settled agriculture had enjoyed huge subsidies and great political support for decades, but it lost out in the end to its 'primitive', 'backward' enemy.

I have argued that the true meaning of Sardinian 'autonomy' lay in Article 13 of the Sardinian *Statuto* with its promise of a 'comprehensive plan for economic and social rebirth'. In fact, nothing much happened for some years, until the combative 'Young Turks' lead by Francesco Cossiga took over DC politics in Sassari, and at the same time Giulio Pastore in Rome proclaimed an industrialization drive in Southern 'development poles'. With Segni as President of the Republic, the DC moving towards 'Centre-Left' coalitions and planning, and the Left parties anxious for industrialization, the Italian Parliament finally granted Sardinia its 'Plan' in June 1962. One hundred billion lire, supposedly of 'new' money, was allocated to industrial development, and a further 300 billion lire to other purposes, over a 12-year period; the main aim was to set up high-technology, often state-owned, industries like petrochemicals, oil refineries and steelworks – the plants that soon came to be called 'cathedrals in the desert'.

This whole strategy – the quintessential strategy of 'autonomy', in my third definition of the term – was of course conceived in Rome, not Cagliari, and was financed and often administered by state agencies: the Fund for the South, ISVEIMER, etc. But the Sardinian political élite embraced it enthusiastically, and Sardinian agencies (especially the *Credito Industriale Sardo*) pumped money into the chemical industry as well. Each new industrial plant from the Centre meant a host of 'subsidiary' contracts (building licenses, housing schemes, roads, etc.) to be allocated by the holders of local political power; and it also meant jobs, to be allocated according to political allegiance. Once again, 'modernization' proved to be perfectly compatible with party-based clientelism.

However, industrial modernization turned out as elusive as its agricultural counterpart. Sardinian regional governments by the late 1960s were complaining they were not consulted enough by the central state agencies; more important, the Plan's defects became all too apparent. The new industries were capital-intensive, i.e. they provided few jobs once the plants had been built; the chemical industry employed only 5700 people in 1971. There was little sign of 'spin-off', but plenty of signs of pollution. Some of the major plants were owned by the State, others by dubious Italian entrepreneurs or by foreign multinationals (e.g. Esso) which picked up vast subsidies, including some from Sardinian taxpayers. These are, of course, familiar problems in recent economic debate; they applied with particular force in Sardinia, and it helped undermine the whole notion of 'autonomy'. In Sardinia, 'autonomy' meant 'the Plan', but the Plan abandoned the mines, ignored pasture, forced 10 per cent of the population off the island, and provided only a handful of very expensive jobs in the 'petrochemical monoculture', an industry with a tacit licence to pollute. Even the politicians soon became uneasy. At this point the first two interpretations of 'autonomy' surfaced once more.

'Resistance' began, as always, in the pastoral areas. True, pasture was becoming more profitable, but the traditional pastoral society was being strongly challenged by modern innovations like schools, television and the car, and young people were emigrating to the mainland in large numbers. In the 1960s, some members of pastoral communities perfected a happy blend of traditional banditry and modern organized crime. Stealing sheep had always been endemic; now they moved into stealing humans. Between 1966 and 1968 there were thirty-three known kidnaps, the best-known gang being led by Graziano Mesina, who became a popular folk hero (Mesina, who remained on the run for eighteen months in 1966–8, was released from prison in late

1991, and soon became prominent again as an intermediary in kidnap cases on the island). Kidnapping was far more profitable than rustling: ransoms of 80 million lire were normal by 1968. It flourished because of the new roads and cars (enabling victims to be transported easily to safe refuges), and because of the new prosperity. Governments reacted to the 'new' banditry (which was actually not all that new, just more profitable) in the traditional manner. Once again, as in the 1890s or 1920s, huge numbers of troops and *carabineri* were sent to the island, and scoured the hills. Once again, spurious sociological theories were fashioned, explaining it all in terms of a 'culture of violence' or of isolation – theories that were used to justify repression, just as Niceforo's had been seventy years earlier.

Banditry was, perhaps, an 'individual' response to social pressures, or to opportunities: but 'community' movements occurred too. In pastoral areas, rioting became normal, sometimes in protest at the army's use of good grazing land for its manoeuvres, sometimes at the proposal to set up a National Park in the Gennargentu, which seemed to threaten grazing rights (the issue is still in contention).

The military issue became (and remains) a particularly significant grievance. Sardinia was regarded by the Italian military as an ideal place for training exercises; by the early 1970s, one-tenth of the island had been compulsorily expropriated for military purposes, or was subject to restrictions at certain times of the year (as were prime fishing grounds). The largest NATO airport in the Mediterranean was at Decimomannu; and the Italian navy's base at La Maddalena was considered as strategically important as in Nelson's day. Above all, from 1972 there was the American (not NATO) nuclear submarine base at Santo Stefano. This base was granted to the USA by the Italian Defence and Foreign Ministries, without any consultation with the Sardinian regional council (or, for that matter, with the Italian Parliament), provoking the first official protest by the Sardinian Establishment against government policy.

The second meaning of 'autonomy' also resurfaced in the 1970s, as a result of the failure of the 'Plan of Rebirth', and as a result of the menacing disorder in pastoral areas. In 1974, after much pressure from Sardinian politicians and a favourable report from a parliamentary commission of enquiry, a new Plan was launched, with far more powers for the regional council, much more 'democratic participation' at the grassroots level, and far more attention to pastoral areas. It gave grants for reafforestation, for reviving the mines, above all for more cheesemaking co-operatives (soon there were thirty of them on the island, producing and marketing about 40 per cent of the *pecorino*). Moreover, rents of grazing land were restricted by law in 1971, and soon inflation greatly reduced them in real terms – a huge benefit to the shepherds, enabling them often to buy land for the first time. Sheep numbers rose from 2 1/2 million in 1970 to over 3 million in 1980. The shepherd had hitherto been squeezed between grasping landlord and exploiting cheesemaker; suddenly he was freed of both. Furthermore, in an effort to curb nomadic pasturage the new Plan provided 260 billion lire for buying up suitable grazing land and selling it to shepherds for winter grazing, a scheme that proved difficult to implement in practice, as land prices were too high. Of course, all these schemes could be seen as an attempt to tame the shepherds and stop them being a menace. Even so, the new policy was the triumph of pasture – politically aided, for the first time since the mid-1920s, and supported by all parties.

However, the real innovation in the late 1960s was the advent, for the first time in Sardinian history, of another meaning of 'autonomy' – an overtly 'nationalist' one, based on strong feelings about Sardinia's language and culture. Like other nationalist movements, this one began with the intellectuals, in particular with Michelangelo Pira's book *Sardegna tra due lingue* (1968). Pira's message was that the Sard language, although in normal spoken use informally and domestically, was in danger: it was not used in schools, in journalism or on television, and it had no official status or encouragement. It needed to be preserved. The argument attracted support from across the political spectrum, including the DC (the archaeologist Giovanni Lilliu was a prominent Christian Democrat supporter). The Socialists soon had their own group, the LUNISS (*Liga de Unidade Nassionale pro sa Indipendencia de sa Sardigna e su Socialismu*). *Neo-sardismo*, with its demand for the use of Sard in schools and the maintenance of Sardinian traditions, became disseminated in short-lived journals. The well-known poet Francesco Masala, who in 1967 had said it was 'absolutely reactionary' to write or even speak Sard, was by 1979 President of the Committee for the Sard Language, and wrote in nothing else. *Neo-sardismo*, focusing on the language question, had some successes, including massive subsidies for folklore societies throughout the island. Moreover, it soon acquired political overtones, namely, a demand for independence, based on self-confident nationalist claims of cultural 'difference' as well as on anti-colonialist (and anti-militarist) hostility to Italian exploitation of Sardinian resources. The PSd'Az adopted this policy in 1979, and soon enjoyed much greater electoral support. The *neo-Sardisti* had, of course, no time for 'autonomy' in any of my senses except the first – the proud Sardinian tradition of 'resistance' to invaders (Cabitza 1968; Lilliu 1970; Pira 1978).

Yet arguably *neo-sardismo* had come too late, and it always remained a minority taste. Most Sardinians, and certainly most members of the Sardinian political Establishment, remained in the 1970s and 1980s firmly committed to 'autonomy' in the sense of 'modernization' , i.e. to the renewed development plan. This was, after all, the tradition of most Sardinian intellectuals: Deffenu, Bellieni, Gramsci and Lussu had all wanted Sardinia integrated into the modern world of industry, literacy and technology. In any case there were, of course, 5000 jobs at stake in the regional bureaucracy and in the various development agencies. A new Sardinian middle-class political and administrative élite had been created since the late 1940s, and it was not going to relinquish its status and income if it could avoid doing so. As for a successful commercial élite, this was relatively small and conspicuously powerless. Thus the content of most political debate remained the region's role in state development projects – a role, however, that always remained fairly minor in practice. The key decisions on her economy continued to be taken elsewhere – by multinationals, by the Italian and US military, by ENI (the state chemical company which took over most of the petrochemical industry), or by the European Community's farm policy. Sardinia was a 'recipient region', economically and politically too weak to bargain effectively with the real arbiters of her fate, except occasionally when a prominent national politician – a Berlinguer, a Cossiga – raised his voice on her behalf. As always, the rhetoric of 'autonomy' was used to disguise the reality of dependence.

Neo-sardismo itself was contained, perhaps 'absorbed' as time went on. It received several important-sounding concessions. A regional law was passed permitting the teaching of Sard in primary schools (although it turned out that this needed approval by the Italian Parliament, as the State has responsibility for education, and the Italian Parliament has not approved it yet; nor has the Italian government signed the European Charter on Regional and Minority Languages). But subsidies were given to folklore and musical groups, and (as argued) the shepherds did well out of the reform of grazing land – a reform which cynics said was designed to tame them and turn them into subsidized form-fillers, like all other farmers in Europe. This scheme worked well for a time: Sardinia now has almost four million sheep. Unfortunately, it has also a cheese mountain and a milk lake, and the CAP reforms of the mid-1980s imposed quite severe quotas on milk, so the picture now looks far more gloomy.

The activities of the PSd'Az probably also helped to contain *neo-sardismo* in the early 1980s. Many enthusiastic young *neo-Sardisti* flocked into the party after it proclaimed independence as a goal in 1979. This, too, worked for a time but eventually failed. Suspicious of incomers, the PSd'Az is a rather sectarian party, whose members tend to stand up at congresses and proclaim their *titoli d'anzianità* (how long they have been members). In such a party the new recruits were given little chance to do anything, and soon became disillusioned. The party also became discredited for its role in the governing Left coalition of the region from 1984 to 1989, and was clearly deserted by many of its erstwhile supporters; in April 1992 it won only 6.7 per cent of the vote at the parliamentary elections. Although it did not run a separate ticket in the 1994 elections, in the 1994 regional elections it received only 5.1 per cent (but it should also be added that other parties running with regionalist platforms increased their showings in both of these elections). In any case, *neo-sardismo* survives today as a cultural movement, worried about the continuing decline of the Sard language among young people and proud of the pastoral tradition of '*resistenza*', but it has little political expression at the moment.

Yet if *neo-sardismo* is in decline, so too are the more traditional interpretations of 'autonomy'. 'Resistance', i.e. banditry, although still found, is not what it was, since the pastoral areas have become more prosperous and far more influenced by modern innovations like education and travel. As for the other two meanings of 'autonomy', they have failed to deliver. Moreover, the debate on them in Sardinia in the early 1990s was complicated by three main factors that called into question the whole feasibility of continued 'modernization' from outside – economic recession, the political crisis of the Italian Republic, and the initially rapid rise of the Northern Leagues.

Recession hit Sardinia particularly badly. Tourist income, of course, fell off. Many of her key industries, like the mines and petrochemicals, are state-owned and loss-making, and thus were affected by spending cuts; the proposed privatization of ENI is an even greater threat, as private owners would obviously close down many plants. Official unemployment figures were 18.8 per cent even in early 1990 before the full impact of the recession hit. Pasturage and agriculture, too, were hit, as stated, by CAP reforms and, in particular, by what Sardinians perceived as the government's failure to protect Sardinian interests when quotas were set at European levels. The classic example is that half Sardinia's olive oil needs are now met by imports, mainly from Greece (which unlike Sardinia has a minister on the Council of Ministers that takes the decision), while the famous olive groves in the *Sassarese* are chopped down. Note that agriculture is an area of 'primary' regional competence according to the *Statuto*, yet in practice negotiations in Brussels on agricultural issues are done by Italian permanent representatives, without any consultation with the regions – this is perhaps the biggest issue in the current debates on 'autonomy'. By the early 1990s, Sardinians were beginning to ask themselves whether mainland Italy could continue to provide the goods. On the other hand, they did not wish to live off their own resources either, and now perhaps could not: the commercial deficit was over £2.5 billion (1988) even during the Italian boom of the mid- to late 1980s.

Political inertia on the mainland was also much resented. I have mentioned the Parliament's failure to approve the Sard language law; let alone, of course, to reform the Sardinian *Statuto* (a Constitutional Law of the Italian Republic) in order to give the region greater powers of its own on cultural matters and, above all, on industrial development. This was the essence of the 'autonomy' debate in the early and middle 1990s. Sardinians, of all parties, are disillusioned with mainland 'development' schemes that have gone wrong, but see themselves as prevented, for legal and constitutional reasons, from undertaking their own industrial initiatives and pursuing their own model of 'modernization'.

Finally, the rise of the Northern League in the early 1990s was even more embarrassing for 'autonomy' as traditionally practised in Sardinia. The League was, in one sense, a natural ally; they would have given the Sardinians all the 'autonomy' they claimed to want. On the other hand, the League would have also cut the cash, which is what really matters. The solution, for politically correct Sardinians, was to denounce the *leghisti* as 'Northern racists' and anti-Southerners, with whom no truck could be had. However, this stance was not really plausible in the long run; if the League had ever been in a position to deliver some form of 'federalism' or independence, this would have been an offer that the PSd'Az, at least, could hardly have refused, although the other parties certainly would have. In 1946–8, a reluctant Sardinian Establishment had to accept 'autonomy', largely because of the Sicilian example; it would been a supreme irony if a stronger form of it had been thrust upon Sardinia by another group of 'separatists', this time from the North. In the event the major players in the 1994 parliamentary and regional elections were nationally based parties and coalitions (the PDS, *Forza Italia* and even the highly centralist *Alleanza Nazionale*). The most significant result of the first set of elections was Segni's failure to win the first-past-the-post seat in Sassari, although he got in on proportional representation, while the regional elections witnessed a good showing by the PPI and the first defeat for Berlusconi after his triumph in the general elections (see Appendix).

To summarize, for a century and a half, from the early nineteenth century onwards, mainland 'Italy' presented to Sardinia a model of economic and social progress that might be resisted, but was rarely challenged intellectually. When it was so challenged, as in the 1920s and from the late 1960s, an alternative model of 'more appropriate' development/modernization was attempted, but on both occasions without satisfactory long-term results. Hence after a century and a half of debate about regional 'autonomy', and almost half a century of 'autonomous' institutions, Sardinia remains very dependent economically, and more than ever dependent culturally – and politically.

Bibliography

Asproni, G. (1974–83), *Diario politico 1855–76* (ed. by T. Orrù and C. Sole), 7 vols, Milan.

Baudi di Vesme, C. (1848), *Considerazioni politiche ed economiche sulla Sardegna*, Turin, 1848, available in G. Sorgia, *La Sardegna nel 1848*, Cagliari, pp.75–267.

Brigaglia, M. (1986), *L'Antifascismo in Sardegna*, 2 vols, Cagliari.

Bulferetti, L. (1967), *Il riformismo settecentesco in Sardegna*, 2 vols, Cagliari.

Cabitza, G. (E.Spiga) (1968), *La Sardegna dauanti ad uma Suolta Decisiva*, Milan.

Cao, M. (1928), *La fine della costituzione autonoma sarda*, Cagliari.

Contini, G. (1971), *Lo Statuto della Regione Sarda*, Milan.

Deffenu, A. (1976), *Sardegna* (periodical); reprinted Sassari (1st ed. 1914).

Fenu, F. (1848), *La Sardegna e la fusione col sardo continentale*, Cagliari, available in G. Sorgia (1968), pp.415–45.

Gemelli, F. (1776), *Il rifiorimento della Sardegna, proposto nel miglioramento di sua agricultura*, Turin, now available as Bulferetti (1967), *Il riformismo settecentesco in Sardegna*, Vol. 2, Cagliari.

Gramsci, A. (1966), 'Alcuni temi della questione meridionale', reprinted in A. Gramsci, *La questione meridionale*, Rome, pp.131–60.

Lilliu, G. (1970), *Autonomia come resistenza*, Cagliari.

Logan, J. (1953), *The Sardinian Project*, Baltimore.

Lussu, E. (1947), 'Speech to Constituent Assembly', 21 July, cited in G. Contini (1971), *La Statuto della Regione Sarda*, Milan, p.478.

Manno, G. (1842), *Storia moderna della Sardegna*, Turin.

Niceforo, A. (1897), *La delinquenza in Sardegna*, Palermo.

Niceforo, A. (1898), *L'Italia barbara contemporanea*, Palermo.

Nitti, F.S. (1905), *La richezza d'Italia*, Turin and Rome.

Pira, M. (1968), *Sardegna tra due lingue*, Cagliari.

Pira, M. (1978), *La rivolta dell'oggetto*, Milan.

Sanna, P. (1978), *Storia del Partito Comunista Italiano in Sardegna*, Cagliari.

Sergi, G. (1907), *La Sardegna*, Turin.

Siotto Pintor, G. (1877), *Storia civile dei popoli sardi dal 1798 al 1848*, Turin.
Sorgia, G. (1968), *La Sardegna nel 1848*, Cagliari.
Todde, G. (1895), *La Sardegna, considerata dal lato economico*, Florence.
Tyndale, J.W.W. (1849), *The Island of Sardinia*, 3 vols, London.

Further Reading

Brigaglia, M (ed.), (1982–8), *Enciclopedia della Sardegna*, 3 vols. Cagliari.
Brigaglia, M. and Sechi, S. (1985), *Cronologia della Sardegna autonomistica*, Cagliari.
Del Piano, L. (1984), *La Sardegna nell'ottocento*, Sassari.
Guidetti, M. (ed.), (1990), *Storia dei sardi e della Sardegna*, Vol. 4, Milan.
Le Lannou, M. (1941), *Pâtres et paysans de la Sardaigne*, Tours.
Ortu, G.G. (1985), 'Stato, società e cultura nel nazionalismo sardo del secondo dopoguerra', *Italia contemporanea*, 161, pp.59–77.
Petrosino, D. (1992), 'National and Regional Movements in Italy: The Case of Sardinia', in J. Coakley (ed.), *Social Origins of Nationalist Movements*, London, pp.124–46.
Pigliaru, A. (1959), *La vendetta barbaricina come ordinamento giuridico*, Milan.
Sabbatini, G. and Moro, B. (1973), *Il sistema economico della Sardegna*, Cagliari.
Sechi, S. (1969), *Dopoguerra e fascismo in Sardegna 1918–26*, Turin.
Sole, C. (1984), *La Sardegna sabauda del settecento*, Sassari.
Sotgiu, G. (1984), *Storia della Sardegna sabauda*, Bari and Rome.
Sotgiu, G. (1986), *Storia della Sardegna dopo l'Unità*, Bari and Rome.

Table 5.1. Regional Council Elections: Sardinia

	1949	1953	1957	1961	1965	1969	1974	1979	1984	1989
PCI	19.4	22.3	17.5	19.0	20.5	19.7	26.8	26.2	28.7	23.3
PSIUP	–	–	–	–	3.7	4.4	–	2.4 (DP, PDUP)	1.0 (DP)	–
VERDI (GREENS)	–	–	–	–	–	–	–	–	–	1.8
PRS (RADS)	–	–	–	–	–	–	–	3.1	1.4	See PRI
PSd'AzSocialista	6.6	–	–	–	–	–	–	–	–	–
PSI	6.0	8.8	9.5	9.6	6.9	{11.8} (PSI + PSDI)	11.7	11.1	10.1	13.9
PSDI	2.9	1.8	2.7	3.1	5.4		5.9	4.6	4.3	4.7
PSd'Az	10.5	7.0	6.0	7.2	6.4	4.4	3.1	3.3	13.8	12.4
PRI	–	–	–	–	–	3.0	2.6	3.3	See PLI	3.9 'Laici' (PRI PLIPRS)
DC	34.0	41.0	41.7	46.3	43.4	44.6	38.3	37.7	32.3	34.9
PLI	2.0	2.0	2.7	3.4	6.1	4.5	2.8	1.9	4.0 (with PRI)	See PRI
PNM/PDIUM	11.6	8.6	5.8	4.9	2.9	3.1	{7.8 DN}	1.0	–	–
			9.0 (PMP, Lauro)							
MSI	6.1	7.7	5.0	6.1	4.6	3.6		5.4	3.9	3.5

Table 5.2. Parliamentary Elections: Chamber of Deputies: Sardinia

	1948	1953	1958	1963	1968	1972	1976	1979	1983	1987	1992
PCI	20.3 Pop.Front	22.3	19.8	22.5	23.7	22.5 (with PSd'Az)	23.5 (with PSd'Az)	31.7	28.8	25.3	14.3 (PDS)
PSIUP	–	–	–	–	5.4	–	1.6 (DP)	3.2 (DP,PDUP)	1.0 (DP)	1.3 (DP)	6.7 (PRC)
VERDI	–	–	–	–	–	–	–	–	–	–	2.3 (Verdi)
PRS (Radicals)	–	–	–	–	–	–	0.8	3.4	1.6	2.6	1.0 (Pannella)
PSI	See PCI, Pop.Front	8.8	12.3	11.1	{10.7}	8.1	9.3	8.9	10.1	11.4	15.4
PSDI	–	1.8	2.0	3.7		3.9	2.6	3.3	3.8	3.1	4.2
PSd'AZ	10.2	7.0	3.0	4.0 (with PRI)	3.6	See PCI	See PCI	1.9	9.5	13.1	6.7
PRI	–	–	3.5 (PMP)	See PSd'Az	2.0	2.5	2.0	1.9	3.1	2.3	5.2
DC	51.2	41.7	47.1	42.5	42.8	40.9	39.9	38.1	31.7	34.3	33.7
PLI	–	2.0	2.7	5.8	4.4	3.3	1.1	1.3	1.4	0.9	2.8
Blocco Naz	8.7	–	–	–	–	–	–	–	–	–	–
PNM/PDIUM	1.6	8.6	3.0	3.7	3.3	{11.3} DN	{7.2}	–	–	–	–
MSI	2.8	7.7	4.7	5.8	4.0			6.3	6.2	4.7	5.2

Table 5.3. Parliamentary Elections (PR): Chamber of Deputies: Sardinia 1994

PARTIES	NUMBER OF VOTES	%	SEATS in Proportional Ballot
PDS	199,337	19.3	1
All Dem	23,381	2.2	
RC	61,690	5.9	
Rete	6,967	0.7	
PSI	31,792	3.1	
Pannella	30,073	2.9	
Verdi	21,385	2.1	
PPI	45,208	9.2	1
Patto Segni	185,322	17.9	1
FI	225,301	21.9	1
AN	125,116	12.1	
Other	28,785	2.8	—
VOTERS		82.5	4

FPTP

PARTIES	SEATS in Single-Member Constituencies
AN-FI	9
Progressisti	4
Patto-PPI	1

Table 5.4. Regional Elections: Sardinia 12 and 26 June 1994

FIRST BALLOT

Provincial Constituencies	Number of Votes	%	Seats	Regional List (First Ballot)	%
FI	195,206	21.0	14	266,605	30.5
AN	102,723	11.1	8		
PDS	167,509	18.1	13	261,117	29.9
RC	55,160	5.9	4		
All Dem & Verdi	26,976	2.9	–		
Lista Sardegna	48,804	5.2	4		
PPI	150,245	16.2	11	133,402	15.3
Patto Segni	85,924	9.3	6	130,075	14.9
PS d'azione	47,071	5.1	4	59,452	6.8
Sardigna Natzione	10,979	1.2	–	23,108	2.6
CCD	14,024	1.5	–		
PRI	8,375	0.9	–		
Other	13,556	1.6	–		
			64		

SECOND BALLOT (16 seats allocated on regional list basis, ballot open to top three lists of regional lists in first ballot.)

FI/AN	36%	6 seats (4 to FI, 2 to AN)
Progressisti	42%	8 seats (3 to PDS, 2 to All.Dem & Verdi, 3 to Lista Sardegna)
PPI	20.7%	2 seats
		16 seats

TOTAL REGIONAL COUNCIL (80 seats)

FI	18	PDS	16	PPI	13
AN	10	Rifondaz	4	Patto Segni Pact	6
		All Dem. & Verdi	2	PSd'Az	4
		Lista Sardegna	7		
Right	28	Left	29	Centre	23

'Lista Sardegna' = Federalist Socialists, 'Rinascita & Sardismo', and Social Christians. Centre-Left Government (minus Rifondazione) confirmed.

Part II

Regionalism in the Italian Republic: Centre and Periphery under Strain

–6–

Federalism, Regionalism and the Unitary State: Contemporary Regional Pressures in Historical Perspective

David Hine

The rebirth of territorial politics in Italy in the 1990s has given unexpected new life to the debate on regionalism. In recent years, the regional authorities set up in 1970 were frequently thought of, for reasons explained later in this chapter, as a rather disappointing experiment in territorial devolution. However, the breakdown of the national party system and the rise of parties with more concentrated territorial strength than in the past has changed the mood considerably. Though it is true that the territorial interests pursued by the new parties and movements are not generally coterminous with the official regions laid down in the constitution (the biggest tension is a broad 'North–South' cleavage), their rise does pose the question of whether, for the first time since the *Risorgimento*, there is a real threat to national political unity, and whether a new form of regional charter can provide an effective response to this threat.

To help answer these questions, we need first to place the modern regional system in historical perspective. In many respects it has always been rather surprising, in a country that was united comparatively recently, that political tensions based on territorial conflict have not been stronger than they have been, and that regional parties and movements have not played a bigger role in national politics. With the exception of certain small areas of the periphery, there have been few significant parties or movements of territorial defence, let alone parties promoting the break-up of the Italian state. Yet economically the country itself has since Unification been quite deeply divided, and compared to other major European states has a far higher variation in socio-economic structures and living standards across its regions (Commission of the European Communities 1990: 238).

Why the unified state has not been subject to stronger centrifugal tensions thus requires some explanation. The constitutional order brought by Unification was certainly not sensitive to regional differences. It imposed a highly centralized unitary state, and a set of policies whose effects on the least advanced areas were frequently harmful. Until 1948 it admitted of no decentralization to a regional tier of government, and very little to the municipal level. The one visible symbolic concession it did bring was to transfer the capital from the economically and culturally dominant North, down as far as Rome, and in this it did at least something to alleviate the sense of colonial annexation of the South by the Piedmontese state.

The real explanation of the relative absence of a reaction to this centralization, however, probably lies, at least for the period from 1860 to 1922, in the cultural dominance of the myth of national popular resurgence on which the *Risorgimento* was based. Among the remarkably small stratum of the population that constituted the politically active class, the Italian people's historic destiny was seen as being to achieve its unity, and though there were a few, such as Carlo Cattaneo, who thought otherwise, the great majority, including the Mazzinian republicans, believed that most forms of territorial decentralization, let alone federalism, would weaken the fragile unity of the new Italian state and therefore undermine this fundamental purpose.

After the First World War the context – though not the constitutional reality – began to change. The Italian state was by now more solid, and had far more administrative tasks to fulfil which called for a measure of decentralization. It also absorbed new territories (Trentino-Alto Adige and Fruili-Venezia Giulia) which had enjoyed substantial autonomy under Austria, and were likely to demand similar status under Italian rule. However, until after the Second World War, the central state was still able to resist these pressures for Fascism was soon in power, and with it a mode of rule based on force not consent, and one which could hardly be other than highly centralist in outlook.

Only after 1945, therefore, was the question of the territorial articulation of the Italian state posed in a genuinely open way. What came forth, not surprisingly, was a compromise which left few parties to the argument satisfied. The compromise made substantial concessions to decentralization, albeit still within the framework of a unitary state. The regional unit was recognized as a necessary one, but the region was not, as in truly federal states, recognized as having a valid claim to representation in the national legislature. Moreover, while there were strong pressures for regional government coming from the periphery (Sicily's early post-war separatist tendencies, Sardinia's island heritage, the special history and problems of Trentino-Alto Adige and Friuli-Venezia Giulia, and the linguistic peculiarity of Valle d'Aosta), and while this gave rise to the concept of regions of 'special' statute, on the mainland the regional theme was far less deeply felt.

Republican Italy thus had a pale imitation of a problem well-known, and much more acute, in the United Kingdom and Spain: the need to differentiate between areas of the country with a strong local identity and strong demands for devolution, and those where identification with the dominant metropolitan culture obviated any such need. The solution adopted in Italy – special structures for just some regions – is by no means uncommon, though one side-effect is obviously an uneven pattern of representation and administrative coverage across the country.[1] Italy thus distinguished between 'ordinary' regions and 'special' regions, and though in constitutional theory the difference was not great, in practice, it proved for over twenty years to be enormous since the ordinary regions were simply not set up. Once again, the imperative of the unitary state was the dominant one, and so it was, as we shall see later, even after the fifteen 'ordinary' regions were introduced in 1970.

The reasons for the delay were rather more complex in Republican Italy than in earlier regimes. Besides the relatively low level of mainland regional sentiment in the dominant regions like Piedmont, Lombardy, Tuscany, Lazio and Campania, there were complex factors connected with overtly partisan issues. The two dominant parties of post-war Italy (DC and PCI) took almost diametrically opposed views of the value of regional government at the outset, but ironically their positions began, almost at once, to reverse themselves, leaving everyone in doubt, and much opportunity for delay and obstruction. The DC had been in favour of a decentralized state as a form of prototype Catholic subsidiarity counterposed to a potentially over-mighty central executive. The PCI had been opposed precisely because it saw a strong central executive as the instrument for profound socio-economic change. In power, the DC saw the benefits to itself of centralized power, and the threat to national unity posed by a 'red belt' across the regions of North-Central Italy. In opposition, the PCI slowly came round to the idea of regionalism as a counterweight to central control. The two forces cancelled one another out and the status quo remained unaltered until 1970: regionalism existed on paper, but remained unimplemented because enabling legislation was blocked in Parliament.

This was not, however, the only reason why the regions took so long to establish. An equally important factor was the absence of deep-rooted regional identification among the relevant populations in most regions. This did not apply to the special regions on the periphery, but elsewhere, while there was an effort to link boundaries to ancient historical entities, those entities had not existed since 1860 at all, and before that date their patterns had been sufficiently varied and ambiguous to make any attempt to recreate them a century later rather difficult. There is no doubting the significance and loyalty of localism in Italian political life, even today, but the unit of loyalty is often the municipality or at most the province, rather than the region. Indeed, territorial contrasts and tensions had historically been as much between *capiluoghi* in the same region, as between regions.

Moreover, municipal localism proved easier to reconcile with a national political system than strongly entrenched regionalism would have done. Local leaders became political entrepreneurs defending local interests inside national parties. This was assisted by an electoral system based on list systems of PR (proportional representation) that focused on choices between national programmes, ideologies and identities, rather than local loyalties. By the time regional tiers of elected government were established nationwide, it was already too late for a distinctive regional class to emerge. The regional unit was largely absorbed into the hierarchy of national party organizations that were by then far too strong to admit of any exceptions.

In retrospect, however, it is clear that underneath the surface of this nationally dominated system, a new form of tension was developing, as the two main governing parties – the Christian Democrats (DC) and Socialists (PSI) – gradually became more Southern-based in terms of membership, leadership and, eventually, electorate. Since both parties originally had their areas of greatest strength in the North, it took many years for this tension to become acute, and to change fundamentally the electorate's view of which territorial interests the DC and PSI really defended. Gradually, however, the DC lost ground in its north-eastern stronghold and from the mid-1970s onwards the growing budgetary deficit put pressures on the party's ability to redistribute resources from the North to the South and satisfy Southern supporters without more prosperous Northern taxpayers feeling this to be at their own expense. A very similar process occurred with the PSI's electorate, though the period of relative Socialist ascendancy in the 1980s did something to halt, and briefly even to reverse the trend, before it returned with a vengeance in the 1990s.

Admittedly, in the long boom of the latter half of the 1980s, these tensions were sublimated by economic growth. Once that boom turned to recession, however, the difficulties became starkly apparent. In the 1992 election the Northern League emerged as one of the major forces in the North. In the South, the governing parties held on better, though a strong challenge was mounted by the DC breakaway movement *La Rete*, and later by the neo-fascist Italian Social Movement (MSI). The national party system was breaking up, hastened by a widespread rejection of the traditional governing parties for their alleged incompetence and corruption. That this dissatisfaction expressed itself in such different forms in different parts of the country (the League in the North; the MSI and *La Rete* in the South), suggested that a new and powerful distributional conflict had taken hold of political life.

By the early 1990s, it was widely believed that the crisis which had overtaken the political system as a result of this heightened territorial conflict, and of the corruption which such tension had indirectly helped expose, required thoroughgoing institutional reform, and that such reform would have to include some form of new devolutionary charter. But what such a charter should include remained very much in the air. For the Northern League, it involved the division of the country into a confederation of three macro-regions (the League prefers the word 'republic'): Padania in the North, Etruria in the Centre, and 'the South', to which the League had as yet been unable to give a name. For most other parties, it meant a strengthening of the existing regional order to overcome the deficiencies which have been evident since the establishment of the ordinary regions in 1970. After the 1992 general election, the Bi-cameral Parliamentary Commission on Institutional Reform worked towards the latter goal and came up with proposals which are examined later in this chapter. First, however, we need to understand in more detail what lessons are to be learned from the experience of regional government as it has been practised over the last two decades.

Italian Regional Experience since 1970

Italian regionalism is not federalism. Exactly what constitutes a federal system is much debated, but it clearly involves not only constitutional entrenchment of state powers within the federation, but also a strong version of state representation at federal level (as in the US Senate, where each state, irrespective of size, is represented by two senators, or the German Bundesrat, where states are in effect represented by their governments).[2] In Italy, the Senate is only in a minimal sense representative of the regions. More importantly, while the powers of the regions are theoretically entrenched in the constitution, in practice they are very imprecise. In comparison with strong forms of coordinate federalism, few powers are devolved, there are virtually no areas of 'exclusive' (as opposed to 'concurrent') legislative power and financial autonomy is extremely modest.

If Italian constitution drafters were fairly clear that they did not want federalism, they had only rather unclear notions of what they meant by regionalism. They knew that it involved direct representation of the people through elected regional authorities, and they thought (though their successors did not stick to this constitutional rule) that a region had to be of a minimum size (one million inhabitants) to be viable. They also identified a range of functions which they thought were best handled by regions rather than the centre, and they set this out in the Constitution too. Article 117 lays out the broad headings under which the region may legislate: municipal boundaries; urban and rural police forces; fairs and markets; public charities, health, and hospital assistance; vocational training and financial assistance to students; local museums and libraries; urban planning; tourism and the hotel industry; regional transport networks; regional roads, aqueducts, and other public works; lake navigation and ports; mineral and spa waters; extractive industries; hunting; inland fisheries; agriculture and forestry, and artisanship.

However, when regions legislate in these areas they have to take account of any basic framework legislation laid down at national level. Much of this framework legislation has proved to be remarkably detailed, even in areas where it was originally intended that the regions would be relatively free to interpret it to suit their own needs and choices. The apparent precision of Article 117 on the powers of the region is thus rather misleading. Large changes have occurred in the regional role over time, and several of the key tasks of today's regions are not mentioned in the Constitution itself. Over time, views of the appropriate level at which to deliver a particular service have changed. In particular, with the modern state engaged in policy on a very broad front, the regions are seen as appropriate agencies for *administrative deconcentration*, even if they still lack real legislative autonomy, and this has happened most notably in the area of health and transport. But the case of health is emblematic in that, while the National Health Service has been regionalized, its vast army of employees, and the key decisions on resource allocation, remained responsible (until the very recent reconstruction) to highly decentralized USL (local health units) well below the regional authority. The administrative powers enjoyed by the regions have thus varied between policy areas and over time. Overall, however, and despite the great enthusiasm with which regionalization has been greeted by many acute observers of Italian politics (Putnam 1993: 184), the region remains a relatively weak administrative unit, as can be readily seen in personnel terms: the provinces and the municipalities in total still employ nine times as many staff as do the regions, while the size of the central state apparatus itself towers over all three devolved tiers (Hine 1993: 259).

The situation on the financial front is little better. Regions have few 'own resources' and have not established distinctive fiscal stances and expenditure patterns. The contrast with Germany, where fiscal revenues are shared out between *Bund* and *Länder* far more equally, is stark (Hesse 1987: 73). Most regional activities involving large sums of expenditure have been specially assigned tasks, with ear-marked funding coming not from 'own fiscal resources', but from special transfers from central Treasury funds. The heavy dependence on ear-marked funds from the centre has exposed regional authorities to the inevitable vicissitudes that have derived from the central government's efforts to keep the overall level of public spending in check. This has been especially marked in the last decade, as the public-sector borrowing requirement has expanded. Various developments – the regionalization of the health service, the growth of spending on agriculture and transport, and changes in funding formulae – have further weakened regional fiscal autonomy. And central government's predictable desire to minimize forward projections of its overall deficit has led to regular, unrealistically tight, estimates of future regional expenditure. When such limits cannot be respected, pressure goes up – exercised mainly through the national party networks whose influence is discussed further below – for additional grants, soft loans, etc. In the end, the dam has generally burst, and special supplementary funding has been forthcoming. When this happens, the short-term problem is alleviated, but at the expense of rational financial planning at regional level, and ultimately at the expense of the credibility of central government's resolve in the face of budgetary strains.

Regional governments have had as a result only limited opportunities to develop their own distinctive spending priorities, but equally, in any given area, too little reason to limit their propensity to spend, as they lack a direct responsibility to voters paying for their services through local taxes. As has been widely observed, the risk in such a system is that the regions develop a culture of dependence rather than self-reliance, and that their link with the electorate is deprived of the fundamental responsibility of making choices and reconciling spending and taxing in an acceptable equilibrium. At the level of central government, this tendency has been reinforced by a concern about the position of the economically or culturally weak regions, and has been used to justify state intervention to impose common standards, or at best centrally determined redistribution, rather than to foster autonomy. Regional legislation, though substantial in output, tends as a result to be very similar from region to region, and reflects the fruit of the bargaining process with central government rather than the autonomous choices of the regional authorities (Onida 1991: 17). As we shall see below, the relationship thereby created is not entirely one-sided, especially since the national political parties are themselves sufficiently fragmented to give regional demands a degree of leverage inside the parties. Indeed, the great range of joint state-region committees that has grown up to service the relationship between the two tiers of government does to a certain degree assist the regions. Overall, however, fiscal dependence and administrative intermeshing with the central state has reinforced the dependency culture, and focused the attentions of regions on their reactions to central government, rather than on their own individual margin of autonomy.

The Parties and the Regional Ideal: Divergent Philosophies and Common Practice

The state of affairs described above has deliberately focused on the weaknesses of the regions, and is mainly a structural account. These weaknesses are closely linked to the initial artificiality of the regional unit of government in most of the country. This is not to say that regional government is in principle undesirable or unnecessary but rather, as we observed earlier, that it does not grow organically out of a long tradition of government at this level, nor, at the outset, out of a genuine sense of popular identification. It is, in this respect, a tier of government imposed from above, and conceived initially in the abstract. Moreover, given the strength of Italian parties within the overall political system, it is not surprising that the imposition reflected the outlooks of the *national* parties – there being virtually none, except on the periphery, which were genuinely regional in character.

However, this is not to say that parties all had the *same* vision of the regional unit of government and its role, or that the parties, being national and centralized in nature, effectively suppressed real regional autonomy. On the contrary, precisely because the parties had very uncertain and ambiguous visions of the regional ideal, they have by their, sometimes unintended, practice managed to counteract some of the tendencies towards regional dependence on the centre described in the previous section. As we shall now see, the complex political relationship established between the state and the regions has probably helped generate, at least at the level of the political élite, some degree of regional sentiment and identity where previously there was rather little.

The most difficult problem faced by the parties in fleshing out the regional ideal has concerned how the region is to be integrated with the goals of the modern welfare state. Should it be, as in Germany, the administrative agent of the federation, employing large numbers of civil servants, and bearing responsibility for many agency-delivered government services? Or should it be a system of government with a lighter touch: a level of policy formulation and participation both to channel ideas upwards to a partnership between regions and the state at national level, and downwards to politically-elected authorities (the provinces and municipalities) below it?

A top-down answer to these questions reflects the unitary state: regions as mechanisms for implementing *national* policies. This view is reflected in the Constitution, which implies a reactive philosophy of administrative decentralism, establishing, at least for the ordinary regions, only shared or concurrent, rather than exclusive, legislative power, with policy agendas being set largely at national level. It was further bolstered by the post-war passion for 'planning'. Planning in the 1950s and especially the 1960s was an essentially technocratic activity: the application of technically correct, welfare-determined, solutions to policy problems. In reality, even in the heyday of comprehensive national plans in the mid-1960s, Italy never approached anything like the planning system used by France; many Italians would have liked to emulate it, but indicative economic plans in Italy were always late, and generally still-born by the time they were officially approved. But in so far as the planning philosophy was influential among policy makers it implied, for the regions, subordination to a grand national design. Regionalism might thus make planning more 'democratic' or responsive to local needs, but it also implied a decidedly secondary role for regional authorities as political entities. They might be suitable subjects for administrative deconcentration, but not for real political autonomy.

A bottom-up answer, in contrast, gives much more political autonomy to the region, and it was this approach which, at the level of public utterances, held sway, albeit for a time, during the 1970s. In reality the planning vogue was not abandoned – particularly since the decade was, far more than the 1960s or 1980s, one which saw the Left in the ascendancy. But planning henceforth went hand-in-hand with participation, and the region was to become the laboratory for the participatory, assembly-dominated, system of government which was supposed to achieve this. The region would not be heavily bureaucratized, but would work closely with provincial and municipal government both in policy formulation and administrative implementation. Regional government would ensure that policy would be implemented by government closely in touch with the citizen, and would emerge in a consensual form with an upward flow of demands and inputs to policy makers, to replace the classic downward chain of command of the unitary state.

With hindsight, the assumptions that drove this interpretation were not fully thought through. The years in which the regions were introduced were in many respects a period of heightened idealism in Italian politics. The belief that participation and broad, if carefully controlled, *political* mediation could solve the over-bureaucratization of the early version of the Italian welfare state was fostered by the Left – then in the political ascendancy – and it was a Left which above all sought to test out at regional level the broad consociationalist coalition that it ultimately wanted at national level as well. 'Participation' in practice frequently meant very broad coalitions of all the main parties in a form of consociational alliance, rather than explicit citizen involvement. As a result it was eventually destined to lose its appeal, as did the vogue for assembly-dominated government at regional level. Spending limits grew tighter, and competition for resources increased. In reaction, spending lobbies became more vociferous and demanding, and resource allocation was marked more by piecemeal incrementalism than consensus-based long-term planning. As the Communist Party learned to its cost, the line between participation and politically directed control of bureaucracy on one side, and bureaucratic and corporatist capture of politicians on the other, is a fine one. In the 1980s, the political system struggled with the effects of a highly corporatist state system in a way that was eventually to return the focus of interest to allocative efficiency and a renewed emphasis on the private sector. Optimism about the political market as a mechanism for allocative efficiency waned as broad and inclusive coalitions seemed to result in mutual vetoes and policy deadlock.

It was not only or even primarily the Left that had this lesson to learn, however. On the contrary, the Left learned the lesson to a considerable degree vicariously, through the experience of the Centre and Right in power. For even at its height in the later 1970s, the PCI was influential in only about half of the regional governments; by the end of the decade, it had lost its role in the national governing coalition, and its bargaining strength even at regional level was being eroded (Leonardi *et al.* 1987: 102–3). But the distinction between Right and Left in the 1970s and 1980s became increasingly blurred as the Christian Democrat Party itself became the real protagonist of the public sector, and of a system of state-directed clientelist bargaining. This system was most visible at national level, but profoundly affected the regional and local levels as well. Christian Democrat practice towards regional government, every bit as much as that of the Left, frequently enabled participation and consultation to degenerate into undiscriminating interest-group incorporation into policy networks. Under the DC, indeed, the country developed one of the largest and most complicated systems of public intervention and interest intermediation anywhere in Europe.

This complex interaction between the interventionist state, the regional tier of government, and party responses to it, created a system presided over by a group of governing parties which lacked the necessary cohesion to manage the resulting strains. The PCI might just have assembled the requisite level of party cohesion to make a reality of its original design, but the *Pentapartito* of the 1980s certainly could not. This generated a margin of manoeuvre for the regions themselves. They may have lacked legislative and financial autonomy, but through the porous and open governing parties in which their leaders participated, they managed to create arenas in which to bargain with Parliament and government in Rome in ways that gave them back a degree of power at the centre. This was most notable in the large number of national committees in which regional interests are represented, in the legal and even constitutional complexity that was generated therein, and in the area of regional finance.

These tendencies are most evident in the regulatory and allocative committees, containing representatives of both the state and the regions, which have become the norm whenever a new task is imposed on the regions. The most senior of such committees, indeed, is a standing one (the *conferenza permanente stato-regioni*) giving the regions permanent access to government on a wide range of policy issues. Over the last fifteen years a hundred such joint committees have sprung up to service the complex interaction of the two levels. The legislation that imposes such tasks is invariably complex and difficult to interpret. It leaves the scope for regional independence juridically unclear. And though, in general, the system of legal and constitutional arbitration that regulates the state-region relationship depends on a judicial order that is entirely national in scope, and although the Constitutional Court has in general (albeit with certain significant exceptions) tended to side with the state not the regions, central government does not generally wish to leave the fate of policies which are often urgent, and important to its overall strategy, to the vagaries and inevitable delays of the legal system. The joint committees therefore become the bargaining arenas in which such potential conflicts are smoothed out. In the process, regional interests can express themselves through national party structures, often in cross-party alliances that have ramifications right up to national level.

A similarly complex set of relationships applies to the question of regional finance. We noted earlier in the chapter that the Centre, in principle, enjoys overwhelming dominance in fiscal matters through the financing formulae determined by the original regional finance legislation (law no. 281, 1970). That legislation effectively limited the size of 'own resources' to 5 per cent of total regional spending. The rest comes as direct transfers from Rome. However, this covers the so-called 'common fund', the fund for regional development, and 'special contributions', and while transfers under the first category are calculated on the basis of territory and population, they also contain a significant redistributive element to take account of various socio-economic indicators of development levels.[3] The formula on which it was based has remained unaltered since 1970, despite an original commitment to review it every three years, and this reflects the strong interest that the less-developed regions have had in not reopening the basic formula, for the long-established 'one region, one vote' principle benefits them considerably.

In regional finance, then, as in other aspects of the state-region relationship, the complexity of policy making reflects the internally diverse nature of both the governing coalition, and its component national parties. Government in Italy came to be characterized by juridicized bargained pluralism, and was not subject to any form of purposeful, single-party programme. Had it been, the balance of power would have lain much more firmly with Rome. But parties were porous and open coalitions of sectional and territorial interests, and their leaders were as much the prisoners as the masters of these interests. Through these open parties, regions and regional party leaders had ample mechanisms to make the territorial distribution of resources an important element in national coalition bargaining. Frequently, indeed, it led to an overloading of the system of national coalition bargaining, as factions and parties in Rome brought the behaviour of regional and local governments into the equation of power they fought over in Parliament and Cabinet.

Thus, although these bargains were struck between members of national parties, their outcomes certainly did not always reflect a dominant centre. On the contrary, the system reflected a form of 'centralized collegiate decision making': centralized in so far as quite detailed decisions were taken *at the centre*, but collegiate in that the regions won for themselves extensive rights to representation in the taking of decisions. The system was untidy, and could be criticized above all for the extent to which it was forced into a pattern determined by the internal power relationships of national parties. Under such a system there was always a risk that regional leaders would abandon the interests of their own regions for the sake of personal or group advancement at national level. Set against this, however, the national parties did at least provide a form of cement to a system that might otherwise have started to fragment much earlier. It eventually did so only when the internal tensions and perceived conflicts of interest between North and South could be suppressed no longer, and when the North–South conflict (at least for Northerners) became entwined with a more widespread frustration with the inefficiency of the Italian public sector.

The Uncertain Steps Towards a New Regional Contract

The experience of the Italian regions over the last two decades raises difficult problems of interpretation in the new political system which has developed in Italy in the 1990s. Had the old party system remained intact, the prescription might have been more straightforward. It would above all have involved an increase in the chain of accountability between regional authorities and the regional electorate. As we have seen, those who benefit from locally produced services are not in a direct sense those who pay for them; the immediate paymaster in regional government is the state not the local taxpayer. Local voters have until recently had little incentive to think in local terms, and have tended to vote on the basis of national party performance. The notion that voters can understand clearly what elected regional (and local) authorities are responsible for, and can distinguish between this and areas where they are mere executants of central direction, is crucial for local democracy. Central government's failure to resist pressures from regions for supplementary finance when budget ceilings prove inadequate can thus only be addressed by a clearer division of powers between the two tiers, and an electorate capable of understanding that division. Greater constitutional clarity than under the present system is necessary, and this probably means a sharper divide between the two tiers, and fewer but more important roles for the regions.

By the start of the 1990s, the case for a new legislative and fiscal relationship between the state and the regions had been widely accepted. Before the 1992 general election the Constitutional Affairs Committee of Chamber of Deputies produced wide-ranging recommendations for such a change (Putnam 1993: 61–2). This work was resumed in the short-lived Parliament elected in 1992. The Bi-Cameral Commission on Institutional Reform produced a wide-ranging document revising no fewer than eighteen articles of the Constitution relating to the regions. The two most fundamental revisions affect Articles 70 and 117: defining the *legislative* roles of state and region. A key change was the so-called 'residual' clause. Under the 1948 Constitution all powers not explicitly exercised by the regions are reserved to the state. Under the new proposals, all legislative powers not defined in the new version of Article 70 as pertaining to the state (the article defines twenty-six which *are* thus reserved) would be either reserved 'exclusively' to the region or would be subject to concurrent powers of both state and region. Thirteen sectors were defined, under

Article 117, as areas of 'exclusive' regional legislative competence. These included agriculture, commerce, industry, tourism, land-use planning and vocational training. In the areas of 'concurrent' legislative authority, the state would write 'organic' or framework legislation ('*legge organiche*'), while the region would fill this out with detailed regional legislation. Only the latter would have direct applicability on ordinary citizens; the state's organic laws would be binding on regions only, not on individuals.[4] However, should the regions fail to fulfil minimum standards of provision defined in the organic legislation, the state would, under Article 118b, have the right to intervene directly in the affected area. (The most obvious such area not defined explicitly as pertaining to either the state or the regions was health.)

In principle, an equally important element of the new proposals concerned a more equitable system of revenue-sharing. A revision of Article 119, dealing with regional finance, was proposed by which the regions would be granted their 'own fiscal resources'. But while the detail was somewhat more explicit and morally declarative than that of the article it was to replace ('Financial autonomy and freedom in the imposition of taxes are necessary elements of regional, provincial and municipal autonomy'), the essence of any future fiscal distribution was devolved to a future 'organic law'. Whether the drafters of that law (were it ever introduced) would have the courage to take substantial revenue away from the national tier, would be critical to its success.

The third area dealt with by the Bi-Cameral Commission concerned institutional questions, and built on extensive, but inconclusive, work undertaken in the 1987–92 legislature by the Parliamentary Commission for Regional Affairs (Camera dei Deputati 1993: 555–7). The Commission's proposed revisions were explicitly aimed at rectifying the extreme political fragility of the regional executives (Fedele 1993: 471–554). It proposed a form of 'constructive vote of no confidence' for the regional president (who was to be installed directly by a vote of the regional council, and thereafter could nominate the members of the regional executive without a further vote of confidence). The regional council could redraft this arrangement by regional statute if it so chose, but could only do so through a two-thirds majority. The same qualified freedom to redraft the regional constitution also applied to regional electoral law; so in principle, regions could be elected on differing bases across the country. However, such constitutional revisions could be subject to an abrogative referendum, at the demand of one-fifth of the members of the regional council, or 5 per cent of the regional electorate.[5]

While the above proposals represented a fairly broad consensus on the need for greater devolution to the regions, they contained inherent ambiguities over exactly how much power was really to be devolved and how solid an institution the new region would be. Despite the brave words of Article 119, the exact fiscal contract remained undefined. The extent to which 'organic' laws would bind regions was also potentially highly corrosive of regional autonomy. Article 70 reserved to the state the power to define the widespread civil rights recognized in the first section of the Constitution – areas where the state retained the exclusive right to legislate. Here too a future set of judgements by the Constitutional Court could prove very corrosive of regional autonomy. Moreover, Article 117 maintained the catch-all proviso that 'Regional laws cannot conflict with the national interest or the interests of other regions'. And finally, it was notable that regions were not to have a provision (operative in the large municipalities) for the direct election of the chief executive and the automatic dissolution of the council should the latter lose her/his majority. Yet without this, and in the absence of a more cohesive and responsible party system, it was far from clear that the constructive vote of no confidence alone could stabilize and strengthen regional executives.

The proposals produced by the Commission were in any case superseded by the events of 1994. They emanated from a dying and discredited legislature, whose members were thoroughly delegitimized by the time of the March 1994 general election. The results of that election did little to clarify the future prospects of regional reform. The Northern League had over the previous five years made the 'confederalization'[6] of the country into three 'macro-regions' a central plank of its electoral appeal. However, by the start of 1994, its interest in regional devolution was rapidly subordinated to the exigencies of national politics. First, in its search for party allies in the new single-seat constituencies introduced by the 1993 electoral reform, the League found itself having to down-play its more radical demands for confederal arrangements, since these were looked on with disfavour not just by a good part of its potential northern electorate, but also by Berlusconi's *Forza Italia*.[7] After the election, moreover, the new right-wing government found itself fundamentally divided over the future of regional devolution. The League inserted into the government programme an unspecific commitment to explore devolution proposals, yet *Alleanza Nazionale* inserted an equally unspecific proposal for a stronger central executive which on the face of it seemed diametrically at odds with the League's position. In reality, the political controversies in which the new government became embroiled almost from the outset precluded any real progress during the eight brief months of its existence. The Northern League set out to weaken Berlusconi and eventually bring him down, but its strategy was almost entirely focused on national political issues, especially those connected with investigations of political corruption, rather than on devolution proposals.

It was therefore perhaps predictable that the main change to regional government in the year following the 1994 general election should emanate from the Dini government, not from its predecessor, and should be a fairly limited change bringing regional electoral law closer into line with the new majoritarian principles introduced at national and municipal level. Under the new law 80 per cent of the seats are elected by proportional representation, but a pool of 20 per cent is reserved for the largest party or coalition list emerging from the proportional contest. The aim is to create a more stable form of regional government. The same goal is served by the provision by which fresh elections are held after two years not five if, during the first two years of its existence, the majority is brought down in a confidence vote. What the new legislation did not touch, however, was the distribution of power between central government and the regions.

The regional elections of Spring 1995 were therefore held under conditions not dissimilar to those of the 1970s and 1980s: a referendum on the state of national politics, rather than a real opportunity for the expression of regional autonomy and diversity. This did not necessarily imply that with the electoral decline of the Northern League the issue of regional devolution had gone away, but it did reflect concerns in all parties about the consequence of moving towards a fundamentally higher level of devolution at the very moment at which the old national party system was in a state of great turmoil, and in which even large parties like the PDS, the PPI, *Forza Italia* and *Alleanza Nazionale* had difficulties reconciling and aggregating the variety of demands of the different regional interests they represented.

As we saw in the previous section, the internal disunity of the traditional parties was in the 1970s and 1980s a factor which gave the regions an opportunity – albeit mainly through arenas at national level – to play a role in forming, rather than simply following, policies determined by the state. It might therefore be thought that the cause of greater devolution would be further served by a more thoroughgoing weakening of the national party system. Not only might regions henceforth have different party coalitions in different parts of the country, they might also have entirely different party systems. However, the old system may be said to have worked (in so far as it did work) precisely because of the presence of national parties, albeit open ones, right across the country. National parties, in the final resort, were the sources of arbitration. *Without* hegemonic national parties there is always a risk that conflicts get out of hand, especially where they become not simply conflicts over resource allocation between single regions but conflicts between much larger areas. In the last three years the national party system has come to reflect precisely this type of 'macro-regional' conflict, with only the PDS and *Forza Italia* still apparently strong forces throughout the country.

Even this risk might not be a significant one in a country that was economically homogeneous, and in which a major increase in regional fiscal autonomy was possible without damaging the poorer regions. But Italy is anything but homogeneous. The Bi-Cameral Commission of the 1992/4 Parliament itself recognized the danger that the demise of a uniform, and hence massively redistributive, fiscal system would pose for the poorer regions. Its remedy was an equalization fund equivalent in total to the sum necessary to bring the regions with lower fiscal yields up to the national average (Article 119b). To avoid a re-erosion of regional autonomy, the payments made from this fund to the poorer regions would come in the form of a 'block' grant, and could not be earmarked for specific activities. However, while such a fund could – as the Commission proposed – have strict upper limits, and could be paid for out of general central government revenues, it would still be likely to be seen as a major form of income redistribution from the rich to the poor. Without national parties to legitimize such measures, and mediate between competing demands, this type of income redistribution might become increasingly unacceptable to the richer regions.

All this presupposes, of course, that a massive process of fiscal decentralization would actually be harmful to poorer regions. The Northern League for one has never accepted this. On the contrary, it argued that social transfers to the South, and the propping up of state-assisted industry and commerce in the area, encourage political clientelism and corruption, and are disincentives to the operation of the private market. It might even be argued that the League's arguments are supported, though not intentionally, by those who believe that deep-rooted, historically determined, cultural differences affect the operation and effectiveness of regional and local government in different parts of the country (Putnam 1993). For if this type of argument is true, transfers of income and wealth will result in a substantial misallocation of resources to authorities less capable of using those resources properly. However, assessment of the League's case is difficult, and to date there is little evidence that it is widely understood. The risk is not that voters in the North and Centre will believe that they can help their southern cousins by denying them resources, but that they simply will not care about the consequences of such a denial.

If the above dangers are real ones, then the current debate on regional reform needs to be handled with some caution. Devolution measures that seemed right in one set of political circumstances may not be so appropriate in new and less predictable ones. The arguments over federalism and the unitary state are recurrent ones that go to the heart of nationhood and national solidarity. And the case for solidarity itself need not necessarily be an altruistic one. Just as prosperous voters discover, sometimes belatedly, that voting for a more regressive taxation system can in the long run work against their own interests (a less-skilled, less-healthy, less-motivated workforce for the national economy, rising homelessness, crime rates, drug problems, inner-city decay, etc.) so richer regions ignore the plight of poorer regions within their national territory at their own peril. Few North Italian industrialists who produce for the national market, for example, and certainly very few of those who produce for the public sector throughout the national territory, would consider that the northern economy would be assisted by separatism or a seriously damaged southern economy. More generally, across the span of 130 years of the Italian state it has been rather rare for there to be a consensus that the real beneficiary is the South not the North.

The potential dangers of a rapid shift towards strong regions and extensive fiscal decentralization in the context of weak national parties are thus considerable. Time will tell whether the reform of the Italian party system currently in progress really can produce a new, rationalized and more cohesive system, built around the principle of alternation in power between government and responsible opposition. There is certainly a risk that it will not. But even if it does, it would not be surprising if, after some experience of incisive decentralization, the focus of political concern turned fairly rapidly back towards the unevenness of provision between services, and the conflicts of interests between regions, that are frequent and inevitable in all federal systems, and lead to cycles of enthusiasm and rejection for further devolution. Likewise, on the budgetary front, a country with as great a budget deficit problem as Italy cannot afford significant measures of fiscal devolution without encountering major conflicts of interest between regions and central governments over borrowing and spending.

None of this is to argue, of course, that the current push towards stronger Italian regions is misconceived. It is hard to argue that it is. But Italy has been through something very similar before, without finding clear-cut answers in simple institutional reform, as the experience of the 1970s shows. The obvious measure, to avoid a re-run of the disappointments of the last twenty years, would be to lock the country into the sort of devolution-based constitution from which central government could not escape. But while that might be feasible in Germany or the United States, it is far from clear that it is wise, in the long run, in Italy. An effective and workable balance between tiers of government takes time to work out, and has to be based on unwritten understandings as well as formal rules. Without first reaching a consensus on what that balance should be, it is far from clear that formal rules will prove lasting. Whether, between North and South, and perhaps also Left and Right, such a consensus on a new blueprint for devolution can be found, remains to be discovered.

Notes

1. The obvious example in the UK is the Scottish and Welsh Offices, Stormont and the ever-looming 'Midlothian Question': the political imbalance inherent in a situation in which regional devolution in one part of the country (region A) would deprive national MPs representing areas lacking regional devolution (regions B and C) of a say in policies subject to devolution in region A, but *would* allow region A's MPs to help determine the same policies in regions B and C. Arguably, Italy had a version of this 'question' during the period in which only the regions of special statute had their own regional assemblies.
2. For a discussion of the concept of federalism see, *inter alia*, Duchacek, (1986); also Wheare (1963).
3. The literature on regional finance is extensive. As an introduction see Giarda (1982), (1990). Also Cerea (1991).
4. The text of the proposed changes were supplied direct to the author by the *Commissione Parlamentare per le Riforme Istituzionali* in an unpublished cyclostyled document entitled 'Articoli Approvati' (Rome, no date). The proposals were discussed in the Italian press at the time of their definition. See, *inter alia*, 'Arriva un po' di federalismo', *La Repubblica*, 28 October 1993.
5. Article 123 of the proposed constitutional revision also makes provision for a wider use of abrogative referendums on regional legislation, along lines set out for parliamentary legislation in Article 75 of the Constitution.
6. Exactly what 'confederation' might mean in the Italian context remains unclear, despite the great outpouring of words that has been expended on it in recent years. Other essays in this collection examine in greater depth the League's proposals for constitutional

reform. The former chief ideologist of the Northern League's institutional design was Gianfranco Miglio. His ideas are set out in Miglio, G. (1992). The fluidity of the League's ideas on federation and confederation can be gauged from the speed with which the constitutional ideas presented by Miglio to the movement's 1993 congress at Assago were repudiated by Bossi and other senior members of the League in the days following the congress. Bossi was reported on 16 December as saying that the unity of Italy was 'safe in his hands' and that the confederal ideas were little more than a 'provocation' to stimulate debate on federalism. See *Corriere della Sera*, 16 December 1993, p.4, and in this volume Allum, Diamanti, Farrell, Levy and Cento Bull.

7. A number of published opinion polls have made this clear. See, for example, *L'Espresso*, 26 September 1993, p.53, and *La Repubblica*, 6 July 1993.

Bibliography

Bartole, S. *et al.* (1985), 'Le regioni, le province, i comuni', in Branca, G. (ed.), *Commentario della Costituzione* (**Vol.** I), Bologna.

Camera dei Deputati (1993), *Forme di governo regionale* (Indagine conoscitiva della Commissione parlamentare per le questioni regionali (settembre 1989–gennaio 1992) e documentazione allegata), Rome.

Cerea, G. (1991), 'I nodi della finanza regionale', in Formez, *Rassegna di Documentazione Legislativa Regionale*, **24** (Atti dell'incontro di studio *Per un nuovo regionalismo prospettive di riforme istituzionali*, Roma, 13 dicembre 1990), Rome, pp.23–43.

Commission of the European Communities (1990), *Fourth Periodic Report on the Development of the Regions*, COM, (90) Final, Brussels, 9 January.

Dente, B. (1985), *Governare la frammentazione. Stato regioni ed enti locali in Italia*, Bologna.

Duchacek, I.D. (1986), *The Territorial Dimension of Politics Within, Among and Across Nations*, Boulder, Co.

Fedele, M. (1993), 'Rapporto di ricerca su "La forma di governo regionale"', in Camera dei Deputati, *Forme di governo regionale* (Indagine conoscitiva della Commissione parlamentare per le questioni regionali (settembre 1989–gennaio 1992) e documentazione allegata), Rome, pp.471–554.

Formez (1991), *Rassegna di Documentazione Legislativa Regionale*, **24** (Atti dell'incontro di studio *Per un nuovo regionalismo prospettive di riforme istituzionali*, Roma, 13 dicembre 1990), Rome.

Giarda, D.P. (1982), *Finanza locale. Idee per una riforma*, Milan.
—— (1990), 'Vicende e problemi della finanza regionale', *Quaderni Regionali*, **IX**, 1, pp.23–32.
Hesse, J.J. (1987), 'The Federal Republic of Germany: From Co-operative Federalism to Joint Policy-Making', *West European Politics*, **10**, 4 , pp.70–87.
Hine, D.J. (1993), *Governing Italy: the Politics of Bargained Pluralism*, Oxford.
Leonardi, R., Nanetti, R.Y., and Putnam, R. (1987), 'Italy: Territorial Politics in the Postwar Years. The Case of Regional Reform', *West European Politics*, **10**, 4, pp.88–107.
Miglio, G. (1992), *Come cambiare: le mie riforme*, Milan.
—— (1991–2), 'Towards a Federal Italy', *Telos*, 90, Winter, pp.19–42.
Onida, V. (1991), 'Sviluppo e declino dell'esperienza regionale', Formez, *Rassegna di Documentazione Legislativa Regionale*, **24** (Atti dell'incontro di studio *Per un nuovo regionalismo prospettive di riforme istituzionali*, Roma, 13 dicembre 1990), Rome, pp.13–22.
Putnam, R. (1993), *Making Democracy Work: Civic Traditions in Modern Italy*, Princeton, N.J.
Putnam, R., Leonardi, R. and Nanetti, R. (1984), *La pianta e le radici*, Bologna.
Rolla, G. (1982), 'La determinazione delle materie di competenza regionale nella giurisprudenza costituzionale', *Le Regioni*, pp.100–30.
Tarrow, S. (1977), *Between Center and Periphery: Grassroots Politicians in Italy and France*, New Haven, Conn.
Torchia, L. (1986), *I raccordi fra Stato e regioni*, Milan.
Vandelli, L. (1984), *I controlli sull'amministrazione regionale e locale*, Bologna.
Wheare, K.C. (1963), *Federal Government*, 4th ed., London.

–7–

The Northern League: Conservative Revolution?

Joseph Farrell and *Carl Levy*

Introduction

There has been much debate whether or not the recent period in Italian history (1992–4) merits the description 'revolution' (Gilbert 1995; Gundle & Parker 1995; Levy 1996). Certainly, all observers would agree that Italian politics have experienced a period of rapid change. The pressure for renovation initially took muted forms. It found expression among the electorate both in the growing level of abstentionism at elections and in the increased willingness to use the referendum as a means of bypassing institutions which were held to be inert and unresponsive to public demands; among the parties themselves, in the proposals for constitutional reform, however tentatively and unconvincingly advanced. A presidential Republic on the French model figured for some time as an item on the programme advocated by Bettino Craxi and the PSI, and after the 1992 general elections, a Bi-Cameral Commission was established under the presidency of Ciriaco De Mita, with a wide-ranging remit. For a time it seemed this body had transformed itself into a *de facto* Constitutional Assembly. It was working under the pressure of the two referendums which were finally held on 18 April 1993 – a deadline which seemed likely to concentrate minds – but the commission's workings were marred by the very self-serving factionalism which was the source of the original discontent, and it failed in its purpose of providing any agreed measures which could have rendered the referendum unnecessary.

The 1992 elections, the 1993 referendums, the activities of Antonio Di Pietro and fellow magistrates and the emergence of new political forces changed the agenda of politics and the political map of Italy out of all recognition. The recent past was already a foreign country, as was noted by the joint authors of *Il crollo*, a pioneering and exhaustive account of the collapse of the old order. Beginning their survey with the fall of the Berlin Wall in 1989, with its not-fully-appreciated implications for Italy's system of unchanging government parties, they wrote: 'Looking at the debris of that '89, and examining one by one the fallen certainties, it requires an effort to recall entirely that climate' (Bellu & Bonsanti 1993: 13). The most significant of the agents of change included *La Rete* founded by ex-Christian Democrat mayor of Palermo Leoluca Orlando, and Mario Segni's *Popolari per la Riforma*, which originally operated inside the DC but later allied itself with the centrist *Alleanza Democratica*, itself set up on 17 October 1992. Whatever the contributions of the others, the most important of the new forces in this period remained the *Lega Lombarda/Lega Nord*.

The League had succeeded where the New Left parties of the 1970s and early 1980s had failed. It made itself credible as an anti-system force in the late 1980s and early 1990s. Under the clever guidance of its leader Umberto Bossi and its erstwhile chief ideologist, Gianfranco Miglio, the League presented itself as above and beyond traditional criteria of Left and Right. It evolved considerably in its brief life from a body with a passion for Lombard dialect and culture, only to declare that these matters were insubstantial and that finance, industry and institutions were what counted; it casually jettisoned policies, for instance on the referendum on proportional representation, which it previously espoused. It presented itself as the paladin of modernity, yet that paladin came bedecked in the armour of the Middle Ages; it constructed for itself a history, choosing the medieval protector of Lombardy, Alberto da Giussano, as its mascot, and the nineteenth-century *Risorgimento* theorist of federalism, Carlo Cattaneo, as the guarantor of its integrity. In constitutional politics, the *Lega* was for a Europe of the regions, hostile to the present institutions of Italy, and pro-federalist in domestic politics. It seemed to be a federalist, anti-system party securely rooted in the quasi-racist attitudes of Northern Italy towards the *Mezzogiorno* and, latterly, immigrants. But later the imperious Bossi decided that the North was a state of mind and that any Italian who espoused the virtues of honesty, hard work and frugality could be a *Legista*. In economics it identified itself with the aggressive market economics and tax-cutting, pro-privatization, anti-big government stance originally championed by Reagan and Thatcher. But, as we shall see, it came to national power in an uneasy alliance with Italy's native son, crony capitalist Silvio Berlusconi, and neo-fascists favourable to continuing Italy's neo-corporatist political economy.

The dramatic and seemingly unbridgeable contradictions in this new political situation may also reveal the limits of the 'Italian revolution' even if the League helped destroy the power base of the DC in the white districts of Lombardy and the Veneto and at least temporarily usurped the votes of the PSI in Milan, thereby emboldening the judges behind the *Mani Pulite* investigations and accelerating the collapse of the *partitocrazia*. But in the flush of enthusiasm for the popular mass mobilization against organized crime in Palermo and Naples and the mass arrests of the politico-business class throughout Italy, commentators were oblivious to the contradictions in these developments.

The First Republic was being replaced, it was argued, by a more virtuous 'Second Republic'. In the aftermath of the general elections of 5 April 1992, Umberto Eco, in one of his weekly columns in *Espresso*, compared the current situation to the fall of the Bastille. In an article which appeared in many publications world-wide, Edward Luttwak, head of the Centre for Strategic and International Studies in Washington, wrote squarely that 'The Italian Revolution – and it is time to call it that – is historically unprecedented in that it is being carried out by exclusively legal means' (1993: 4). Others more recently have dissented from this view, interpreting the events as a house-cleaning operation, and underlining the fact that the so-called revolution had no specific ideology to differentiate it from the system it sought to replace. Indeed the victory in the general election of March 1994 saw the Italian electorate choose the most right-wing government since 1945. Italians still refused to allow an alternation of government in which the major left-wing party (PDS) would be the senior partner in a government. The Italians had moved from the right of centre to the right (Bobbio 1994). The media tycoon Silvio Berlusconi (Lyttelton 1994; Mannheimer 1994; Revelli 1994), whose own political base was inherited from the Socialists and Christian Democrats, and whose political and business successes can be traced back to the patronage of Bettino Craxi, was joined by his two outsider partners, the Northern League and the National Alliance, in an inherently unstable coalition government which did not last until Christmas. The experience of the first general election in the so-called Second Republic illustrates the limitations of any interpretation of the recent events as revolutionary.

But is it accurate to describe the victory of Berlusconi and the rise of the neo-fascist-dominated National Alliance, whose support was found largely in parts of the South, as a restoration? It is certainly the case that the mixed first-past-the-post and proportional representation electoral system did not reduce the number of parties in Parliament and may have deepened in the long run the territorial cleavages which the Northern League and the National Alliance represented (Diamanti & Mannheimer 1994; Parker 1994). Berlusconi's neo-liberalism, endorsed by the

Northern League before the election, was not so readily supported by them in government. The neo-fascist and corporatist roots of the National Alliance had meant that it was always cautious about Thatcherism Italian style (Ignazi 1994; Valentini 1994). Berlusconi had engaged in two separate marriages of convenience with his chief coalition partners. But once in power, the Northern League sued almost immediately for divorce. If controversy over pensions reform and Berlusconi's continual battles with the judiciary and the President of the Republic undermined the credibility of his government, it could be argued neither these problems in themselves, nor the curious inability of the media mogul to manage government or communicate with the population, would have caused his rapid eclipse and replacement by a government of technocrats.

It was the Northern League which pushed him from power. If a restoration had been under way under Berlusconi, the *sans culottes* of the Northern League, cleverly guided by Umberto Bossi, stopped its progress. The former chief ideologist of the Northern League, Gianfranco Miglio, gloried in the description of himself as a 'Jacobin', and in the early 1990s, the *Lega Lombarda* used to employ with relish the tag 'barbarians' originally applied to it polemically by certain sectors of the press. But to what extent did the Northern League become part of the very machinations of Roman politics it used to decry in its colourful, vulgar and racist language? In order to answer this question in the remainder of this chapter we will first summarize the developments of its political fortunes and ideology up to 1994 and then review how its position changed during the experience of national government.

The Evolution of the Northern League

The exact nature and collocation of the *Lega Lombarda* and the *Lega Nord* has become subject to much dispute but its record in the late 1980s and early 1990s has established beyond a reasonable doubt that the leagues answered a need. The *Lega Lombarda* grew not only without the support of the media, but indeed in the face of a campaign of vilification which had not been equalled in Italy since the anti-Communist fervour of the 1940s and 1950s. In spite of that handicap, the *Lega Lombarda* grew to prominence at a rate which had few precedents or parallels in the politics of the Italian Republic before the meteoric rise of Berlusconi and his *Forza Italia*. It was not the first of the Leagues in Northern Italy. The *Liga Veneta*, founded by Franco Rocchetta, put up candidates in its own name at the European elections in 1979, and succeeded having a candidate elected to each house of the

Italian Parliament at the 1983 General Elections (see Allum & Diamanti in this volume). Both Rocchetta and Bossi admitted their ideological debt to the *Union Valdotaine* of Bruno Salvadori, which belonged to an earlier generation of regionalist politics (Bossi 1992: 31–5; Diamanti 1993: 43–54). As a movement, the Lombard League, originally known as the *Lega Autonomista Lombarda*, was founded on 12 April 1984, although the first issue of its periodical, *Lombarda Autonomista*, containing the basic manifesto, had been published two years previously, on 1 March 1982. On 4 December 1990, six of the leagues operating in Northern Italy – the *Liga Veneta*, *Piemont Autonomista*, the *Lega Emiliana-Romagnola*, the *Alleanza Toscana*, the *Unione Ligure* as well as the *Lega Lombarda* – signed a pact in Bergamo, which was subsequently formalized at a congress in Milan on 10 February 1991, giving birth to the *Lega Nord*. Bossi was nominated secretary and Rocchetta given the largely ceremonial office of president. The Northern League was declared officially a federal rather than an integrated movement, and Bossi, in spite of some dissent, remained also secretary of the Lombard League.

At successive elections, the *Lega* was constantly on the ascent. As the *Lega Lombarda*, it made a partial appearance at the 1985 local elections when its candidates stood for selected councils in the province of Varese, winning representation in two councils, Varese and Gallarate. It first presented candidates nationally in the general elections of June 1987 when it stood in seven of the nine constituencies in Lombardy, taking 3.0 per cent of the vote for the Chamber of Deputies and 2.5 per cent for the Senate, which gave the *Lega* one seat in each house. In the European elections in 1989, the *Lega* took 6.5 per cent of the popular vote in Lombardy, but in the regional elections the following year its share of the vote had risen to 16.4 per cent. At the general elections in 1992, operating as the *Lega Nord*, it took 8.7 per cent of the national vote for the Chamber of Deputies (8.2 per cent in the Senate), but in Lombardy itself its vote reached 20.5 per cent. It had fifty-five members of the Lower House and twenty-five Senators. Its vote continued to rise, and at the local government election in the Lombard city of Mantua on 27 September 1992, its vote of 33.9 per cent established it as the leading force in the region. (It could be added that in those elections a further 6 per cent went to the *Lega Alpina*, a group led by Bossi's sister and which ran with a title and logo deliberately similar to that of the League. Most commentators agreed that the majority of the votes it attracted were probably given in error.) In the local elections of June 1993, it became the largest party in the Milan City Council with its candidate, Marco Formentini, elected mayor.

The general elections of March 1994 will probably be seen as a watershed in the history of the Northern League. An inherent weakness in the Northern League was revealed in the mayoralty elections of late 1993 when it stood alone in the second round of the double ballot system and was defeated by the Progressives in Venice, Genoa and Trieste. The need to form alliances with kindred parties was also present in the different electoral system used in the 1994 general elections. At first Bossi toyed with the idea of forming an alliance with Segni but he then turned to his alliance with Berlusconi who formed two separate agreements with the *Lega Nord* and the *Alleanza Nazionale*. With 8.4 per cent of the national vote, or 0.3 per cent less than in 1992, the Northern League benefited disproportionately from its electoral pact with Berlusconi who assigned 70 per cent of the first-past-the-post seats in constituencies they jointly contested thereby ending up with the largest number of seats in the Lower Chamber (116) and in the Senate (105). But the limits of the real electoral power of the Northern League were revealed. In Milan, where the Northern League had just won a straight fight with the Left in the mayoral election of 1993, its percentage of the vote dropped from 41 per cent (in the first ballot) to 16 per cent in just three months (*Corriere della Sera*, 30 March 1994: 4). In the 211 electoral colleges in Northern Italy in which the Northern League contested the election, it received similar results from 1992 in only 31 (15 per cent), it fell in 116 (55 per cent) and grew in 64 (30 per cent). The result was the concentration of the Northern League's vote in well-defined areas of the North (Diamanti 1994: 57–60). The Northern League returned to its areas of original success and was driven from the metropolitan centre of Milan. Diamanti has located the sources of greatest strength for the League in twenty-seven colleges of which fifteen were located in the Veneto, four in Lombardy, three in Friuli and five in Piedmont. The heartland of the Northern League vote was located in provinces such as Belluno, Treviso, Vicenza, Verona, Brescia, Bergamo, Como, Varese, the hinterland of Milan and Cuneo. In these provinces, where the Northern League achieved more than 25.5 per cent of the vote, it seemed to be returning to its first strongholds. Not only had the Northern League been stymied by Berlusconi in Milan, its vote fell substantially in the province of Turin, in Liguria, in Emilia-Romagna and in Trieste and Bolzano. The Northern League failed to make an impact in the red subcultural area or in the special regions.

The concentration of the vote in certain areas of the North reflected the sociological basis of its supporters. The nature of the Northern League's support had come full circle from its origins in the 1980s. The first sources of support for the Northern League were located in the white regions of the Veneto and Lombardy. Here the small-business sector felt betrayed by growing corruption within the Christian

Democrats, the diversion of patronage from its Northern to its electorally critical Southern supporters and the increasingly effective collection of taxes from Rome. But as the Northern League became more successful, its electoral support diversified so that many commentators began to argue that it had become a regionally specific catch-all party (Leonardi & Kovacs 1993). The Northern League began to attract younger manual workers and educated middle-class professionals. Nevertheless, the bedrock support for the Northern League remained amongst the self-employed and white-collar private-sector employees living in Lombard and Venetian provincial towns. The results of the 1994 general elections merely reconfirmed this picture. The Northern vote of the centre right has been split between the Northern League's heartlands in the Northern industrial periphery and Berlusconi's strongholds in the other North: metropolitan, secular and dominated by the service industries (Diamanti 1994: 60). Particularly in Milan, Berlusconi inherited the Socialist *craxiano* vote. The net result of the general elections of 1994 was to allow Bossi to focus the Northern League on certain interests and, although it lost votes, this assured him of a solid core of supporters. Even before the Berlusconi government was formally inaugurated, Bossi realized that his greatest enemy was the Prime Minister himself. This meant that at the very moment when the outsider Northern League had entered government in Rome, Bossi set out to reaffirm the anti-governmental nature of its mission. In the following months Bossi sought to turn the Northern League as coalition partner in government into an opposition within government but at the same time seeking out allies within the formal parliamentary opposition itself.

Bossi's behaviour caused splits within the Northern League but he was moderately successful at retaining support within the parliamentary group. The new, clearly defined, electorate of the Northern industrial periphery also allowed him the freedom to return to the original message of the Northern League. Although the Northern League vote in the European elections of June 1994 saw its share drop to below 7 per cent, the Northern League recovered somewhat in local elections held in the autumn. It is hard to speculate about the future of the Northern League with Berlusconi's future and his movement in doubt and the dissolution of the neo-fascist *Movimento Sociale Italiano* into the 'post-fascist' *Alleanza Nazionale*, but the leadership and the ideological flexibility of the Northern League may see it once again play a national role in Italian politics. We will now turn to the programmatic statements and ideology of the Northern League up to 1994.

The rise of the Northern League alarmed politicians and mystified commentators. Vittorio Moioli's work, *I nuovi razzismi* (The New

Racisms), was a valuable source of data and statistics, but the author, an official of the PCI before its dissolution, perhaps exaggerated when he described it as merely an updated form of racism (1990: 45). He shared with Renato Mannheimer, the editor of the multi-authored, *La Lega Lombarda* (1991), the insistence of understanding the rise of the Lombard League in the context of the fall of support for the traditional parties – Christian Democrat, Communist and Socialist – which had dominated Italian politics in the post-war era. Roberto Biorcio's contribution to the early discussion explained the Lombard League's appeal by including aspects of Moioli's and Mannheimer's observations in a new synthesis. He advanced the view that *leghista* ideology could be regarded as a combination of 'populism and regionalism', linked to a similar re-emergence of populism in European politics all over the continent. Biorcio (1991: 70–1) wrote:

> A series of political movements which have emerged in the last decade – associated with the figures of Slobodan Milosevic, Boris Yeltsin, Jean-Marie Le Pen and (in recent years) Lech Walesa – seem to present, apart from the major differences of the national situations, a series of traits in common: the rupture of the symbolic codes typical of traditional ideologies and political forms, the appeal to 'common sense' against politicians and intellectuals, the charismatic personalities. . .In the Lombard League are to be found all the characteristics typical of classical populist movements.

Therefore, in the early discussions of the *Lega* its ideology was defined as racist (towards Southerners and Third World immigrants) and populist, associated with a protest vote in the North as the old *partitocrazia* crumbled. But to this could also be added an inchoate but widely expressed fear that the *Lega* represented a revival of Fascism or, in a modified and slightly more sophisticated version, the Italian face of the anti-immigrant, extreme-right, neo-fascist mood which had emerged in several European countries in the 1990s. Bossi was often portrayed as a Mussolini figure, while in Strasbourg, a group of Green and ex-Communist MEPs denounced the *Lega* as an extreme-right racist party, explicitly linking them with the French *Front National*, the Belgian *Vlaams Blok* and the German *Republikaner Partei* (*La Repubblica*, 29 October 1992: 9). However, even before the aftermath of the general elections of 1994 demonstrated that the ideology and practice of the Northern League were more ambivalent than previously believed, a more nuanced approach was adopted by political scientists. Ilvo Diamanti (also see the excellent account by Gilbert 1995: 46–65), while confessing his enduring antipathy towards the *Lega*, rejected the previous analyses based, in his words, as a facile, *parti pris* 'banalization and stigmatization of the entire movement' (1993: x; also see Sales 1993). The *Lega* retained a distance from the Italian Fascist tradition which would assume increasing importance in defining its ideological and political space during 1993 and 1994.

In Search of an Ideology

The ideology of the *Lega* up to 1994 demonstrated an unstable mixture of regionalism, anti-statist neo-liberalism and varying degrees of racism. In the early 1990s the Northern League's regionalism and federalism seemed to be bolstered by European developments. Although the terms the 'Europe of the Regions' and 'subsidiarity' were only gradually being translated into policy with the negotiations surrounding the Maastricht Treaty and the ensuing difficult period of ratification, the Northern League's demand for the transfer of power to the regional level seemed to be re-enforced by these developments. In fact this aspect of Northern League ideology always remained the most abstract.

The attacks on centralism and *étatisme* were more successful and were later used by Berlusconi to steal the Northern League's thunder. While the three-tier system of local government, with town or city councils, provinces and regions, not to mention the special statute regions, appeared to give Italy a highly decentralized structure, the devolution of real power only became apparent in the 1980s. Putnam noted that 'Over the last two decades the region has become an authentic, autonomous and increasingly distinctive arena in Italian politics' (1993: 46). But Leonardi also detected greater resistance on the part of central government in the second half of the 1980s to devolve tax-raising powers to this tier of government (1992: 234–5). This could be partly attributed to the uneven performance of regional governments and the party political control of hiring of its staff (Putnam 1993: 63–82). Hine (1993: 257–61), however, added a deeper understanding by stressing the enduring connection between Roman politics and the regions. Italian national politicians were extraordinarily concerned about the composition of local authority coalitions. No local politician in Turin, Milan or even in small towns and villages in the peninsula could form an alliance which was not given the approval of the party HQ in Rome. The fracas caused by the 'anomalous' anti-*Mafia* coalition formed by Leoluca Orlando when he was Christian Democrat mayor of Palermo was sneeringly tagged the *imbroglio di Palermo* by the Socialist party (*Partito Socialista Italiano*: 1988). It was unusual only in that it provided a public and well-documented case study of the rage of the national party leaders at a local government which had genuinely acted autonomously. While the information made public in the course of the *Tangentopoli* investigations provided many more cases; no one will now sustain that the Sicilian region had any autonomy from the Andreotti faction.

This party political control of the regions from Rome was merely one aspect of the Northern League's critique of the 'First Republic'. The promiscuous relationship between industry and the state was well-known even before the Milan magistrates made the precise mechanisms public (della Porta 1992). The same dependence on political authority was present in cultural life, in research bodies, in the universities, in the press and in broadcasting (Turani 1980; Mastropaolo 1991). (Thc parties notoriously divided up the public broadcasting authority, RAI, to give the Christian Democrats, the Socialists and the ex-Communists control of one channel each. And they also allowed Berlusconi to gain a virtual monopoly over private Italian television.) Indeed, although the Lombard League set out as a body with a passion for the Lombard dialect and culture, basing its regionalism in a putative ethno-linguistic identity, by the early 1990s this had been replaced by a critique of the political structures of the Italian state. This concept of the State represented the kernel and convergence of many *leghista* policies. Distrust for the capacities of the State, the *Lega*'s pro-privatization, *laissez-faire* coincided with its desire to dismantle the centralist Italian state and replace it with a federal system.

Lega-style market economics and regionalism were predicated on a weak, decentralized state. The unitarian state created by the *Risorgimento* was brought into question by Bossi and the *Lega*, but the basic policy was for the most part federalist not separatist. By the standards of the pro-independence Scottish National Party, of *Plaid Cymru*, of *Esquerra Catalana*, of *Herri Batasuna*, the constitutional demands of the *Lega* were modest. The first point of its programme, carried in every issue of the Lombard League's own periodical, *Lombarda Autonomista*, remained the establishment of 'self government for Lombardy, which moves beyond the centralized state towards a modern federal state capable of respecting all the peoples which constitute it'. The separatist card was always a bluff. Even at the public meeting in Curno on 26 September 1993, when Bossi threatened that if elections were not called by the following April he would withdraw the *Lega*'s elected members from Rome to establish their own parliament, he added the rider that this body would constitute the 'first parliament of the Republic of the North in a federal Italian state'. Indeed, the disenchanted Miglio argued in his memoirs that the Northern League's more radical proposals had been discredited by the second half of 1992 when its campaign for the non-payment of taxes lost steam and the political drive for federalism would have to await the possible opportunities afforded from the change from above which the *Tangentopoli* scandals seemed to bring in its wake (Miglio 1994).

Blueprints for devolution had been produced with an insistent rapidity by the *Lega*'s leadership. When the Lombard League operated on its own, its objective was autonomy for Lombardy, but after it allied with other leagues to form the Northern League, the policy was refined to one of the federal division of Italy into three macro-regions or Republics covering Northern, Central and Southern Italy. Some *Lega* spokespersons advocated a higher number of constituent states, with separate parliaments in Sicily or Sardinia, and there remained the capacity for tension between the demands of the various regional components of the Northern League, particularly since all started from a belief in the cultural uniqueness of their own region (see Allum & Diamanti in this volume). The nature of the federal, or confederal, state envisaged was given its fullest expression in the motions approved at the founding conference of *Lega Nord* in Milan. It was intended that the powers of these new bodies would be wide-ranging, including exclusive control in the fields of fiscal policy, industry, trade, civil and criminal law, education and health and social services. The central government would retain control only of defence, financial and monetary matters as well as foreign policy (Miglio 1990; 1991–2; 1993).

After the Northern League issued its federalist proposals, the exact shape of the Central Republic was ignored in debate, since it had no real historical identity, and all attention was focused on the proposed Northern and Southern Republics. But debates about the nuts and bolts of devolution were quickly overtaken by controversy over the League's racist sentiments. Opponents of the League claimed that the decentralization of power would institutionalize the most fundamental and damaging divisions in Italian life and politics. Cardinal Martini of Milan entered the debate with his co-authored book, *Nord/Sud, L'Italia da riconciliare*, in which he stated that any separation of the South would be 'morally unacceptable' (Agostino & Martini 1992: 35). The Cardinal argued that the appeal of the League lay in its pandering to economic egoism and to a quasi-racist public sentiment in Northern Italy *vis-à-vis* Southern Italians. While Bossi quickly disowned the Trentino branch of the League when on 27 October 1992 it 'invited' Southerners to leave Northern Italy and return home, the suspicion lingered that the repeated assertion of the gulf between 'European' Italy and 'Mediterranean' Italy was merely the salon face of racism. In its most sophisticated form the Northern League's programme spoke of a 'two-velocity' Italian economy which federalism would make possible, where the developed, industrial, free-market economy of Northern Italy and the state-dependent, welfare-oriented economy of the Southern part of the country would be unshackled one from the other to allow the two to move at the pace appropriate to each. These suggestions were understood within the imperatives of the Maastricht Treaty and the competitive pressures the European Union and globalization placed upon the Italian economy. As the ex-New Leftist Giulio Savelli wrote: 'It is clear that the North cannot accept the burden of permanently subsidizing the South and must – especially at the moment when European integration is coming closer – remove from its shoe a stone which reduces its competitiveness with its tenacious adversaries' (1992: 123).

In its early days, the *Lega* used slogans like '*No allo strapotere meridonale*' (No to the overwhelming power of the South) and continued to use posters depicting Sicilian peasants, recognizable by the distinctive beret or *cupola*, as thieving the tax revenues paid by honest Lombards. The other celebrated poster (in dialect) '*Lombard tas*', (Shut up Lombard), carried the same message, that the honest Lombard had been cowed into paying silently and submissively taxes which were to the benefit of others. Umberto Bossi himself was entirely candid, and unapologetic, about his deliberate manipulation of anti-Southern sentiment in the early days of the Lombard League:

> We decided to exploit the anti-meridionalism widespread in Lombardy, as in other regions of the North, to attract the attention of the wider public and of the mass media. I did give a somewhat crude twist to certain vital phrases (Bossi 1992: 168).

The opportunism which Bossi has always demonstrated was reflected in his shrewd political leadership and the flexibility of his ideology. The League has sometimes been described rather mistakenly as a new social movement (Ruzza & Schmidtke 1991–2: 64). In fact, it has had a traditional, indeed Leninist-like, party structure and decidedly materialist and traditionalist values (Diamanti 1993: 13–15). Bossi always had great powers to determine policy in the League. The cardinal points of League ideology had been far less than consistent, with various elements diminishing and increasing in importance for tactical reasons largely decided upon by Bossi and his inner circle. What had been important for the success of the League was its populist style, but one which was closely aligned to discontents within certain areas of Northern provincial Italy. If the more recent though perhaps fleeting success of Berlusconi has been explained by invoking the post-modernism of the televisual soundbite and the target group (Mannheimer 1994; Paolucci & Barbesino 1994; Riotta 1994), the Leagues used hand-to-mouth amateur forms of communication to recruit support. The leafleting of football games or the recruitment of support in the relatively apolitical (neither white nor red) leisure associations of civil society in provincial Lombardy and the Veneto in the 1980s were initial sources of immense success. Bossi shaped the image of the League by using down-to-earth, indeed vulgar and sexist, language to appeal to a disproportionately male middle social strata of the Northern industrial periphery who were alienated by the tortuous political language of the Christian Democrat and Socialist political élites (Ruzza & Schmidtke 1993).

We have examined the *Lega*'s interrelated pronouncements on neo-liberalism, federalism and Southerners in the period up to 1994. To what extent were the Northern League's demands for greater regionalization, federalism or separatism merely convenient ideological covers for the charismatic leadership of a protest party seeking access to power in Rome? Mannheimer, Biorcio and Moioli all considered they had demonstrated that support for the *Lega* was based on a transitory protest vote when they discovered that many interviewees were more concerned with the malfunctioning of the party system than with regionalism. On the other hand, Gianfranco Miglio has claimed in his own memoirs of the League that Bossi probably never read the sources he cited in his autobiography, *Vento dal Nord*, and that his and the inner circle's federalism was merely a method of gaining national power (Miglio 1994). It is hard to deny the validity of many of these claims but an analysis of how the outsider party operated in Rome might at least demonstrate that the leadership of the *Lega* retained a unique bundle of ideas that differentiated it from *Forza Italia* and the *Alleanza Nazionale*.

The Northern League in National Government: 1994

In Spring 1994 the Northern League's position in central government seemed fairly secure. Roberto Maroni (Umberto Bossi's right-hand man) was appointed as one of Berlusconi's two Deputy Prime Ministers and to the powerful and formerly Christian Democratic position of Minister of Interior, and other League representatives had been given ministerial posts in EU and regional affairs (Domenico Comino), industry (Vito Gnuti), institutional reform (Francesco Enrico Speroni) and the budget (Giancarlo Pagliarini).

The first controversy to erupt was, predictably, over the Northern League's programme for a federal Italy. The result of this dispute placed Bossi and the Northern League in a fairly moderate position. In the immediate weeks after the elections, certain League ideologists were suggesting that the Republic of Italy change its name to the Italian Union. In Gianfranco Miglio's conception of a confederation, powerful macro-regions (Padania, Etruria and Sud) would have replaced the present regions and have left the central state with only the duties of foreign policy and defence (Miglio 1991–2; 1992). This resulted in a short-lived but vociferous debate in the leading Italian newspapers (Marroni 1994). Almost immediately, however, Miglio resigned from the Northern League in disgust and set up an alternative movement which claimed to protect the true aims of the League movement that had been betrayed by Bossi, Maroni and Formentini (*La Repubblica* 19 May 1994: 14–15). Moves towards confederation or outright separatism were disowned by the League's leadership.

After this controversy, the details of what type of regional and federal policy to endorse was overshadowed by arguments between Bossi on the one hand and Berlusconi and Fini on the other. However, there were figures in the Berlusconi camp who did endorse certain reforms proposed by the Northern League. While *Forza Italia* was not prepared to propose an upper house of the regions, its representatives seemed to be sympathetic to allowing the regions to raise more of their own resources and therefore be more closely accountable to regional electors. There was also some hint in Spring 1994 that another approach building on the electoral reforms and greater powers granted to urban conurbations (Hine 1993: 277–81), which have increased the accountability and durability of municipal government in Italy, seemed like a more logical way forward and appeared to find approval amongst such League heavyweights as the Mayor of Milan, Marco Formentini, and the Progressive Mayor of Venice, Massimo Cacciari (Da Rold 1994). The Minister of Finance, Tremonti (*Forza Italia*), had already written about this form of fiscal federalism, although the chief problem he identified was that devolution of powers at the regional level might suffer from the lack of voters' identification with regional government. He therefore sought greater fiscal freedoms for local and municipal government (Tremonti 1994; Tremonti & Vitaletti 1994). Finally, it also remained to be seen how the proposed decentralization of certain government ministries to the regions could be effectively managed by these entities (*La Repubblica* 21 May 1994: 14), although just before the fall of the Berlusconi government, Tremonti did issue a White Paper with some interesting proposals.

If policy making on the devolution of powers to the region or municipality was stalemated in the rest of 1994 due to other issues, it is still possible to assess how the Northern League fared in local and regional government. In the regional government of Lombardy the Northern League quickly became enveloped in a series of scandals over its own usage of the spoils system it had denounced (*Corriere della Sera* 9 & 10 January 1995; *La Repubblica* 25 February 1995). With

Bossi already facing a possible prison sentence in connection with a kickback scandal surrounding Ferruzzi/Montedison, this compromised the League's image (*Financial Times* 25 May 1994: 2). But perhaps the clearest test of its new politics was the track record of Formentini as Mayor of Milan. The first year was not impressive. He generated a good deal of opposition after increasing municipal bus fares. His attempt to evict counter-cultural *autonomisti* from their long-squatted social centre at Leoncavallo was appreciated by his supporters even if after their removal they found a new locale in the Greco area of Milan. There were also systematic and insensitive attempts to move migrants out of social housing and off the streets which was met by approval by many Milanese. However, the net results of Formentini's first year in office were disappointing because his promises to create new urban planning policies did not materialize and his popularity fell amongst Milanese.[1]

While the Northern League failed to impress at the local and regional level, it was within national government that it chose to leave its real mark on Italian politics. Here, some of the League ministers and deputies retained their outsider populist style and the followers of Bossi's line did seem to sharpen their position against the Right. The tensions between the Northern League and its other two chief coalition partners – *Forza Italia* and the National Alliance – centred around four issues: neo-fascism, Berlusconi's legal and financial problems, his clashes with the President of the Republic and pensions reform. From the very beginning Bossi sought to include anti-fascism as part of the League's *nordista* identity. Indeed, in an interview in the wake of the elections Bossi explained that anti-fascism was a characteristic of the ethnic culture of the North whereas neo-fascism was an inherent part of the Southern *ethnie* (*Corriere della Sera* 30 March 1994: 4). Historians of the rise of Fascism might have found this statement more than slightly bizarre, but Bossi's demarcation of the League's anti-fascist and democratic position continued apace throughout 1994. The League took a much more supportive line than Berlusconi during the commemorations of the Liberation on 25 April. Throughout the rest of the year Northern League and National Alliance deputies came to physical blows in the Chamber on several occasions. At times Bossi warned that either Fini would inherit Berlusconi's voters and power or that Berlusconi (Bossi's '*Berluskaiser*') himself was the real fascist threat and would use Fini's supporters and his control of the media to turn Italian politics in an authoritarian direction (Graham 1994: 6; *Financial Times* 18 July 1994: 2; *Financial Times* 1 September 1994: 2). At the same time, through figures such as Cacciari, the League developed ties with the PDS and the Progressives (*La Repubblica* 21 May 1994: 12).

Later in February 1995, after the Berlusconi government had fallen and the League split, the PDS party secretary, Massimo D'Alema, even addressed the founding meeting of the Bossite new Northern League-Federal Italy and received a sympathetic hearing (*Corriere della Sera* 13 February 1995: 2). Addressing the same conference, Bossi was proud to demonstrate that the League's actions had prevented a government with neo-fascists in its cabinet presiding over the fiftieth anniversary of the Liberation (*Corriere della Sera* 13 February 1995: 2). The Left itself had not been immune to some of the League's arguments. There had been previous attempts to theorize about the acceptability of a greater regional identity in red subcultural strongholds such as Tuscany (Caciagli 1993). And in an interesting journalistic account of League support in the 'Deep North', Gianna Pajetta demonstrated that in local governments the Left could work quite comfortably with a League mayor (Pajetta 1994).

Although Bossi continually squabbled with the National Alliance, his real target of abuse was Berlusconi himself. Throughout 1994 Bossi and most of the Northern League insisted that he advance new media laws to curb Fininvest's near-monopoly of private television and they also insisted that he divest control of his vast fortune into a blind trust (for a summary of the events of the autumn of 1994 see Gilbert 1995: 182–8). Pressure was also maintained on Berlusconi as he sought to obstruct judicial enquiries into his business empire's affairs. Bossi was in the forefront of the confrontation in the summer, when Berlusconi's attempt at limiting the judges' powers of detention led to a temporary mass resignation by them. Although Di Pietro resigned and under an appeals court ruling some of the investigations were switched to judges in the smaller town of Brescia, Berlusconi's position was becoming increasingly untenable throughout the autumn, while Bossi maintained his opposition to Berlusconi's tampering with the judiciary.

Concurrently, the attempts to reform Italy's generous pension system was met by widespread popular opposition because it seemed as if the poorest and least advantaged pensioners might lose the most. The trade union confederations mobilized the largest series of peaceful demonstrations since 1945 (Levy 1994: 74–7); and although the Northern League was not prominent in these demonstrations, the largely left-of-centre tone of this mass protest encouraged Bossi to press home his war against Berlusconi. When in late November Berlusconi was formally notified that he might soon be indicted, his position reached a crisis point. During a vote of confidence at the end of December the League deserted the government.

Even if Roberto Maroni was more sympathetic to Berlusconi and distanced himself from Bossi's outsider style, he too could not support the continuation of the present crisis which seemed to threaten Italy with a run on the lira and a serious constitutional clash between judiciary, Prime Minister and President. He had done a rather efficient job at the Interior Ministry by cleaning up long-standing right-wing subversive activities within it, while also taking a strong line against the violent Naziskins and giving support to newly elected anti-crime mayors in Sicily when they were threatened by the *Mafia* (Balzoni 1994: 14–15). Although Berlusconi felt that he should be allowed to form a new government or seek a general election to reconfirm his mandate of March 1994, President Scalfaro invoked his constitutional powers and formed a temporary government of technocrats to address the pressing political and financial reforms. Maroni refused to support a potentially anti-constitutional struggle with the President and Berlusconi lost power. But at the end of the day the Berlusconi experiment failed because of the obstinacy of Bossi.

Conclusion

By January 1995 the Berlusconi government had been replaced by one led by apolitical technocrats, and the League itself had split. Even during the brief episode of government, the Northern League was losing parliamentarians either to Berlusconi or as independents. At the time of the schism 50 of 177 League members of the two chambers of the Italian Parliament had realigned. The dissidents under Roberto Maroni created a new pro-Berlusconi party called the Italian Federalist League; Bossi's Northern League became the Northern League-Federal Italy (Graham 1995; Hill 1995). While the Northern League-Federal Italy may become a harmless part of Italian political folklore, the evolution of the Northern League has been extremely complex and ambiguous but nevertheless significant for recent Italian history. It has demonstrated itself to be more than a mere tax revolt party. Although it retains racist impulses and represents many traditionalist Catholics in the old white subculture of provincial Lombardy and the Veneto, the larger faction of the old League has been wooed by the Progressives and may end up in an electoral coalition with them. It stubbornly defends its own type of anti-fascist and democratic identity, and although its attempt at being a different and less corrupt party was tarnished by proceedings against Bossi himself and corruption in the Lombard regional government, the League has proven its ability to undermine the old Christian Democrats and Berlusconi's first attempt to inherit their mantle of power.

The future of Bossi's League will depend on whether or not *Forza Italia* will fragment and release 'captured' *leghista* voters. Although a reconstituted *Partito Popolare* might be a possible competitor for these votes, a more serious adversary will be Fini's newly founded 'post-fascist' National Alliance. A straight fight between a right-of-centre coalition dominated by the National Alliance, which has formally cut its ties with the Fascist tradition, and the Progressives, might see the left of centre relying upon the Northern League-Federal Italy to win the wavering Northern provincial middle classes to its electoral coalition. But even if Bossi and the Northern League-Federal Italy are crushed in the centre between two larger right and left-wing electoral coalitions (and the results of the regional elections in April 1995 did not bode well) and are therefore forced back into the political wilderness, it seems probable that once the current political and financial crises are resolved, the question of devolving power to the regions and cities will finally be addressed, since there are now too many new and powerful figures on the Left who would also endorse some reform. Therefore, in retrospect, the leagues will at the very least be viewed in later years as a curious, perhaps disturbing, but nevertheless important element in the evolution of Italian political system in the 1980s and 1990s.

Note

1. We would like to thank Dr John M. Foot of Churchill College, Cambridge for this information.

Bibliography

Agostino, (Bishop) A. and Martini, (Cardinal) M. (1992), *Nord/Sud*, Rome.

Balzoni, A. (1994), 'Il ministro leghista scopre la mafia', *La Repubblica*, 19 May, pp.14–15.

Bellu, G.M. and Bonsanti, S. (1993), *Il crollo*, Bari.

Biorcio, R. (1991), 'La Lega come attore politico', in R. Mannheimer (ed.), *La Lega Lombarda*, Milan, pp.34–82.

Bobbio, L. (1994), 'Dalla destra alla destra, una strana alternanza', in P. Ginsborg (ed.), *Stato dell'Italia*, Milan, pp.654–60.

Bossi, U. (with D. Vimercati) (1992), *Vento dal Nord*, Milan.

Caciagli, M. (1993), 'Tra internazionalismo e localismo: l'area rossa', *Meridiana*, **16**, pp.81–98.

Da Rold, G. (1994), 'Progressisti in tormento', *Corriere della Sera*, 10

May, p.5.
Della Porta, D. (1992), *Lo scambio occulto*, Bologna.
Diamanti, I. (1993), *La Lega*, Rome.
—— (1994), 'La Lega', in I. Diamanti and R. Mannheimer (eds), *Milano a Roma. Guida all'Italia elettorale del 1994*, Rome, pp.53–62.
Diamanti, I. and Mannheimer, R. (eds), (1994), *Milano a Roma. Guida all'Italia elettorale del 1994*, Rome.
Gilbert, M. (1995), *The Italian Revolution*, Boulder, Co.
Ginsborg, P. (ed.), (1994), *Stato dell'Italia*, Milan.
Graham, R. (1995), 'Italian duo who are no longer in league', *Financial Times*, 10 February, p.2.
Gundle, S. and Parker, S. (eds), (1995), *The New Italian Republic. From the Fall of the Berlin Wall to Berlusconi*, London.
Hill, A. (1995), 'Italian wake becomes a rebirth', *Financial Times*, 13 February, p.3.
Hine, D. (1993), *Governing Italy: the Politics of Bargained Pluralism*, Oxford.
Ignazi, P. (1994), 'Alleanza Nazionale', in I. Diamanti and R. Mannheimer (eds), *Milano a Roma. Guida all'Italia elettorale del 1994*, Rome, pp.43–52.
Leonardi, R. (1992), 'The Regional Reforms in Italy: From Centralized to Regionalized State', *Regional Politics and Policy*, **21**, 1–2, 1992, pp.217–46.
Leonardi, R. and Kovacs, M. (1993), 'The Lega Nord: the rise of a new Italian catch-all party', in S. Hellman and G. Pasquino (eds), *Italian Politics: A Review*, **8**, London, pp.50–65.
Levy, C. (1995), 'From Fascism to "Post-Fascists": Italian Roads to Modernity', in R. Bessel (ed.), *Fascist Italy and Nazi Germany: Comparisons and Contrasts*, Cambridge, pp.165–96.
—— (1994), 'Italian Trade Unionism in the 1990s: the Persistence of Corporatism?', *Journal of Area Studies*, **5**, pp.62–79.
Luttwak, E. (1993), 'Italy's Ancien Regime', *London Review of Books*, **15**, 19 August, pp.3; 6–7.
Lyttelton, A. (1994), 'Italy: The Triumph of TV', *The New York Review of Books*, 11 August, pp.25–9.
Mannheimer, R. (1994), 'Forza Italia', in I. Diamanti and R. Mannheimer (eds), *Milano a Roma*, Rome, pp.29–42.
—— (ed.), (1991), *La Lega Lombarda*, Milan.
Marroni, S. (1994), 'La rivoluzione della destra', *La Repubblica*, 9 April, pp.2–3.
Mastropaolo, A. (1991), *Il ceto politico*, Florence.
Moioli, V. (1990), *I nuovi razzismi*, Rome.

Miglio, G. (1993), *Come cambiare: le mie riforme*, Milan.
—— (1994), *Io, Bossi e La Lega – diario segreto dei miei quattro anni sul Caroccio*, Milan.
—— (1990), *Per Un'Italia federale*, Milan.
—— (1991–2), 'Towards a Federal Italy', *Telos*, 90, pp.19–42.
Pajetta, G. (1994), *Il grande camaleonte*, Milan.
Paolucci, C. and Barbesino, P. (1994), 'Berlusconi's Dream: Contesting Modern Representation Through the Re-Presentation of Society', unpublished paper, presented at 'Alternative political Imagination: The Logics of Contestation', Goldsmiths' College, University of London, 8–9 April.
Parker, S. (1994), 'The March 1994 Parliamentary Elections: An Overview', *ASMI Newsletter*, **25**, pp.28–35.
Partito Socialista Italiano (Palermo), *L'Imbroglio di Palermo*, No date or place credited but Milan, 1988.
Putnam, R. D. (1993), *Making Democracy Work*, Princeton, N.J.
Revelli, M. (1994), 'Forza Italia: l'anomalia italiana non è finita', in P. Ginsborg (ed.), *Stato dell'Italia*, Milan, pp.667–70.
Riotta, G. (1994), 'Il segreto della vittoria è "la strategia da judo"', *Corriere della Sera*, 30 March, p.3.
Ruzza, C.E. and Schmidtke, O. (1991–2), 'The Making of the Lombard League', *Telos*, 90, pp.43–56.
Ruzza, C.E. and Schmidtke, O. (1993), 'The Roots of Success of the Lega Lombarda: Mobilization Dynamics and the Media', *West European Politics*, **16**, 2, pp.1–23.
Sales, I. (1993), *Leghisti e sudisti*, Bari.
Savelli, G. (1992), *Che cosa vuole la Lega?*, Milan.
Tremonti, G. (1994), 'Democrazia fiscale, ecco che cosa dobbiamo fare', *Corriere della Sera*, 20 May, p.17.
Tremonti, G. and Vitaletti, G. (1994), *Il federalismo fiscale*, Bari.
Turani, G. (1980), *Padroni senza cuore*, Milan.
Valentini, C. (1994), 'Alleanza Nazionale: la componente "storica" del Polo delle Libertà', in P. Ginsborg (ed.), *Stato dell'Italia*, Milan, pp.667–70.

–8–

The Autonomous Leagues in the Veneto[1]

Percy Allum and *Ilvo Diamanti*

Introduction

The rapid, and seemingly irresistible, rise of the autonomous leagues took the Italian political class more or less by surprise. Indeed, before the 1992 elections most Italian politicians were convinced that the leagues were an ephemeral phenomenon and of little national consequence. 'I do not think', reasoned in 1990 *il dottor Sottile*, alias former Treasury Minister and PSI Vice-Secretary, Giuliano Amato, 'that the Northern League (*Lega Nord*) on the basis of its separatist constitutional rantings and dancing round the bonfire of the Italian flag, is destined to see its electoral support grow.' At much the same time, Interior Minister and DC Party boss, Antonio Gava, was boasting: 'I'm not afraid of the Northern League. We have swallowed Giannini's *qualunquisti* and Lauro's monarchists. We'll swallow Bossi and his *leghisti* too.'[2] But, all this was before *Tangentopoli* and the collapse of the Christian Democrat power system.

The 1992 parliamentary elections demonstrated, if that was necessary, that the leagues, and the Northern League in particular, were a political force to be reckoned with, above all in Northern Italy with 80 parliamentarians (55 deputies and 25 senators) elected in April 1992. Moreover, the subsequent local government elections in various northern provincial capitals, culminating in the capture of the mayoralty of the city of Milan in June 1993,[3] confirmed that the Northern League's success was not that of a 'flash party', like that of the *Poujadistes* in France in 1956. Nevertheless, up to now, its success was territorially circumscribed, not penetrating beyond the 'Gothic Line' and so dramatically reproposing the historical regional cleavage between North and South, rich regions and poor regions, that the electoral results of the post-war period had suggested was disappearing.[4]

The League Phenomenon

The initial electoral successes of the leagues occurred in what has been called 'opulent periphery', that is to say the white provinces of the Veneto, Lombardy and, to a lesser extent, Piedmont (Table 8.1). These are the areas of the post-war wave of industrialization in the North – small businesses developed during the 'economic miracle' and after – characterized by a high level of social integration and dominated politically by Christian Democracy. This origin is significant, although it has tended to be lost to view as a result of the Northern League's widespread advance in the 1992 elections. It points to the nature of the leagues' appeal: the response of prosperous and socially integrated populations to what is perceived as a 'threat' to their lifestyle and well-being.

Table 8.1. Ten Italian Provinces with Highest Vote for the Leagues in 1983, 1987 and 1992 (in percentage of votes cast).

1983*		1987		1992	
Treviso	(7.4%)	Bergamo	(7.3%)	Bergamo	(27.6%)
Vicenza	(5.9%)	Varese	(7.2%)	Brescia	(26.4%)
Belluno	(4.9%)	Como	(6.3%)	Varese	(25.9%)
Verona	(3.7%)	Torino	(5.5%)	Vicenza	(24.9%)
Padua	(3.6%)	Cuneo	(5.1%)	Como	(24.9%)
		Vercelli	(5.0%)	Treviso	(24.5%)
		Sondrio	(4.7%)	Verona	(23.7%)
		Vicenza	(4.5%)	Sondrio	(21.7%)
		Treviso	(3.8%)	Pavia	(21.3%)

* List only in the Veneto
(Sources: Diamanti & Riccamboni 1992: 64, and Diamanti 1993a: 31)

This 'threat' was visible in at least three guises, all of which were felt to be improper interferences in the territorial development of these areas, and became the basis for a generalized attack on the Italian political and constitutional system. The first was public intervention, particularly by the organs of the state, which was judged to be inefficient and wasteful. Moreover, it was claimed to be directly responsible for an iniquitous fiscal policy that was harmful to the 'productive' North and advantageous to the 'parasitic' South. In the words of Senator Speroni, leader of the Northern League's parliamentary group: 'The people want to be alright and don't want to pay taxes for those who are incapable of looking after themselves. We want autonomy so that we can look after ourselves with our own resources and without having to forgo them in favour of the South' (*Il*

Gazzettino, 14 April 1992). Such sentiments inspired the various leagues' electoral slogans: '*Somaro lombardo, paga*' (Lombard donkey, pay); '*Governo terrone, governo ladro*' ('Southern' government, robber government); '*Soldi dal Nord; mafia dal Sud*' (Money from the North; *Mafia* from the South).

The second was the traditional parties and their power system which, it was argued, were responsible for the general degeneration of political life and the state institutions. 'We are the poison in the parties' veins', proclaimed Umberto Bossi, leader of the Northern League in an interview in *La Repubblica* (5 October 1992), adding, 'The people are now convinced, and I feel it in the street even in Rome, that they have destroyed democracy; that there isn't just a economico-financial crisis, but also a very serious political and social crisis which is caused by the parties.' Franco Rocchetta, went further, claiming that the *Mafia*'s real power resided in Rome 'in the heart of the parties' (Rocchetta 1992–3: 140).

The third threat to the local well-being of these areas was immigration, both from the South and from the Third World, which, it was maintained, by facilitating a rapid rise in criminality, was undermining the high level of social and cultural integration they had achieved and so the good order of society. It was impossible to assimilate the immigrants because, as Bossi argued, '. . .the cultural differences are too great. The difference in skin colour is detrimental to social peace. Imagine if your street, your public square, was full of people of colour, you would feel no longer part of your own world' (*Epoca*, 20 May 1990). Southerners were foreigners, that is culturally different, like all other nationals: 'I have no more affinity with a Neapolitan' – maintained the Venetian, Rocchetta – 'than with a Frenchman or an Armenian' (1992–3: 141).

The South (as Rome writ large), in the Northern League's perspective, is projected as a metaphor summing up and reproducing, in an exaggerated form, all that is wrong with Italian society and politics. In addition, it is also intended to convey, thanks to its Mediterranean (even Afro-Oriental[5]) overtones, the conviction that Italy's place in Europe is being compromised by unscrupulous politicians, resulting in the country's possible exclusion from European markets which are now more important to Northern industry than the market in the South. In other words, the metaphor incarnates 'a corporate and egotistic vision of its (the North's) own interests that exploded just at the moment when it was felt that the South was no longer functional to the North' (Sales 1993: 287).[6] Scapegoating the South and Southerners was, in fact, the basis of the slogans daubed on so many monuments and walls in Lombardy and the Veneto: '*Fora i romani dal Veneto*' (Get the Romans out of the Veneto); '*Roma, KanKaro d'Italia*' (Rome, Italy's cancer); and the most sinister of all, '*Forza Etna, fai il tuo dovere!*' (Come on Etna, do your duty!). Moreover, it was a sentiment which the Northern League leadership continued to fuel from time to time: 'The only thing that grows in the South is the *Mafia*' (Bossi, 2 December 1990); 'The State bosses (*boiardi di Stato*) are all of Southern extraction. . .Even in Milan the corrupt politicians were all people who came from Rome. Rome is corrupt to the marrow. Milan is not. Our politicians when they go to Rome become corrupt. The Romans are corrupt from morning to night. But, the *leghisti* will not be corrupted' (Miglio, *Tg1 Dossier*, 21 September 1993).[7]

The success of the Northern League was in its ability to translate the groundswell of dissent towards the political system in general, and the functioning of the state institutions in particular, which had been building up in the North, into electoral support. Two factors are particularly relevant for explaining the acceleration in this support that occurred in the early 1990s. The first is the crisis of the traditional sources of organization and values that had secured grass-roots' socio-cultural integration and had given direction and stability to electoral choice hitherto. This crisis has two aspects: on the one hand, the development of 'secularization' and so a changed relation of the population to the Church and organized religion with faith now conceived as a personal, rather than a social, matter at the local level;[8] and on the other, the collapse of the old Cold War divisions (East vs. West; socialism vs. liberal democracy) and with it the mobilizing capacity of 'anti-Communism' at the national level, after the fall of the Berlin Wall in 1989.

Such dissent and tensions were not new – as suggested, they had been building up over the previous twenty years – but they had earlier been overshadowed by the major international cleavage. The disappearance of the latter brought the former out into the light of day. The result was that the factors that had rewarded the Christian Democrat Party as the obligatory political reference for Catholics and moderates ceased to operate because the party was now seen as part of the problem because it was identified with the state. It was not that the Christian Democrats' vices were not well known; indeed, they were.[9] But once the reasons for overlooking them had disappeared, the party began to pay the price for its increasingly obvious shortcomings: inefficiency was the price of mediation elevated into a closed system. It is no coincidence that the price of this inefficiency was greater fiscal pressure on the taxpayer, including special one-off taxes, to meet the startling deterioration of the public finances.[10] The revelations of the *Tangent-*

opoli scandal completed the party's humiliation. The result was that the Northern League appeared to be on the way to becoming 'the new mass party in the North, establishing that fiduciary relationship with its electorate that was the traditional parties' strength' (Magna 1993: 31).

The second factor was the ability of the leagues' leadership (and this means above all Bossi's leadership of the Northern League) to rally this social discontent and channel it against the central state, its institutions and the traditional parties, so as to present themselves as a sort of 'anti-party' movement. In this the leagues were powerfully aided and abetted by the traditional parties, which, by attacking the leagues without modifying their customary corrupt behaviour, succeeded in legitimating the opposition role of the leagues. By choice, making a virtue out of a necessity, the leagues did not use the traditional means of political communication (television, radio, national press), but resorted to more informal and indirect means of propaganda and 'promotion' (posters, handbills, face-to-face conversations in bars, buses and other public spaces). Paradoxically, this worked to their advantage in the sense that it reinforced their image of being a 'pure' political force 'uncontaminated' by power. The paradox lay in the fact that by ignoring the media, the leagues became, in fact, the most discussed political force in the media, that is to say in the 'messages' of their opponents, the traditional parties. The result was to establish and emphasize their role as the real opposition to the '*partitocrazia*' ('partyocracy', alias the Italian parties and party system).

In this connection, mention must be made to the leagues' use of language. Dialect was used in a deliberate attempt to break the symbolic codes of 'traditional' party politics. The leaders spoke in the everyday language of the people which contrasted with that of the coded messages of the politicians' 'politesse'.[11] Bossi's language was always direct and to the point, even blunt. Indeed; it was the language of the bar-room, usually sexist and often phallocratic. Former DC Prime Minister Giulio Andreotti was described as a typical example of the political class: 'with stooping shoulders and therefore without balls'; while former Justice Minister and PSI Vice-Secretary, Claudio Martelli was 'not very virile because of his "gay" look'. Moreover, when former Immigration Minister, Margherita Boniver, suggested that certain members of the Northern League were arming themselves with a view to secession, Bossi patronizingly replied at the Curno Assemby (October 1993): 'Don't worry "good-looker" (*bonazza*), the *leghisti* don't need arms, because they always go out armed. They always carry this shaft (*manico*)', and illustrated his words with an appropriate gesture (*La Repubblica* of 28 October 1993). Not surprisingly, such talk evoked an immediate response from the man in the street in the

Northern regions: 'Bossi tells the politicians to their face what we are saying'; 'when Bossi speaks it is though we were speaking'; The Northern League says and thinks what the Lombards say and think. . .' (Biorcio 1991). The contrast with traditional 'politesse' served to reinforce further the idea of the leagues as a political movement apart representing something different. It was neatly summed up by a Paduan leader of the Venetian League: 'One day – it was in the early eighties – I saw a hand-written poster of the League. I was struck by the things that it said and by the way that they were said. I don't say that I decided then. But, that way of saying things, so different from the official political speeches, was the decisive stimulus' (Diamanti 1993a: 51).

The Particularity of the Leagues in the Veneto

During the late 1980s and early 1990s, attention focused on the Lombard League-Northern League (*Lega Lombarda-Lega Nord*) not only because of the strength and suddenness of its success, but also because of the importance of Lombardy in Italian economic and political life: Milan is Italy's economic and financial centre as well as the self-proclaimed 'moral capital' of the country, at least, before the *Tangentopoli* scandal broke. Thus, there was a natural tendency to identify the phenomenon of the leagues with the sole Lombard League-Northern League.

However, the Venetian League (*Liga Veneta*) is of interest in its own right. Moreover, its longer history points up certain not insignificant differences. Firstly, the Venetian League was founded in 1980, while the Lombard Manifesto of Autonomy dates from 1982 and the Lombard League itself only from 1985, although both were prepared by the activity of regional cultural associations in the previous decade. Indeed, later Rocchetta (1992–3: 134–6) claimed to have launched the idea of the Venetian League in a church at Danzig in Poland in 1968!

Secondly, the longer electoral history of the Venetian League has meant that it has been more eventful than that of the Lombard League (see Figure 8.1). It first presented candidates at the 1979 European elections in an 'autonomous' list under the auspices of the *Union Valdotaine* gaining 8,000 votes. However, it had its first real success in the 1983 parliamentary elections when, to the general surprise, it won 4.2 per cent of the vote in the region, with high points of 6–7 per cent in the provinces of Treviso and Vicenza, and elected one deputy (Achille Tramarin) and one senator (Graziano Girardi). This success was followed by a period of electoral stagnation and decline (2.7 per cent in the 1989 European elections), and then a second success at the 1990 regional elections (5.9 per cent) and the triumph of April 1992 (25.5 per cent).

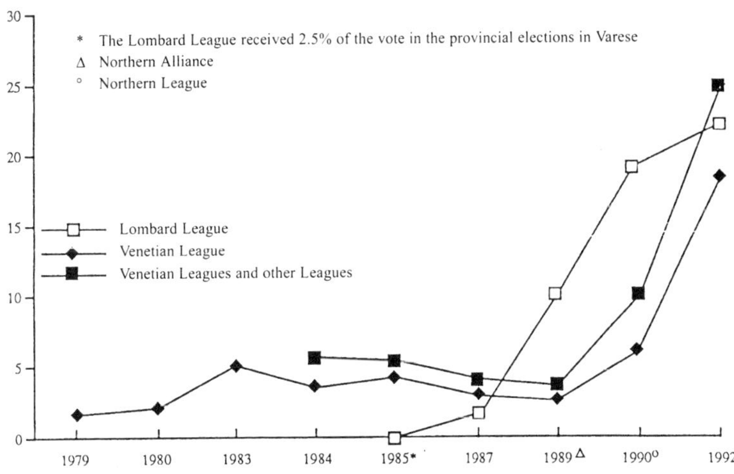

Figure 8.1. The Votes of the Lombard League in Lombardy, the Venetian League and other Autonomous Leagues in Venetia 1979–92

This second success was very different from the first. In fact, the longer history of the leagues in the Veneto has resulted in a significant organizational differentiation in relation to Lombardy. It was the fruit of a series of schisms that led to at least four autonomous leagues active in the Veneto at the present time (Figure 8.2). Beside the original Venetian League (part of the federal Northern League after its foundation), which remained the largest and most deep-rooted (575,000 votes or 17.8 per cent in 1992), three other leagues established themselves in the late 1980s and early 1990s): the Union of the Venetian People (*Unione del Popolo Veneto* – UPV) constituted in 1987 as a result of splits in the Venetian League's ruling group (50,000 votes or 1.5 per cent of the vote in 1992); the League of Civic Lists of the Autonomous Veneto (*Lega delle Liste Civiche dell'Autonomo Veneto* – LAV) founded in 1990 round the progressive civic lists of former PSI Mayor of Venice, Mario Rigo (150,000 votes or 4.7 per cent of the vote in 1992); and finally, the Autonomous Venetian Regional Movement (*Movimento Veneto Regione Autonoma* – MVRA) constituted by a group of former Christian Democrats in breach with the original ruling group of the Venetian League since 1983, and linked to the Alpine Alliance (*Alleanza Alpina*), a group of Lombard League dissidents (50,000 votes or 1.5 per cent of the vote in 1992).

The original nucleus of the Venetian League was formed in the Venetian Philological Society (*Società Filologica Veneta*) in the 1970s. It was an association that, as its name indicates, organized seminars and research into Venetian language, culture and history. They were subjects, so the members claimed, that the Italian scholastic system ignored because they contradicted the *Risorgimento* tradition of Italian history taught in the schools. The society's activity suscitated a certain local interest and brought together the group that was to found the Venetian League in 1980 (Rocchetta, Tramarin, Bergami, Beggiato, Marin, Gardin, etc.). However, the event that gave a political focus to the group's activity was the solicitation of the *Union Valdotaine* to all ethnic and regional groups to join together in a single list to help elect a MEP at the European elections of 1979. The Venetian Philological Society joined and named Achille Tramarin as its candidate in Italy's North-East constituency.Without any promotion or electoral propaganda, the list and Tramarin's candidature won 8,000 votes (0.3 per cent). This was a totally unexpected result that convinced the group that there was a larger basis of political support for the '*Venetista*' programme than they had previously suspected.[12] Hence, in January 1980, the group decided to found the Venetian League as a movement with the objective of politically asserting the Venetian regional identity.

The Venetian League, thus, emerged as a result of an experience and reflection on themes and questions outside traditional politics, and pursued specifically outside the traditional party organizations and networks. This latter point is particularly significant as the social profile of the Leagues' (UPV as well as LV) leaders – young, male, middle class, secondary or higher education – demonstrates that political experience in the Leagues is for almost all their first experience of political activity. None the less, like the founders of the Venetian League, most had been active in voluntary associations, particularly in the leisure, sporting and cultural fields, which gave them an intimate contact with the problems of the local population. Such activity indicates the existence of a latent demand for participation outside the traditional party career system, awaiting the opportunity to express itself and which constitution of the Leagues provided. A parallel with the role of the Social Democrat Party in England in the mid-1980s readily suggests itself. The result in both cases was a growth in political participation at all levels.

The original focus was on the Venetian region as a territorial and cultural unit. The appeal to the region as a territorial identity – '*il popolo veneto*' (the Venetian people); '*la nazione veneta*' (the Venetian nation) – was chosen to stress the movement's difference from the representative logic of the traditional parties, and specifically to that of the dominant party, Christian Democracy. It was not that territorial demands did not have a place in the traditional parties' programmes. Indeed, for the Christian Democrats in the 1970s, thanks above all to former minister and regional party boss Toni Bisaglia (who died in 1984), the mediation of regional interests in relation to the state was a major aspect of national politics (Bisaglia: 1988). But – and this is the important point – it remained within the traditional framework, characterized by universal values (freedom, democracy, justice, etc.), and within the logic of national integration. The relations between national centre and regional periphery were developed in terms of mediation and *not* conflict.[13]

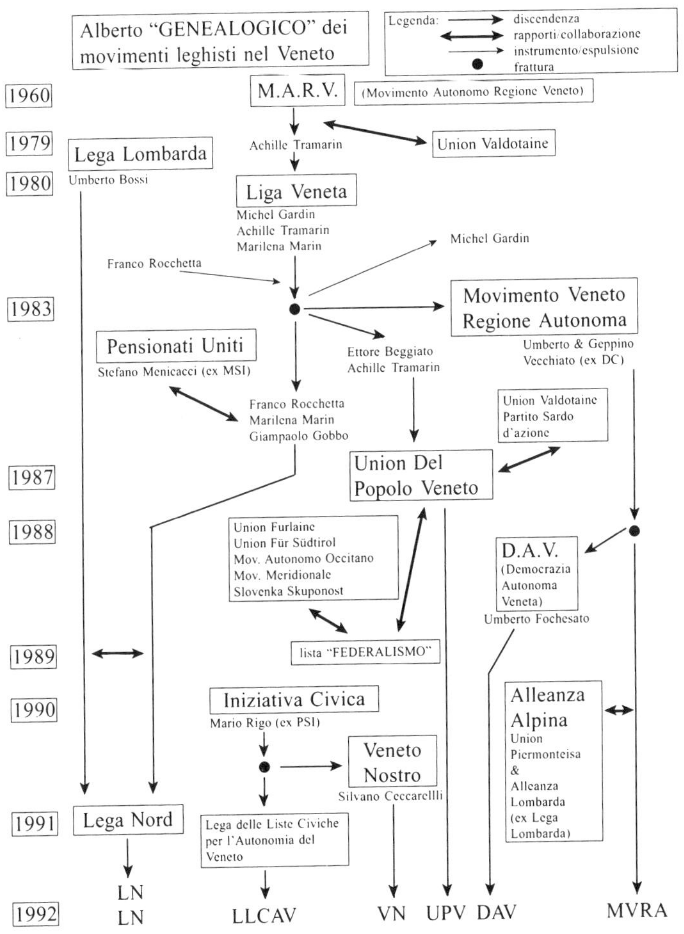

Source: Il Mattino di Padora of 8 April 1992.

Figure 8.2. Genealogy of the Autonomous Leagues in the Veneto

In the case of the Venetian League, and the cultural experience that formed it, the territorial (regional and cultural) factor was, on the contrary, a specific value in itself.[14] It was the premise on which the demands and representation towards – but implicitly *against* – the Italian national state were formulated. Hence, for example, Rocchetta's attempt to get the 'Venetian language' (*lingua veneta*) recognized on an equal footing with Italian in the Venetian Regional Assembly in 1985;[15] or the Venetian League's long polemic against the *Risorgimento* and the 'swindle plebiscite' of 22 October 1866, which attached the Venetian region to Italy, culminating in the public demonstration against Senator Spadolini's celebration of it in 1986. The Venetian League's opposition to all traditional parties was based on the latters' acceptance of the national state as the political frame of reference. This regional bias (*pregiudizio*) was reinforced by alliances with other ethnic and regional forces (*Union Valdotaine* initially, Lombard and the other leagues, later). Moreover, it fitted in naturally with the notion of the 'Europe of the Regions' in opposition to the 'Europe of National States', supported by the majority of traditional political forces, because it was also believed to be a vehicle for a much greater regional autonomy: 'Further from Rome, nearer Europe' (*Più lontano da Roma, più vicino all'Europa*')[16] was the slogan.

Mention must be made of the interlude between the Venetian League's 1983 electoral success and its post-1989 revival. The period 1984–7 was a period of schisms and stagnation, which led to the setting-up of a rival organization, the Union of Venetian People in 1987. The struggle was personal and organizational and *not* strategic (Rocchetta and his now former wife, Marilena Marin, against Tramarin, elected deputy in 1983, and Beggiato), which had a number of folkloric episodes. Basically, what was at stake was who controlled the movement. In view of its 'anti-party' nature – unpaid voluntary activity undertaken from conviction in contrast to that carried out for personal interest characterized by professionality and bureaucracy – the movement had a low level of institutionalization, but compensated for it by a high level of identity, and so naturally a power structure concentrated round small groups and family ties that tended to accentuate internal conflicts.

Despite Rocchetta's public claim that the movement was democratic, the absence of organizational rules for a long time has meant a lack of internal democracy. In the early 1990s, the leaders of the UPV stated that 'The Venetian League is closed up like a hedgehog, dominated by Rocchetta and his family'; 'It is a sect'; 'At the beginning, I joined the Venetian League [said a former member from Rodigo]. Later on I was elected Provincial Secretary. Rocchetta arrived to say that internal elections were not valid; that the leaders designate the Secretary. So I left' (Diamanti 1992: 238). Indeed, Rocchetta admitted that the Northern League applied a severe selection process: 'Everybody can join as long as they can prove the sincerity of their commitment. We ask a lot of our members. But, on the other hand our movement is democratic – it freely elects its leaders – and, above all honest' (1992–3: 138). However, there were many indices,[17] not the least by Rocchetta himself, that Bossi controlled the movement (and in the Veneto through Rocchetta's former wife, Marilena Marin,[18] Secretary of the Venetian League) with an iron fist.[19] Indeed, an attentive observer, the journalist G.-P. Pansa defined the Northern League in these terms: 'It is a centre-right movement, neo-Thatcherite, very centralist, strong and well organized with internal rules of iron' (in *Il 2000 Vicenza* of 14 November 1993: 7).

At all events, after the schisms, the leaders of the Venetian League decided to develop their relations with other regional movements. In 1985, they gave (from its public party funding) an interest-free loan of fifty million lire (£25,000) to Bossi's newly-founded Lombard League; for the 1989 European elections, they forged an electoral alliance (Northern Alliance – *Alleanza Nord*) with Bossi and the Lombard League. The next step was the fusion with the Lombard League, Autonomist Piedmont (*Piedmont autonomista*), and the leagues of Liguria, Emilia-Romagna and Tuscany, to form the Northern League (whose name was suggested by Rocchetta), signed in Autumn 1990. In February 1991, the first congress of the federal Northern League was held at Pieve Emanuele when Bossi was elected federal Secretary and Rocchetta federal President of the new movement.

Each of the 'regional' leagues was represented in the Northern League's Federal Council. The statutes lay down that the number of representatives is proportional to the electoral strength of each league. Thus, for example, the Venetian League had five representatives in Winter 1992 – less than the Lombard League but more than the others – because the former had more votes than the Venetian League when the Northern League was formed in 1991. In addition, each league had its own National Council and enjoyed widespread autonomy (Rocchetta 1992–3: 137–8). This said, there was little doubt, however, that not only did the Lombards dominate the Venetians in the Northern League,[20] but also that Bossi dictated its strategy, not the least because of its success in the early 1990s. After all, the Lombards were in the van in the take-off of 1989–90, prelude to the triumph of 1992.

The difference of electoral history, that is to say, the rapidity and size of the Lombard League's success in relation to the slower and more contradictory development of the Venetian League, owed something to regional differences and everything to Bossi's leadership. It is no coincidence that the initial electoral success in Venetia in 1983 occurred as a result of the 1980–2 economic recession. However, it must be stressed that the impact of the social contradictions was less than in Lombardy because of the greater socio-economic integration, lower levels of immigration and lower criminality. In addition, the Venetian labour market demonstrated greater resilience due to the informal mechanisms of small business and the deeper social roots and organizational structures of the Church that animated networks (voluntary associations of all kind) which mitigated the worst effects of the recession. Hence, the discontent was absorbed after the initial protest in the mid-1980s; this was not the case in Lombardy in late 1980s and early 1990s.

As regards the greater leadership capacity of the Lombard League thanks to Bossi, it was not just a case of personal charisma (although there was also an element of this), it was above all a question of strategy, of conception and of proposals. The strategy of the Venetian League was based, as noted, on an ethno-regionalist model: the region as the source of values and historical identity. This limited the possibility of communication with the grass roots which had more urgent and immediate material problems. Bossi's strategy, on the other hand, was based on a very different model, that of an 'anti-institutional' party. He quickly played down the symbolic elements and privileged the instrumental ones, conceiving territorial identity as a basis for the representation and conflict of interests. Lombardy, rapidly replaced by the North, was merely a marker for the conflict of the productive against the improductive sectors, market logic against welfare logic, efficiency against iniquity. Hence, the Northern League became the party of civil society against the state, of the producers against the parasites. Coherent with this strategy, Bossi announced at the Second Congress of the Northern League at Jesolo in November 1992 that too much weight had been given in the past to the ethnic element and it should be toned down in the future:[21] this coincided with the formation of the Northern-Central-Southern League lists for local government elections in the South in December 1992, where, however, they had no success. The year 1993 was to be, according to Bossi (*Corriere della Sera* of 3 January 1993), the one when the Northern leagues, as the movement of constitutional reform, would enter the government and succeed in penetrating the South:[22] a far cry from the leagues' original point of departure.

In this connection, the electoral recovery of the Venetian League-Northern League in the Veneto in 1990 and the triumph in 1992 were largely explicable in terms of the pull exerted by the 'Lombard model'.

It was a clear demonstration of the Venetian League's leaders' acceptance of the superiority of Bossi's strategy of the 'anti-institutional' party based on the North/South-civil society/state (political system) cleavages, capable of mobilizing all sectors of the Northern electorate. However, as indicated, it was not the only strategy available because, if the Venetian League-Northern League won two-thirds of the Leagues' votes in the region, a third of the electorate still opted for the other movements (LAV, UPV, MVRA), which pointed to the continued relevance of the other strategies. Two others have been identified. The first is the 'ethno-regionalist' model mentioned above which rests on the notion of the region as the source of values and historical identity; it is capable of mobilization in the original areas of league support (the 'white industrial periphery'). This model was adopted by the UPV and MVRA (3 per cent of vote in Venetia in 1992). The second model is the 'localist' model based on civic lists which enabled the movement to differentiate its appeal and was the strategy traditionally operated by the Christian Democrats in the Veneto. It was pursued to good effect by the LAV (4.5 per cent of the vote in 1992) (Diamanti 1993a: 76–7).

The significance of the persistence of territorial identity and localistic feeling that the Lombard model does not cater for was difficult to assess. Diamanti (1992) found, for instance, that the federal hypothesis was stronger among UPV leaders than among those of the Venetian League-Northern League. Indeed, the former accused the latter of preferring a confederation to a federation of sovereign regions. Moreover, the Venetian League leaders were more reticent: they saw federalism as a general political orientation, that is, as 'anti-state', rather than a specific political objective. This was probably due to Bossi's influence, that is, his selection of instrumental objectives to attract a socially differentiated electorate rather than spell out clear proposals that might repel significant groups. Regional autonomy in this light was an instrument that emphasized the 'anti-party' and 'anti-state' strategy that he has espoused. Nevertheless, that Bossi had some fears of the consequences of the persistence of these other traditions,[23] can be assumed from his exhortation: 'Either the North is mature and makes no mistake with its vote or, with the false Leagues, it remains the slave of Rome' (quoted in Diamanti 1993a: 77). When asked whether he was sure that his supporters would follow his brusque tactical changes, he was forced to reply: 'The *leghisti know* that the basic project has not changed: for this reason the Northern League is as solid as a rock. *And then there is me*: as long as there is a leader like me, no one need fear being betrayed' (*Corriere della Sera* of 3 January 1993).

Conclusion

The leagues in the Veneto, as in Lombardy, extended their support in the early 1990s far beyond the 'opulent periphery'. They invaded the big city centres and eroded the support of the traditional parties. And most of this occurred before the full impact of the *Tangentopoli* scandal was felt. It has been argued that the leagues profited from a combination of three sentiments – territorial identity, intolerance of strangers and alienation from traditional political forces (Mannheimer 1991: 9–10) – in a particularly favourable conjuncture (end of the Cold War, economic recession, etc.). The question now is whether the leagues have, as Bossi believed before 1994, planted the roots of a new kind of collective identity, or whether they represented, as many believe, a protest movement against the fiscal consequences of the post-war system of power. Although the Northern League made spectacular gains in terms of seats won in the 1994 parliamentary elections as a result of the new mixed majority electoral system, it actually lost votes (*circa* 0.3 per cent or 300,000 votes) in relation to 1992. Indeed, the suggestion was that it no longer was a party of the North as it was in the early 1990s (this was contested by Berlusconi's *Forza Italia*), but simply that of a part of the North, the 'opulent periphery' of small businesses and Catholic political traditions where it originally emerged in the 1980s (Diamanti 1994). In all events, the future of the leagues, and the offshoots of the original Northern League above all, depends as much on what they do, and more still on the capacity of their adversaries, the other parties, to respond adequately. Today, it depends on the future of Berlusconi and *Forza Italia*. What is at stake is the eventual institutional nature of the Second Republic.

Notes

1. The text is the result of a common reflection of both authors, while more specifically, Percy Allum is responsible for the first section and Ilvo Diamanti for the second. In addition, Percy Allum would like to thank the Leverhulme Foundation for the award of a fellowship that enabled him to spend time in the region in 1993 to collect material used in this study. This text was written in Spring 1994.

2. The first quotation is from *Corriere della Sera* of 22 September 1990, and the second from the Neapolitan edition of *La Repubblica*. For a panorama of politicians' and media views of the leagues from 1985 to mid-1993, see Fusella (1993).
3. The local elections held in June 1993, were the first held under the new system of direct election of mayors of large and medium-sized towns by a two-ballot majority, introduced by law n.84/93.
4. This was confirmed by the parliamentary elections of 27 March 1994, in which the Northern League held its vote in the North (where with 118 seats it was the largest single party in the Chamber), but was totally absent from the South, see (Diamanti & Mannheimer 1994); and (Parker 1994).
5. Such views have a long history: typical are those of Cavour's representative in Naples in 1861, Carlo Farina: 'Italy indeed! This is Africa: compared to these boors the bedouins are the flower of civic virtue . .'; or Lord Rosebury, some years later: 'Naples is the only Oriental city without a European quarter. . .'
6. Bossi was very explicit in an interview in *La Repubblica* (13 January 1993): 'If Germany puts its affairs in order and the East takes off and we still have this welfare-dependent South, everyone understands that sooner or later the division of Italy will happen. But it will not be me who will provoke it. It will be the economic situation, international competition.'
7. Quoted in Giusti (1993: 100, 35, 41) respectively.
8. For instance, 'half of the Vicentines believe that "it is better to find God individually than through the Church" and only 5 per cent believe that "the Church should give concrete guidance on political and social problems". . .Therefore, the most significant fact revealed is the progressive decline of the social role of the Venetian Catholic Church: it is no longer capable of inspiring the social and political behaviour of the majority of the Venetian people, as it had in years past' (Cortelazzo *et al.* 1984: 88–9).
9. As many public opinion polls of the 1970s and 1980s revealed, but they were not considered, at the time, 'a good reason to be against it [the DC]', see, for example Marradi (1978: 69).
10. The public spending deficit reached about 10 per cent of GDP and the public deficit over 100 per cent of GDP in 1992. These figures are to be compared with the Maastricht Treaty permitted figures of 3 per cent and 60 per cent respectively! See Allum (1993: 4). G. Baget-Bozzo is very explicit: 'The tax revolt is the real League struggle, not that for the Republic of the North' (quoted in *Corriere della Sera* of 23 November 1993: 6).
11. The *locus classicus* of Italian politicians' 'politesse' is probably

Christian Democrat Secretary Aldo Moro's pronouncement of the 'opening to the left' in a television interview in November 1961: 'I confirm what I have said. . .that there is a common opinion in the party, that there really is a closure to the right, that is we do not believe that a left-right opposition, which would be fatal to our country and in which the DC would be unnaturally on the right and which would disrupt the equilibrium of Italian political life, is useful, not so much for the fortunes of our party, but useful to Christian Democracy. . .Thus, in these circumstances, excluding this formula and the parties' decisions remaining unchanged, the theme [of the Congress] is precisely the one which I have indicated, that is the formula to which I do not see there is any concrete and stable political alternative. . .', quoted in Allum (1973: 260).

12. This is very different from the situation in the 1950s, when the Vicentine writer, Guido Piovene (1957), observed in the course of his *Viaggio in Italia* (1953–6): 'Then I ask myself what is the Veneto for the Venetians? It has nothing to do with a national sentiment. . .It is neither politics, nor activism, and indeed in the Veneto there isn't a trace of separatism. But there exists in the Venetian's heart a fantastic belief, that there land is its own world, an admirable sentiment, almost a private dream, that has no equal in the other regions of Italy, not even where separatism has caught on. *Venetismo* is a potent living fantasy that does cause trouble in Parliament'(23).
13. In many ways, Bisaglia anticipated the League's main constitutional proposal before it was formulated. In an interview in 1982, he replied to a question on what should be done to develop the region in the interests of the whole country, 'The main obstacle is the centralist vision that still prevails in Italy. . .If it was possible, I would say that the Veneto would be ready to participate in a "federal state". But not Italy, it is not ready. The main obstacle is the excessive imbalance between the general [lack of] cohesion [of the regions] and that of the Veneto. The State is afraid of this' (Bisaglia 1988: 24).
14. Rocchetta explained in an interview given a few years ago (in *Il Gazzetino* of 15 December 1993: 3) the Venetian League's vision in these terms: 'I have always considered language as an important element of identity, but I have also stressed that the Venetian identity is not a question of folk dances or of local curiosities, but rather derives from a richness [in its culture],. . . which today is confirmed also by CENSIS and is among the most advanced examples in Europe.'
15. It failed to win the support of the other political groups.

16. For a development of the Venetian League's views towards Europe, see Diamanti (1993b).
17. 'In any case, the internal controversies that preceded the vote [for the local elections of June 1993], makes one believe that selection of candidates has been based on the criteria of fidelity to the leader and personal reliability' (Magna 1993: 31).
18. Rocchetta's comment, after she had frustrated his candidature as Mayor of Venice, was devastating: 'Do you know what they call her? Semiramide. Remember Dante?' "Ell'è Sremaramis di cui si legge/che succedette a Nino e fu sua sposa/ella terra ch'il Soldan corregge. . ." 'I could be mistaken but this how the present structure functions. She controls a great deal in a Veneto reduced to a fiefdom.' (*Corriere della Sera* of 7 December 1993: 4).
19. Rocchetta's public grievances regarding Bossi's leadership were two-fold: (1) Bonapartism: 'I would say Bonarpartism more than Caesarism. Besides, for many years he has had this myth of Napoleon and the Cisalpine Republic with Milan as capital'; and (2) his loss of contact with the rank and file: 'I see Umberto more than ever surrounded by dwarfs and ballerinas, as Farassino calls them, body guards, functionaries and would-be functionaries. By now he is unapproachable. . .' (Interview in *Corriere della Sera* of 7 December 1993: 4). Hence, his advice to Bossi, 'Do not distance yourself too much from the rank and file of the movement, stay in contact with normal people. . .' (*Il Gazzettino* of 15 December 1993: 3).
20. Lombard centralism, not to say chauvinism, was another of Rocchetta's grievances against Bossi and the Lombards: 'This insistence on Milan, Milan, Milan Milan. . .' 'But isn't it going well there?' 'Not so well'. 'In Liguria they say to you that for them it would be fine if Rome was replaced by Milan. But in Piedmont there is resistance[to this proposal]as there is here with us. I see historical precedents that can only be damaging.'. . . 'Yes, but four out of five are Lombards. . .Why?' 'Just a moment. We have won a lot of localities and we could have also won in Venice. But you have asked me why they have chosen low profile candidates here, in Genoa, in Turin? Many are also asking this within the League. . .' (interview in *Corriere della Sera* of 7 December 1993: 4).
21. 'Rocchetta is a supporter of ethnic themes, while Bossi never misses the occasion to explain that is a waste of time' (G. Passalacqua in *La Repubblica* of 7 December 1993: 8).
22. The *Leghisti* were convinced that the South was theirs for the taking ('The South is diffident, they think that the League ends at Florence or at the most Rome. One feels defeated in advance. But under the

surface is a crazy desire for the League', Santino Rizzo of the Southern League in *L'Indipendente* of 9 May 1993), so they combined seduction ('the word *terrone* ['Southerner'] is disappearing from the League's dictionary. It has already been deleted from my dictionary for some time', Bossi in *La Stampa* of 2 October 1992) from time to time with suggestions that the Southerners are their own worst enemies ('The South is condemned by its own *meridionalisti* ('Southernists'), Bossi on the *Maurizio Costanzo Show*, Canale 5, 15 May 1993). But their success was negligible.

23. Rocchetta was conscious that he represented an alternative but he claimed that he had no intention of leading a rebellion. However, after the 1994 elections the conflict with Bossi came to a head: Rocchetta (Under-Secretary for Foreign Affairs during the short-lived Berlusconi government) was not only dismissed from his post of President of the Northern League, but also expelled by Bossi, and in the autumn of 1994 founded his own league, *La Liga Nathion Veneta*. It appears to have no grass-roots support.

Bibliography

Allum, P. (1975), *Politics and Society in Post-War Naples*, Turin.

—— (1993), 'Chronicle of a Death Foretold: The First Italian Republic', *Reading Papers in Politics*, **12**, Reading.

Biorcio, R. (1991), 'La Lega come attore politico: dal federalismo al popolismo regionalista', in R. Mannheimer (ed.), *La Lega Lombarda*, Milan, pp.34–82.

Bisaglia, A. (1988), 'Il politico come imprenditore, il territorio come impresa', interview with I. Diamanti, in *Strumenti*, **2**, pp.11–26.

Cortelazzo, M.A., Isnenghi, M., Pace, E. and Renzi, L. (1984), 'Il ritorno di San Marco. Retroterra, ideologia, possibilità politiche della Liga Veneta', *Venetica*, **2**, pp.78–99.

Diamanti, I. (1992), 'La mia patria è il Veneto: I valori e la proposta politica delle Leghe', *Polis*, **2**, pp.225–35.

—— (1993a), *La Lega. Geografia, storia e sociologia di un nuovo soggetto politico*, Rome.

—— (1993b), 'L'Europa secondo la Lega', *Limes*, **4**.

—— (1994), 'La Lega', in I. Diamanti and R. Mannheimer (eds), *Milano a Roma. Guida all'Italia elettorale del 1994*, Rome, pp.53–62.

Diamanti, I. and Riccamboni, G. (1992), *La parabola del voto bianco. Elezioni e società in Veneto (1946–1992)*, Vicenza.

Fusella, A. (1993), *Arrivano i barbari. La Lega nel racconto dei*

quotidiani e periodici, 1985–1993, Milan.
Giusti, M. (1993), *Bossoli*, Rome.
Magna, N. (1993), 'La Lega: Partito di massa e di governo locale', *Politica e Economia*, **24**, 2, pp.28–32.
Mannheimer, R. (ed.), (1991), *La Lega Lombarda*, Milan.
Marradi, A. (1978), 'Immagini di massa della DC e del PCI', in A. Martinelli and G.-F. Pasquino (eds), *La politica nell'Italia che cambia*, Milan, pp.66–103.
Martinelli, A. and Pasquino, G.-F. (eds), (1978), *La politica nell'Italia che cambia*, Milan.
Parker, S. (1994), 'The March 1994 Parliamentary Elections: An Overview', *ASMI Newsletter*, Spring, pp.28–35.
Piovene, S. (1957), *Viaggio in Italia*, Milan, (new edition).
Rocchetta, F. (1992–3), 'L'Italie existe-t-elle?' interview with M. Lazar, *Politique Internationale*, 58, Winter, pp.129–47.
Sales, I. (1993), *Leghisti e sudisti*, Bari.

–9–

Ethnicity, Racism and the Northern League

Anna Cento Bull

Introduction

The Northern League has often been described as a party with a racist or quasi-racist ideology, although the party has systematically rejected such accusations. Bossi himself admitted in his autobiography (1992: 99, 174) that the Northern League exploited anti-Southern and anti-immigrant feelings in order to gain attention from the media and from the public. He seemed to be saying that although the Northern League itself was not racist, quasi-racist sentiments were diffused among Northern Italians and provided the stimulus for the rise of the Northern League. A more appropriate definition, according to Bossi, would be that of ethno-federalism – ethnicity being defined somewhat ambiguously as being based on both cultural and genetic characteristics.

In this chapter I will examine the ideology of the Northern League *vis-à-vis* immigration, racism and ethnicity, aiming at establishing whether the party can be defined as racist or quasi-racist. I will also explore the articulation between racism and Fascism or neo-fascism comparing the Northern League to some of Europe's right-wing extremist parties, such as the French National Front.

To establish whether the Northern League has been racist or quasi-racist, however, is but the first step in understanding the nature of this party. Racism and xenophobia do not exist in a vacuum nor do they represent a uniform and homogeneous phenomenon. Racism can take on different forms, and the only way to understand a particular form is to relate it to the socio-economic structure and political environment within which it occurs. In the case of the Northern League, I will argue that the racism it has espoused arises from a specific society and economy which can be defined as tightly communitarian. In other words, when Bossi said that the Northern League has mainly exploited embedded anti-Southern feelings he is telling us something about

Northern and Lombard society that needs to be further explored.

As well as relating the ideology of the Northern League to Lombard society and economy, the question needs to be addressed as to why the diffused quasi-racist attitudes of so many Northern Italians only found political expression and representation in the late 1980s and early 1990s and not in the 1950s and 1960s, when immigration from the South to the North undoubtedly created tension and ill-feelings among the 'indigenous' population. Whereas the anti-immigrants attitude of the Northern League can be at least partly explained by the recent wave of extra-European immigration, this explanation does not hold for the anti-Southernism of the Northern League. To a large extent, as we shall see, anti-Southernism and anti-foreign immigration can both be linked to the ethno-regionalist aspirations of the party, but this still begs the question why a pseudo-Lombard ethnicity has achieved political prominence at a time when linguistic and cultural differences within Italy are on the wane.

To sum up, this chapter will address the articulation between racism, anti-immigration, ethnicity and fascism with reference to the Northern League; it will relate the ideology of the League to the Lombard society and economy and will attempt to explain why ethnicity, racism and anti-immigration simultaneously found political expression in Northern Italy in the late 1980s and early 1990s.[1]

Defining Racism and Ethnicity

The starting point for an analysis of the ideology of the Northern League must be a working definition of both racism and ethnicity. It did not take me long to realize that there exist highly contrasting definitions of these two concepts.

Strictly speaking, race and racism refer to the use of phenotypical criteria in the process of social categorization, while ethnic group and ethnicity refer to cultural criteria (Lyon 1972: 257–8; van den Berghe 1981: 29). The traditional definition of racism is that of a doctrine claiming that race determines culture, in other words, 'the doctrine that a man's behaviour is determined by stable inherited racial characters deriving from separate racial stocks having distinctive attributes and usually considered to stand to one another in relations of superiority and inferiority' (Banton 1970: 18). This kind of racist ideology has increasingly been discarded in Western Europe because it has incurred social stigma and also because it was born out of the experience of nineteenth-century colonization, when Europe attempted to justify and legitimize its role as colonizer.

The Northern League rejects all accusations of racism as slander precisely because it publicly equates racism with traditional racism. Yet racism has now been redefined to take into account the new forms it has assumed as a result of the new migrations of the twentieth century. The 'new' racism emphasizes cultural rather than phenotypical differences although in many cases both are used. As Miles pointed out, referring to the migration of European groups such as the Italians and the Irish to Britain, despite the fact that their phenotypical characteristics were not very dissimilar from those of the indigenous population, they were made to experience a process of ideological, political and economic exclusion. Therefore one has to conclude that 'in the absence of phenotypical differences. . .other factors (e.g. cultural) can be made to play the same role' (Miles 1982: 64). According to Miles, in practice phenotypical and cultural characteristics tend to be combined in the new racism. Thus the Irish in Britain were the object of discrimination for being both physically and culturally different from the natives.

In this context ethnic groups are often used as a substitute for race – whether the emphasis is on cultural or phenotypical criteria, a rigid distinction is made between Us and the Other (or Others); this process is defined by Miles as one of racialization rather than racism. Racism occurs when the Other (or Others) is considered to have privileged and illegitimate access to resources and/or is judged to possess negatively evaluated characteristics (Miles 1989: 73–84). Both Us and the Other(s) are considered as static and organic communities whose cultural characteristics are inbred and unchangeable. The 'new' racism thus puts the emphasis on a 'right to differ' and can be summed up in the slogan 'each community in its own natural environment', which implies a rejection of all migrations which are seen as subverting the natural order of things. Alternatively, for those migrant groups which have already settled in their host country, the emphasis is often placed on assimilation and integration.

According to Taguieff, there exist two major types of racism which can be defined as 'universalist-equalitarian' and 'communitarian-differentialist'. The former stems from a process of hetero-racialization, i.e. racialization of the Other who needs to conform to the host society and become 'invisible'; the latter stems from a process of auto-racialization, i.e. racialization of the Self which is judged to be threatened by alien ethnic groups (Taguieff 1988). However, as Silverman rightly stresses, the two forms of racism 'are not opposites, they are part of the same process' (Silverman 1992: 124). Indeed, migrant groups are often categorized and labelled according to their 'degree of assimilability', i.e. on the basis of a pseudo-scientific analysis of their cultural and ethnic distance from the host population. Thus van den Berghe maintained that those ethnic groups which are visibly different from the indigenous (or the dominant) population, have a different religion, speak an unrelated language and/or are large in size have the least potential of being assimilated into the dominant group (1981: 218–24). Van den Berghe cites the example of African-Americans in the USA which, he argues, are the only group excluded from the 'melting pot' process. According to Silverman, however, there is no scientific basis to the discourse of assimilability, as can be seen in the European case. Silverman argues that in France before 1945 Southern Europeans were considered non-assimilable, whereas Northern Europeans were deemed to share a common culture. Nowadays Southern Europeans are considered integrated and assimilated and the process of exclusion is directed at the North Africans, who have become the new 'non-assimilable' ethnic group (Silverman 1992: 105–7).

The Northern League: Racism or Ethno-Centrism?

On the basis of the above definitions and analyses of racism, how are we to judge the Northern League? Has it been a racist or quasi-racist party? The answer has to be affirmative, at least if one accepts the definition of 'new racism', i.e., a racist ideology based on cultural rather than biological differentialism. The Northern League has promoted a process of auto-racialization of the Lombard people and in so doing has taken on board aspects of the 'communitarian-differentialist' racism. The 1992 political programme of the Northern League stated explicitly:

> Our party's strongly critical attitude towards migratory policies stems from our specific concept of mankind. A human person is not simply an economic agent: he or she is also made up of affections, cultural values and identities which can find their best expressions in separate historical and environmental communities. Immigrations, having a purely economic value, break up this equilibrium which forms a vital part of human nature. The theorization of a 'multi-racial society' as the predestined future for mankind is both vain and openly instrumental (*Lega Nord-Lega Lombarda* 1992).

This process of racialization is accompanied by a racist subtext, i.e. by the attribution of negatively evaluated characteristics to the Other and/or by the assumption that the Other was having illegitimate and privileged access to resources. Interestingly, the Northern League has held both convictions (but particularly the former) in relation to Southern Italians, whereas it tended to view other immigrant groups in the context of their access to resources. This is partly due to the fact, as we shall see, that Southern Italians are attributed with a very specific negatively evaluated culture (which can be subsumed under the term '*mafiosità*') whereas the other ethnic immigrants are seen as possessing potentially threatening but as yet unidentified and undefined cultural specificities.

As well as holding views of the communitarian-differentialist type of racism, the Northern League also advocated assimilation and integration for those immigrants who have already settled in Italy. The Northern League's position, almost undistinguishable in this respect from that of the French National Front and other right-wing extremist parties, was that all ethnic groups should live in their 'natural' environment; however, should there for economic reasons be migrations from one ethnic group to another, preference should be given to those groups which are more 'assimilable'. Both Le Pen and Bossi judged the Africans from the Maghreb to be among the least assimilable ethnic groups; interestingly, neither specified the reasons why this should be so and one suspects that phenotypical as well as cultural differences play a part (how much did Bossi know about Maghrebian culture?). As Bossi wrote, 'I am convinced that the extra-Europeans who originate from certain parts of the world, particularly Arabs from the Middle East and Maghrebians, do not have the least intention of integrating and accepting our customs' (1992: 149).

From this point of view I would disagree with Baget-Bozzo who wrote in *La Repubblica* (26 March 1992) that Le Pen and Bossi differ because the former discriminates on the basis of skin colour, whereas the latter discriminates on the basis of cultural differences. What is true is that Le Pen's racism is more openly based on skin colour because the main target of the National Front were the immigrants from North Africa, whereas Bossi's racism was based predominantly, although not exclusively, on cultural differences because the main target for his party is the Southern '*mafiosità*'. When the Northern League was mainly concerned with the Southern '*mafiosità*' cultural criteria prevailed, but when Bossi discussed the issue of immigration his racism was quite similar to that of Le Pen. In his autobiography, for instance, Bossi argued that the Southern immigrants have by and large been able to integrate into Northern Italian society, whereas Maghrebians and Arab fundamentalists are two non-assimilable ethnic groups (1992: 160). This flatly contradicts what the League says or implies about the Southern immigrants in different contexts.

There are, therefore, similarities between Le Penism and *Leghismo* as far as racism is concerned. Nevertheless, the two movements are by no means alike. The National Front is characterized by the articulation of racism and fascism on the one hand and racism and nationalism on the other. The former is totally lacking in the Northern League, and the latter has been reshaped as an articulation between racism and ethno-regionalism, leading to very different political proposals. As Griffin stated:

> In itself racism implies no specific political programme, even though it may inform any number of them. As such it is questionable whether racism can be treated as a political ideology at all. Fascism, on the other hand, is an ideology which does involve a political programme, albeit in most cases a utopian and nebulous one, for the creation of some sort of New Order. It is thus to be seen as a form of ultra-nationalism (i.e. radically anti-Liberal nationalism) which pursues the goal or chimera of the nation's rebirth from the phase of decadence which the fascists believe it is destined to become terminal without their intervention. In other words it can be summed up in the binomial 'palingenetic ultra-nationalism', where 'palingenetic' refers to the myth of imminent regeneration from decay (Griffin 1992: 2–3; see also Griffin 1991).

The imagery and language typical of Fascist and neo-fascist ideologies were absent from the Northern League. According to Griffin, however, the party represented a subtle corruption of liberal principles in so far as 'the subtext of the attacks on the parasitic nature of Roman bureaucracy, the South and the Mafia is the myth of Northern Italy's social homogeneity and its imminent regeneration within a new order, albeit an economically and politically Liberal one.' Griffin adds that 'one does not have to be an expert in the history of Northern Italy, home of countless invasions, immigrations and occupations, of a highly variegated regional and linguistic culture and highly contrasting economic activities, to see through the myth of its socio-economic uniformity' (Griffin 1992: 16).

Here is where I disagree with Griffin, for two main reasons. First, the Northern League did not envisage Northern Italy as needing a resurgence after a period of decadence: the party's emphasis on a Lombard as opposed to an Italian ethnicity rested on the belief that Lombardy (and by extension Northern Italy) was still healthy while the country south of Rome, suffered from an incurable disease. The only way to save the healthy part of the body was to cut off the rotten limbs before the malaise spread everywhere. This is not to say that for the League corruption was limited to the South; however, in the South *Mafia*, *mafiosità* and corruption were embedded in society and culture; Northern society, by contrast, was still clean and healthy although in the grips of a corrupt 'Southernized' political class. The Northern League's position was in this respect beyond fascism and beyond nationalism as well as deeply pessimistic: there could be no resurgence but only a process of separation of the good from the bad.

Secondly, and more importantly, socio-economic homogeneity, seen by Griffin as pure invention on the part of the Northern League, is indeed a reality for those areas of Lombardy and the Veneto where the strength of the party originated. Of course the Northern League created a myth out of this homogeneity and as a result it has invented a Lombard ethnicity but the myth was not entirely without foundations. Indeed, it is interesting to see how much Le Penism and *Leghismo* differ in this respect. Le Penism treats national identity as given and thus creates a myth out of French ethnicity which is totally devoid of content, so much so that among the threats against French identity the party programme cites fast food and the Americanization of the French language (Le Pen 1985: 26). This is not surprising, since, as Miles remarked, 'If the main nationalist project in Europe of the nineteenth century was the creation of a sense of imagined community, during the twentieth century it has increasingly become one of reproducing the sense of imagined community in a rapidly changing material context. . .' (Miles 1989: 116). By contrast, the Northern League embarked on the ambitious programme of creating a sense of imagined community *ex novo*. Thus the myth of Lombard ethnicity is much more complex and sophisticated than Le Pen's myth of French identity and was built around a core of fairly specific cultural characteristics, what the Northern League referred to as 'the Lombard neo-Calvinism'. Among these were a strong work ethic, entrepreneurship and personal risk-taking, a spirit of sacrifice, a high propensity to saving, trust and solidarity and law-abidence. These were seen as virtues, of course, and were contrasted to the vices typical of other ethnic groups, especially Southern Italians. Yet it is not simply a question of the myth of the productive and efficient Northerners *vis-à-vis* the parasitic and inefficient Southerners. The cultural characteristics upon which the Northern League erected the myth of Lombard ethnicity have often been identified by both economists and sociologists as belonging to a specific type of economy and society. It is this society and this economy that now need to be analysed.

A Racialized Economy and Society

Traditional modernization theories argued that the process of industrialization would be accompanied by the related phenomena of urbanization, political mobilization and cultural uniformity:

> The traditional view of social development was that these processes would sever ties with local communities and that 'tribal' affiliations would give way to new attachments at national level. Urbanisation would lead to a

> convergence of economic and social systems towards a global pattern, consisting of a comparatively small number of relatively homogeneous 'nation-states' (Richmond 1988: 151).

Much of the industrialization of Northern Italy did not follow this route – it was accompanied by limited urbanization, and although political mobilization and cultural uniformity were high, they were also at odds with the formation of a centralized 'nation-state' (Cento Bull & Corner 1993). Continuity with the old rural economy and society, on the other hand, brought minimal social conflict and disruption (Fuà & Zacchia 1983).

This type of industrialization has been defined variably as 'diffused entrepreneurship', 'areas of localized production', 'localized industries' 'industrial districts' or even the 'Third Italy', a term coined by Bagnasco in 1977 with reference to a model of economic development different from the ones which characterized North-Western or Southern Italy (Bagnasco 1977; Garofoli 1983; Becattini 1987). Very briefly, the various terms just mentioned refer to geographical concentrations of small manufacturing units operating in closely-knit communities characterized by an overlapping of business and family ties, low social and political polarization and a high degree of entrepreneurship. Lombardy, the Veneto, Emilia-Romagna, Friuli, Tuscany and to a lesser extent the Marches and Umbria are the regions affected by this type of industrialization. Leaving aside the industrial organization of such communities of small firms, their socio-economic characteristics are primarily the preservation of the family as an economic unit and limited modernization, i.e. the persistence of primary ties and localistic, community-based allegiances (Cento Bull & Corner 1993). The political culture that goes hand-in-hand with this model of industrialization was identified as a territorial political subculture. By this term Trigilia referred to 'some areas dominated by a specific political tradition, where a complex network of institutions – parties, interest groups, cultural and welfare associations – are well rooted in the local society and of the same politico-ideological origins' (Trigilia 1986: 13). A territorial subculture indicates only limited integration into the national body politic and indeed both the Catholic and socialist subcultures in Lombardy and the Veneto and in Emilia-Romagna put up a defence of the local/regional society against the process of modernization, urbanization and proletarianization seen as endorsed by the Liberal State.

What has all this to do with racism and ethnicity? The answer is that the process of industrialization typical of the regions with a strong political subculture rested on the preservation of a tightly communitarian society which was built upon the distinction between Us and the Other. Let me bring out the social roots of this communitarian-differentialist type of racism, which the Northern League has in recent times politically exploited and 'ethnicized'.

Small-scale industrialization in Lombardy and the Veneto brought with it a heavy predominance of the manufacturing sector, small-size industrial plants, a high degree of social mobility, class collaboration and a low level of political polarization. Trust and solidarity – two essential components of a market economy – were in these areas born out of living in the same village, speaking the same dialect, sharing family as well as business ties, having comparable social statuses. As Piore and Sabel put it: 'The cohesion of the industry rests on a more fundamental sense of community, of which the various institutional forms of cooperation are more the result than the cause' (Piore & Sabel 1984: 165).

It has been the tendency of all scholars interested in the Italian phenomenon of small-scale industrialization to focus on the social cohesion, cooperation and trust underpinning these communities of small firms. Perhaps the time has now come to view trust and social cohesion as part of a dual process of inclusion/exclusion. Or, to put it differently, when trust and solidarity are community-based the community becomes racialized: it is another version of Us against the Other. The Other is whoever does not belong to the community. A sharp division exists between those who are seen as belonging to the community and those who are considered 'outsiders' (Becattini 1989: 114). The 'outsiders' are not necessarily physically outside the community as long as they are outside the community of small manufacturing producers, i.e. as long as they are not employed in manufacturing or related activities. This explains why occupations in the public sector and in public administration have always been viewed with contempt and judged to be foreign. 'Outsiders' are also those who do not speak the local dialect. It is interesting to note here that the dialect is still widely used in business transactions involving local entrepreneurs: it is, therefore, yet another factor conducive to trust.

As a fairly recent survey by the CGIL among nearly 3,000 factory workers and union representatives employed in thirteen plants across the Lombard provinces revealed, widespread prejudices existed against both Southern Italians and coloured immigrants (CGIL Lombardia-AASTER 1991). A third of the workers contacted agreed with the statement 'Immigrants take away our jobs and houses', while another third agreed with the statement 'Southern immigrants pollute the local culture.' The two statements reflect two different types of racism, the one based on considerations of the immigrants' allegedly privileged access to resources, the other on cultural differentiation. The respondents did not necessarily subscribe to both types of racism: altogether, nevertheless, half the respondents agreed with at least one racist statement (CGIL Lombardia-AASTER 1991: Table 7.1).

These sentiments were particularly diffused among workers employed in plants located in areas of small-scale industrialization, as opposed to the large urban conurbations. They were also more frequently expressed by workers who identified strongly with their local community (CGIL Lombardia-AASTER 1991: 51). The researchers argued that most prejudices against Southern Italians and foreign immigrants stemmed from a specific process of exclusion which was common to many Lombard communities. People, they wrote, are generally considered foreigners when they come from a different geographical area, when they are in 'foreign' occupations and/or when they do not share the local productivist/entrepreneurial ethos (CGIL Lombardia-AASTER 1991: 38).

In this respect immigrants from Southern Italy are considered foreign on all three counts since a) they come from outside the area; b) they are considered to be employed primarily in the public sector, and c) they come from a non-industrialized society and do not appear to readily share the productivist ethos of the indigenous population. By contrast, the immigrants from non-European countries are generally employed in the local factories and are therefore judged to perform a useful role (Ambrosini 1992). The process of exclusion is activated against them when they are considered in excess of the needs of local industry and join the ranks of the unemployed or – even worse in the eyes of the locals – the ranks of beggars and petty criminals.

The process of racialization, therefore, and to a lesser extent racism itself, is in Lombardy both widespread and built into the local socio-economic structure. It is thus fairly accurate to describe the League as a political party which has exploited racist sentiments already present among the Lombard population, particularly in areas of diffused industrialization. Let us consider anti-Southernism, for example. Recent research has shown that Southerners comprise a majority of the civil service and public administration employees (D'Orta & Diamanti 1994: 5). It has been recently argued that one of the main components of the Northern League's anti-Southern attitude is 'the transfer of southern employees to public-service jobs in the North' due to 'the high rates of unemployment in the South and the lack of enthusiasm on the part of northeners to take up lower paying public-sector jobs' (Leonardi & Kovacs 1993: 58).

A DC-sponsored survey in the late 1980s among 243 Lombard League sympathizers and voters indicated that racist sentiments were sharply in evidence among League supporters. In particular, it claimed that coloured immigrants were held in higher esteem than Southern immigrants (Cesareo, Rovati & Lombardi 1989). The survey was dismissed by the Northern League as irrelevant and totally unreliable. One can sympathize with the Northern League in this case, since it may be argued that by asking 'race-ethnic' questions one gets 'race-ethnic' answers. Nevertheless, my own research on the Northern League, based on the province of Como, shows that in areas of diffused industrialization it is possible, without even asking ethnic-sensitive questions, to link voting behaviour directly to racialization. I surveyed, in the early months of 1994, 6 per cent of the working population of Erba (Como), a town of 30,000 inhabitants where the League at the 1992 general elections obtained results on a par with the provincial average and which is representative of areas of small-scale industrialisation, with 50 per cent of people employed in industry, a quarter in commerce and a quarter in services and the public sector (ISTAT 1992: 43). In all, 450 people were contacted, of whom roughly 50 per cent were employed in industry, 25 per cent were self-employed, and 25 per cent worked in services and in the public sector. People surveyed were asked, among other things, where they and their parents were born and what party they voted for at the 1992 elections. The 'racialization effect' can be seen in Table 9.1.

Table 9.1. Votes to the Lombard League in April 1992 (Erba survey)
(Province of Como = 28% Erba = 26%)

		All Northerners with Northern parents	Southerners and/or with Southern parents
Industrial employees	43%	67%	7%
Self-employed	42%	61%	0%
Service employees	41%	46%	0%
Public sector employees	16%	22%	0%

Source: Preliminary results of 1994 survey by questionnaires.

As Table 9.1 shows, the effect of racialization on voting behaviour was strongest among those social groups (industrial employees in small and medium-sized firms and self-employed) which are especially sensitive to the cultural values of small-scale industry. Of all industrial employees surveyed (185 usable replies), 43 per cent voted for the Northern League, but the figure rises to 67 per cent if only Northerners with Northern parents (79 respondents) are considered, and decreases to 7 per cent in the case of Southerners and/or people with Southern parents (30 respondents). Among the 79 self-employed contacted, 42 per cent voted for the Northern League, rising to 61 per cent in the case of the 54 Northerners but falling to 0 per cent in the case of the 6 Southerners in this category. As for the public sector, 16 per cent contacted voted for the Northern League (51 usable replies), going up to 22 per cent if people from the North and with Northern parents are considered (25 respondents), but down to 0 per cent in the case of the 10 respondents from the South and/or with Southern parents (for similar findings, though without a breakdown for social categories, see Mannheimer 1991). The Northern League, at least in Erba, successfully became the political voice of the 'indigenous' population, to the exclusion of all 'outsiders'. This probably explains why the 'racialization effect' weakened among those social groups (such as public sector employees) which, as we saw, tend to be considered 'outsiders' irrespective of their geographical origins.

As I wrote elsewhere, the Northern League has taken over from the DC the representation of the interests of the local small-business model of development (Cento Bull 1992; 1993). The Northern League had been able to translate the xenophobic and inward-looking culture of the Lombard communities of small firms into the myth of Lombard (and North Italian) ethnicity. The party's economic programme was heavily in favour of small and medium-sized firms and the Northern League explicitly linked the cultural values of small-scale industry with its own concept of Lombard ethnicity. As one of the party's official documents reads: 'By defending small and medium-sized firms and the artisanal sector, we believe we are defending all citizens because behind this mode of production there is a society rich in important values such as: the family, friendship, a humane environment, social cohesion etc.' (Campagna Abbonamenti 1993, *Lombardia Autonomista*, 27 January 1993: 14). The same concept was expressed elsewhere as follows:

> The Northern League intends to represent the interests of small and medium-sized firms, not just for their mode of production, but also for the type of society which is behind these same firms. A society which is not multi-racial and therefore disintegrated, but is instead characterised by a continuity of relations between citizens and institutions, so that the citizen feels part of society. It is this union which guarantees democracy (*Lavoro e federalismo*, Supplement to *Lombardia Autonomista*, no. 22, 15 July 1992: 1).

In the pages of *Lombardia Autonomista*, the Northern League's official paper, there used to appear a cartoon entitled 'La famiglia Brambilla', which symbolized Lombard ethnicity and was described as counting among its ancestors a Longobard and the grandfather of Alberto Da Giussano. Not surprisingly, Mr Brambilla's occupation turned out to be that of owner-manager of a small manufacturing workshop.

By 1993–4 the Northern League showed signs of wanting to distance itself from an all-too-close identification with the localistic culture of small-scale industry. Thus the party's emphasis on cultural differentialism was no longer as crudely racist as its supporters'. The party claimed to endorse the views of well-known and respected economists and sociologists, who increasingly view economic underdevelopment in the South as a function of cultural and social relations (See for example Trigilia 1992; Putnam 1993). The difference, of course, is that the Northern League sees the cultural difference between North and South as genetically based rather than historically determined. Nevertheless, the party's position remained ambiguous. The road to 'respectability' and 'legitimacy' no doubt lay in abandoning a deterministic and organic (and therefore quasi-racist) view of cultural formation.

Why the Ethnic Revival?

Lastly, I would like to put forward some ideas regarding the timing of the political exploitation of racist feelings and cultural ethnicity. To repeat the question I asked in the Introduction, why in the late 1980s and early 1990s did ethnicity and racism find political expression in Northern Italy, particularly in the areas of diffused industrialization? Why now and not in the 1950s and 1960s? I would like to suggest that the recent evolution of the communitarian society and economy described earlier combined with a changing national and international political climate to produce an ideology and a party which made sense of the world for some sections of the population.

At the level of the Lombard economy and society, economic recession and a process of tertiarization of the economy provided a stimulus for renewed expressions of xenophobia. The 1950s to the 1980s were years of uninterrupted growth for all 'areas of localized production', accompanied by full employment. Even the 1970s did not disrupt expansion, since the Italian response to the recession of that decade was to decentralize production from the large to the small plants: industrial districts benefited as a result. Immigration from the South thus took place at a time of growth for the manufacturing sector, when many Lombard people would not consider employment in the poorly paid public sector.

By contrast, at the end of the 1980s, industrial recession was accompanied by the introduction of new labour-saving machinery and the shedding of labour. The much-despised public sector was no longer so despised and resentment grew against the Southerners for their 'privileged' access to resources in that sector, as well as for the inefficiencies of public administration. These same inefficiencies were tolerated when the economy was expanding, but were now viewed as an intolerable burden upon local industry, striving to maintain its competitiveness in the international markets.

The process of tertiarization of the economy also created a sense of loss of identity, the feeling that the local model of development and its cultural values were declining. This was reinterpreted and presented by the Northern League as an imagined ethnic community under threat. Parallel to the rise of the Northern League was the decline of Christian Democracy, seen as betraying its traditional role of defender of small-scale industrialization and taking on the interests of a new state-dependent bourgeoisie (Cento Bull 1993).

The replacement of Christian Democracy with the Northern League, however, could not have been possible without the end of the Cold War and the weakening of the Communist/proletarian culture. The end of the Cold War meant the end of the Communist threat and of the need to give priority to the anti-Communist alliance. Industry, both large and small, in the Catholic-dominated areas had regarded the Communist threat as the primary threat to the capitalist economy. The Southern electorate and the DC thus lost their primary *raison d'être*, indeed they were directly blamed for the weakening of the traditional model of small-business development.

In this context the degeneration of the Italian political system played an important part in the ethnic revival fostered by the Northern League. Given the Northern League's role as defender of the cultural world of small-scale industry, this degeneration was successfully interpreted (and exploited) by the party not in neo-fascist and ultra-nationalist terms as needing a resurgence from decay, but rather in ethnic terms as a Southernization of Italian politics, as the domination of the non-industrialized over the industrialized half of the country. From this point of view, as I noted earlier, the Northern League has nothing to do with the revival of extreme right-wing and ultra-nationalist parties in Western Europe. The non-industrialization of one half of the peninsula and the Southernization of Italian politics were both seen as two negative effects of nineteenth-century nationalism and Fascist ultra-nationalism.

In many ways this interpretation has been a master stroke on the part of the Northern League, because it has offered the Lombards a scapegoat for the corruption scandals which have hit their own society and their own regional capital. The origins of '*Tangentopoli*', according to the Northern League, lie in the Southern '*mafiosità*' which has polluted the Northern political system and now threatens to destroy Northern 'clean' society. The fight was on between 'Lombard neo-

Calvinism' and 'Southern *mafiosità*'.

Here is also a clue for the possible way forward for the Northern League and its successors: a further refinement of its as yet still ethnocentric and quasi-racist ideology. The party has recently started to present North and South, Neo-Calvinism and *mafiosità*, as non-ethnic but purely cultural concepts. In other words, the Northern League now stated that Neo-calvinism and *mafiosità* were distributed throughout the country, cutting across geographical and ethnic divisions. If this were the case, it could represent, together with the abandonment of the idea of genetically-determined cultures, the final step towards political legitimation, the adoption of an ideology no longer characterized by a racist subtext. Nonetheless, in 1994 the Northern League deliberately kept its options open and its ideology vague. At times North and South are used as purely cultural referents, at other times as ethno-cultural concepts, just as at times Bossi's ideology is ethno-cultural and at other times more explicitly ethno-racist.

One of the reasons for keeping the party's ideology deliberately vague must be the uncertainty of Italy's political future and of the Northern League's own prospects, even before its schism in 1995. The Northern League was a territorially-based subcultural party which has become a governing party without succeeding in widening its appeal much beyond the Northern provincial industrial districts. Not long ago, the Northern League seemed to be putting the onus of its own political transformation upon the South by challenging it to prove that *mafiosità* was not ethnically based and asking it to turn its back to the DC: 'Our is a request for federalism not for secessionism, although there may be risks of secessionism if by 1995 the Northern League is not well established in the Centre and South, too' (*Lombardia Autonomista*, 27 January 1993: 14). Since the party failed to make considerable inroads in the South (and Centre) in the general elections in 1994, it is clear that the transition from a regionally to a nationally based party (or parties) is not an easy one and indeed it may well prove impossible to achieve. In this context the temptation of entrenching behind the ethnic/communitarian boundary and relying on the support of a racialized electorate remains strong.

Note

1. This research project on the Northern League was funded by a grant from the British Academy in 1992. I would like to thank them for their generous support.

Bibliography

Ambrosini, M. (1992), 'Il lavoro degli immigrati. Analisi del caso lombardo', *Studi Emigrazione/Etudes Migrations*, XXIX, **105**, pp.2–20.

Bagnasco, A. (1977), *Tre Italie. La problematica territoriale dello sviluppo italiano*, Bologna.

Banton, M. (1970), 'The Concept of Racism', in S. Zubaida (ed.), *Race and Racialism*, London, pp.17–34.

Becattini, G. (1987), *Mercato e forze locali: il distretto industriale*, Bologna.

—— (1989), 'Riflessioni sul distretto industriale marshalliano come concetto socio-economico', *Stato e mercato*, **25**, pp.118–28.

Bossi, U. (with D. Vimercati) (1992), *Vento dal Nord*, Milan.

Cento Bull, A. (1992), 'The Lega Lombarda. A New Political Subculture for Italy's Localized Industries', *The Italianist*, **12**, pp.179–83.

—— (1993), 'The Politics of Industrial Districts in Lombardy: Replacing Christian Democracy with the Northern League', *The Italianist*, **13**, pp.204–29.

Cento Bull, A. and Corner, P. (1993), *From Peasant to Entrepreneur. The Survival of the Family Economy in Italy*, Oxford.

Cesareo, V., Rovati, G. and Lombardi, M. (1989), *Localismo politico: il caso Lega Lombarda*, Varese.

CGIL Lombardia-AASTER (1991), *Le passioni e gli interessi dei localismi lombardi*, Milan.

D'Orta, C. and Diamanti, E. (1994), 'Il pubblico impiego', in S. Cassese and C. Franchi (eds), *L'Amministrazione Pubblica Italiana. Un profilo*, Bologna, pp.39–56.

Fuà, G. and Zacchia, C. (eds), (1983), *Industrializzazione senza fratture*, Bologna.

Garofoli, G. (1983), *Industrializzazione diffusa in Lombardia*, Milan.

Griffin, R. (1991), *The Nature of Fascism*, London.

Griffin, R. (1992), 'The ultra-right in Western Europe: structural causes and the threat to liberal society', Report to the Institute of Jewish Affairs, Commission on Neo-Fascism, November (Unpublished, quoted with permission of the author).

Hainsworth, P. (ed.), (1992), *The Extreme Right in Europe*, London.
Harris, G. (1990), *The Dark Side of Europe. The Extreme Right Today*, Edinburgh.
ISTAT (1992), *7 Censimento generale dell'industria e dei servizi al 21 ottobre 1991*, Rome.
Le Pen, J.-M. (1985), *Pour la France. Programme du Front National*, Paris.
Lega Nord-Lega Lombarda (1992), *Programma elettorale. Immigrazione*, Milan.
Leonardi, R. and Kovacs, M. (1993), 'The Lega Nord: the rise of a new Italian catch-all party', in S. Hellman and G. Pasquino (eds), *Italian Politics: A Review*, **8**, London, pp.50–65.
Lyon, M. (1972), 'Race and Ethnicity in Pluralistic Societies', *New Community*, Vol. 1, pp.256–62.
Mannheimer, R. (ed.), (1991), *La Lega lombarda*, Milan.
Miles, R. (1982), *Racism and Migrant Labour*, London.
—— (1989), *Racism*, London.
Moioli, V. (1990), *I nuovi razzismi*, Rome.
—— (1991), *Il tarlo delle leghe*, Trezzo sull'Adda.
Piore M. and Sabel, C. (1984), *The Second Industrial Divide: Possibilities for Prosperity*, New York.
Putnam, R. (1993), *Making Democracy Work. Civic Traditions in Modern Italy*, Princeton, N.J.
Rex, J. and Mason, D. (eds), (1986), *Theories of Race and Race Relations*, Cambridge.
Richmond, A.H. (1988), *Immigration and Ethnic Conflict*, London.
Silverman, M. (1992), *Deconstructing the Nation, Racism and Citizenship in Modern France*, London.
Taguieff, P.-A. (1988), *La Force du Préjugé: Essai sur le Racisme et ses Doubles*, Paris.
Trigilia, C. (1986), *Grandi partiti e piccole imprese: Comunisti e democristiani nelle regioni a economia diffusa*, Bologna.
—— (1992), *Sviluppo senza autonomia*, Bologna.
van den Berghe, P.L. (1981), *The Ethnic Phenomenon*, New York.
Vimercati, D. (1990), *I Lombardi alla nuova crociata*, Milan.

Appendix: Note on the 1995 Regional Elections[1]

The results of the 1995 Italian regional elections, held in the fifteen ordinary regions on 23 April, demonstrated the continuing importance of national politics for regional electoral contests. The surprising defeat of Berlusconi's supporters was considered a blow to his attempt to regain the premiership (his national vote declined from 30.1 per cent secured in the European elections of 1994 to 22.4 per cent). However, a few weeks later he recouped some of his lost prestige by winning a referendum which would have threatened his media empire. Centre-Left coalitions formed governments in nine regions: Abruzzo, Basilicata, Emilia-Romagna, Lazio, Liguria, the Marche, Molise, Tuscany and Umbria. In the remaining six regions, the Centre-Right formed governments in Apulia, Calabria, Campania, Lombardy, Piedmont and the Veneto.

The national vote of the *Lega Lombarda* continued to decline. It was now surpassed by *Rifondazione Comunista*, meanwhile the major nationally based parties remained the key players. Within the *Lega* heartland regions of Lombardy and the Veneto, their result was mixed at best. *Forza Italia* and its right-wing partners continued to marginalize the *Lega Nord*. With over 34 per cent of the Milanese vote, even if Berlusconi's party had declined somewhat from the European elections, Bossi's and Formentini's party suffered even sharper losses: from just under 16 per cent of the vote in the general election of 1994, to just over 12 per cent in the European elections and down to just over 9 per cent in the 1995 regional elections. Indeed, the highly centralist and neo-fascist *Alleanza Nazionale* received over 13 per cent of vote in Italy's major urban centre. Although the *Lega Lombarda* retained (eroding) support in the industrial periphery, here too both *Forza Italia* and *Alleanza Nazionale* threatened the hegemony of Bossi's party (indeed in Como the *Alleanza* outstripped the *Lega Lombarda* 17.1 to 15 per cent)! In Lombardy as a whole the *Lega Lombarda* saw its vote drop from 22.1 per cent in the general election of 1994, 17.7 per cent in the European elections of 1994, and 17.5 per cent in the regional elections of 1995. A similar story was told in the Veneto, here the *Lega Nord-Liga Veneta* saw its support decline from 21.6 per cent in the general election of 1994, 16.6 per cent in the European elections of 1994, to 15.6 per cent in the regional elections of 1995 (however here one must also include *Nuova Italia-Autonomia Veneta* with another 2.8 per cent). Locally in the Veneto the *Lega Nord-Liga Veneta* retained its strongholds in Treviso and Vicenza but suffered continued losses in Padua, Rovigo and Verona.

The net effect of the *Lega*'s losses was unclear. With the Centre-Left and the Centre-Right heading for possible deadlock in a future general election, the position of *Rifondazione Comunista* and the *Lega Nord* might be crucial. The Centre-Left will have to choose carefully whether to woo the workerist Left or Bossi's followers.[2]

Table A.1. Regional Elections 1995: National Results (15 Ordinary Regions)

Parties	% of Vote
Forza Italia-Polo Pop.	22.4
AN	14.1
CCD	4.1
Pannella	1.3
Lega	6.4
PDS	24.9
Verdi	2.9
Patto e Laici	6.7
Popolari	5.9
Rif.Comunista	8.4
Others	2.9
Total	100.0

Notes

1. Electoral data and interpretation taken from *Corriere della Sera*, 25 and 26 April 1995.
2. The general elections in April 1996 saw the *Lega Nord* make a good recovery. It received over 10 per cent of the national vote and perfomed very strongly in the Veneto. The new Centre-Left government will be dependent on either the *Lega Nord* or *Rifondazione Comunista* to pass legislation. Bossi's new militant secessionist line will certainly accelerate measures for the decentralization of government.

Index